Introduction to the
History of Cameroon
Nineteenth and Twentieth Centuries

Edited by

Martin Njeuma

St. Martin's Press
New York

First published in the United States of America in 1989

Printed in Hong Kong

ISBN 0-312-03644-2

Library of Congress Cataloging-in-Publication Data
Introduction to the history of Cameroon : nineteenth and twentieth
  centuries / edited by Martin Njeuma.
    p. cm.
  Includes index.
  ISBN 0-312-03644-2
  1. Cameroon—History. I. Njeuma, M. Z., 1940-
DT574.I58   1989   89-10420
967.11—dc20   CIP

For Limunga, Embelle and Bonbankal

Contents

Contributors

Professor Martin Z. Njeuma
Department of History, University of Yaoundé, B.P. 755, Yaoundé, Cameroon

Dr Lovett Z. Elango
Department of History, University of Yaoundé, B.P. 755, Yaoundé, Cameroon

Dr Verkijika G. Fanso
Department of History, University of Yaoundé, B.P. 755, Yaoundé, Cameroon

Dr Fred E. Quinn
5702 Kirkside Drive, Chevy Chase, MD 20815, USA

Dr Jonathan Derrick
15 Courthill Road, London, SE13 6DN, UK

Daniel Abwa
Department of History, University of Yaoundé, B.P. 755, Yaoundé, Cameroon

Dr Emmanuel Chiabi
Department of History, University of Yaoundé, B.P. 755, Yaoundé, Cameroon

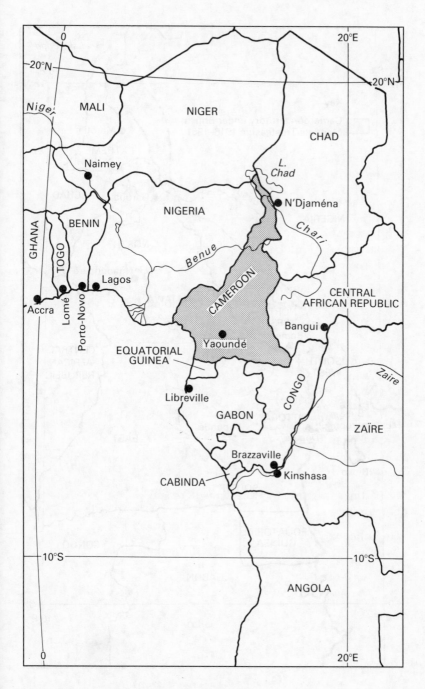

Fig. 1 The location of Cameroon in Africa.

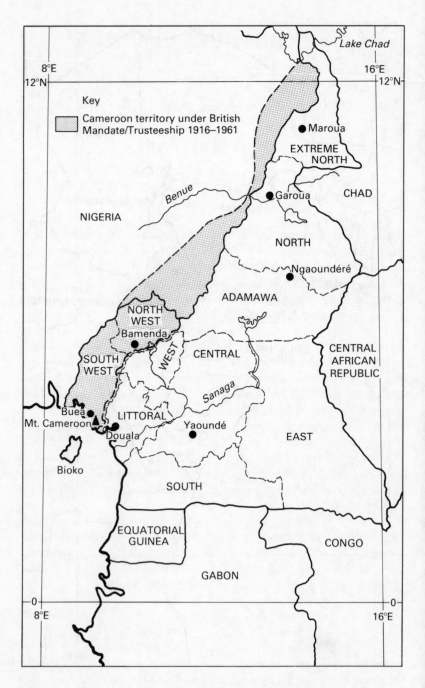

Fig. 2 Cameroon showing national boundaries since 1916, and provinces.

Acknowledgements

Much of the planning of this book was done during a year's stay at Northwestern University, Evanston, Illinois, as a Fulbright research scholar. I wish here to express my deep appreciation to Professors Mobel Smythe-Haith, African Studies Program, University of Northwestern, Ndiva Kofele-Kale, Governor's State University, Chicago, and Dana Greene, St Mary's College of Maryland for being particularly generous with their time and for discussing specific and general problems. In England, I received assistance from three very knowledgeable scholars on Cameroon studies, Mrs Elizabeth Chilver and Shirley and Edwin Ardener. (It is with deep regret that I learnt about the death of Mr Ardener just before going to press.) They encouraged me in various ways and some of their points of view helped me to see more clearly the criteria for selecting the essays. I am greatly indebted to two of my former students – Emmanuel Nguematcha and Joseph Mbembe, who spontaneously decided to translate the English contributions into French, and with the assistance of Daniel Abwa prepared the French version of this book for publication.

I cannot forget the technical assistance I got from Mrs Mette Shayne and Hans Panofski, both of the Africana Library, Northwestern University. They put their entire professional competence at my service for the assembly of rare articles and theses on Cameroon. They taught me how to draw from the 'memory' of the library computer and went out of their way to xerox or order documents specifically for my use. They should find in these pages the expression of my profound gratitude.

I received full, cordial and timely co-operation from the contributors whose essays appear in this book. They followed my instructions carefully and used them as a framework for their contributions. Sometimes we found it necessary to spend much time and money clarifying points of views over the telephone. I received help of various kinds from members of my research team: Lovett Elango, Thierno Bah, Verkijika Fanso, Fritz Mosima, Albert Dikoume, Daniel Abwa, Julius Ngoh, Abubakar Njiase-Njoya, Anthony Ndi, Robert Nkili, Wang Sonne, Denis Fomin and Nichademus Awason. I thank them all and hope that the spirit of collaboration will continue.

Last, but not least, I have dedicated this book to my wife and daughters as a small token of my appreciation for their generosity and equanimity during my long absence from home in order to realise this and other projects.

Preface

When I first announced my intention to undertake this project to my professional colleagues, their immediate response was that the book was better late than never. This response reflected a justified feeling that writing modern Cameroon history is long overdue. Why this should be so can be explained in many ways, but at the heart of the matter, it seems to me, is a language problem. The fact that Cameroon has had three different colonial regimes within three-quarters of a century has created a formidable language problem for historical scholarship.

Practically all the present generation of Cameroon historians lack the multi-lingual training required to exploit the documentation for a broad-based history which takes account of the German, French, British and local indigenous literature. They have all trained abroad in France, Britain, Germany and America where special language training was not emphasised in historical studies. Even those who have studied at the University of Yaoundé have followed programmes which were tailored to fit the systems in the former metropolitan countries. Consequently, historical scholarship is still lopsided and handicapped by a narrow language competence.

The aim of writing a history is that the public immediately concerned can read and draw inspiration from the account, but publishers are more interested in the size of this readership. Before they undertake publication of a book they must first ascertain that the book will sell to cover costs. In Cameroon schools and the public at large, monolingual publications in either French or English attract only sections of the potentially small readership, and works written in German without translations into either English or French are read by only a handful of Cameroonians and mostly for reference purposes. Thus many scholarly works of first class quality on Cameroon lie virtually forgotten in libraries because it is feared that if published, they cannot attract a wide enough readership. This situation is likely to persist as long as the Cameroonian historians do not face up to the challenge of the language problem.

The present work was conceived with these problems in mind. It aimed at writing Cameroon history by involving as many scholars as possible in a collective effort. I tried to ensure that the essays selected maintained a certain degree of coherence and continuity in the main story. Moreover, as far as possible, preference was given to essays whose authors firstly demonstrated competence in the use of more than one language and secondly wrote in a different language from that of the people under study. In this way, the essays are based on more research data and are of value to a wider cross-section of the various linguistic groups.

For this same reason, the bibliography has been arranged according to language to facilitate reference and further reading. The idea of sub-dividing the bibliography by subject matter (for example, exploration, religion, education, etc.) was considered, but dropped because it was felt that such an arrangement would confuse the non-specialist.

Finally, the essays which were originally written in French have been translated into English and vice versa. The overall effect, it is hoped is that what has been a language handicap for one generation of historians will become an asset for those of the future generation.

The logical starting point was to make use of recently defended doctoral theses on aspects of Cameroon history. The selected essays being published here for the first time are therefore based on original and primary sources (written records and oral interviews). All but two of the contributors are Cameroonian historians who have completed major research projects in the fields represented here and are presently teaching and writing about Cameroon history.

Viewed as a whole, the studies cover a time-span of about 150 years from about 1800 to 1954. Chronologically, there are two parts: the first focuses on events of the nineteenth century, while the second examines developments up to and beyond the Second World War. In respect of geographical coverage, the studies touch on virtually all the provinces of modern Cameroon, though at different periods.

The common theme is how disparate peoples originally living in small and scattered communities and politics, often isolated from each other, were drawn into ever larger political entities, the process culminating in European colonial rule. Using a phenomenological model it could be said that in the nineteenth century, geographical and ecological conditions conspired with historical events to unite

Cameroonian societies into two major areas of cultural diffusion: a savannah north, largely under the influence of Islam; and a forest south, under growing European and Christian influence. Muslim and European influences went hand in hand with the adoption of the languages of the primemovers of change — the Fulbe and Europeans respectively. The results were that ordinary communications and social interactions among divers peoples in various regions were made possible. Many people were huddled into new forms of symbiotic living. It was now possible to break out of the walls of ethnic exclusiveness and begin new cosmopolitan relationships, particularly in the embryonic urban centres.

In the twentieth century, through military conquest, or the threat of it, Germany, then France and Britain, imposed colonial rule over both the savannah and forest peoples, and began the integration of Cameroon peoples into a modern nation. Not only were internationally recognised frontiers established and secured but also, as the colonial administrative apparatus expanded, the pre-European communication networks were developed and reoriented to the capital cities, the seat of the imperial governments. Institutions such as schools, courts of law and the civil service, which catered for the common interest, broke down isolation and forged new types of loyalties and co-operation. Beyond certain limits, the people had little or no choice to do or not to do what they liked; the Europeans hemmed them in, as it were, on all sides.

Within Cameroon the army, the Christian Missions, the colonial administration, traders, and planters co-operated in checking and controlling the activities of the bold charismatic leaders who could sway the people against the injustices of the colonial system. Outside Cameroon, the international atmosphere was less than sympathetic to these indigenous initiatives. The imperialists waxed strong. United by a sense of racial superiority against Black peoples in general, the colonial powers forged an unusually strong diplomatic solidarity and acted together in order to maintain their stranglehold on Cameroonians. Ironically, this strength and the attempts to further consolidate their positions through limited native education and economic initiatives, forced the Cameroonians to learn more about themselves as human beings and to start distinguishing their interests from those of their oppressors. The challenge was there to overcome and Cameroonians gradually learnt the hard lessons of patriotism and the love of Fatherland as they participated and suffered together in the ensuing nationalist struggles. Though not immediately perceptible, the ultimate result was that the seeds of unity in diversity, the sense of a common destiny for all Cameroonians, sprouted and grew, like the proverbial mustard seed, in the resistance to and throwing off of colonial rule.

The essays tell the story in various ways. Njeuma describes the origin and growth of Islamic communities in the northern half of the country from the Adamawa plateau in the south to Lake Chad in the north. The major influences came from the Fulbe *jihads* and the formation of Fulbe dynasties in several newly created lamidates in the region. The 'Holy' wars turned out to be a uniting force, though they began by asserting differences between Muslims and non-Muslims. After a brief interlude of exploration, trade and diplomacy, the British and Germans launched a series of invasions which were the prelude to colonial rule, which effectively started early in the twentieth century.

Elango and Fanso examine the outcome of trade and politics on the Cameroon coast. Elango takes up the story of the encounter between 'King' Bile and the British consuls on the Cameroon coast and its sequel is a paradigm of relations between African Chiefs and British consuls during the so-called period of 'informal sway'. The British were interested in abolishing the slave trade by concluding treaties with coastal chiefs and the coastal chiefs wanted British military power and diplomatic support to strengthen the base of their authority. For more than three decades after 1833 Bile ruled over a Bimbian state whose prosperity was founded on trade and friendship with the British. But this incurred the jealousy of rival politics which challenged the primacy of Bimbia over them. Bile's diplomacy, however, triumphed when after his death, his son succeeded him. But the short-lived succession ended in 1882 when the new town of Victoria (founded in 1858) had by then completely eclipsed Bimbia in the political imbroglio which entangled the region.

Fanso shows how the interaction of contemporary colonial diplomacy, trade and politics contributed to the German annexation of Cameroon in July 1884. The annexation was a victory for both German and Duala diplomacy. It hurt the British who at first stoutly resisted the annexation and tried to limit German authority to areas under the effective influence of the Duala chiefs who had signed the treaty with Dr Nachtigal, the German imperial commissioner. But the British, like the French, failed to reverse the tide against the Germans. Thus between 1885 and 1887, the story is one of negotiated disengagement from Cameroon by the British. This left the Germans supreme in the territory.

German rule over Cameroon lasted from 1884 to 1916. The impact of German administration, especially where it concerned the use of military force, trade and the recruitment of labour, was felt throughout the country. Quinn examines some of the salient features of German rule among the Beti. What emerges from the investigation is that German authority in the area was very much what Hans Dominik and his indigenous protégé, Karl (Charles) Atangana, made of it. All resistance to German brutality and innovation was crushed by force of arms while Atangana consolidated his position as Paramount Chief (*Oberhäuptling*) of the Ewondo and Bane.

The most outstanding feature of the history of the Duala ruling élite is the passage from English missionary influence to German and French colonial rule. For over one decade after the French took over from the Germans, much tension characterised the relations between the Duala élite and the French administration. By the 1930s the storm had abated with the collapse of organised Duala protests. Derrick highlights élite activities during this period by showing how they participated in the private sector of the economy, in sports as well as in traditional festivals. The élite emerge as individuals with personal and collective ambitions who live astride two worlds: the traditional and the colonial.

Abwa dwells on the ambiguity and contradictions in French colonial policy in Cameroon, using a Muslim state, Ngaoundéré, as his model. The French, he argues, did not radically depart from the previous German Muslim policy which consisted in reinforcing the powers of the Lamido, the central person in the lamidate administration. However, moved by the desire also to 'protect' the interests of non-Muslim populations, the French authorities undertook reforms in local administration. This involved increasing supervision or control, even 'liberating' the non-Muslim communities from Fulbe sub-imperialism. Thus during the period under review, one cannot categorically speak of French rule as having been either direct or indirect.

Finally Chiabi reviews the major events which led to and have conditioned British rule in Cameroon. He demonstrates how the failure of Britain to acquire a 'viable' territory in Cameroon after the First World War led to the frustration of attempts to integrate Cameroon into the neighbouring Nigerian colonial system. Developments in Cameroon were consequently slow and throughout the period under discussion, politically-conscious Cameroonians felt cheated, neglected and dispossessed. After the Second World War, the British administrators tried to harness the growing discontents in the society, through reforms in native administration, with a view to involving both the westernised élites and the traditional rulers in politics. The essays of Derrick, Abwa and Chiabi do not dwell on the subject of nationalism, but the accounts provide essential background material for explaining the origin and character of Cameroonian nationalism.

Certainly, not all the sub-disciplines of history have been included here. Much more could and needs to be done. But what has been presented here should provide food for thought as well as a stimulus not only to students of history, but also to those in the human sciences whose approaches can be enlarged by a proper historical perspective. In any case, it is hoped that this pioneering effort at presenting Cameroon history by bringing together a series of special-ised studies in a single volume will encourage the production of more ambitious collaborative works.

Martin Z. Njeuma
Ndogbianga
November, 1984

Chapter One
The lamidates of northern Cameroon, 1800–1894

Martin Njeuma

The nomenclature 'northern Cameroon' or even 'Cameroon' is inexact in the context of the nineteenth century. Cameroon (the savannah region) became a legal entity in 1894 after the end of the period covered by this study. In that year the British, German and French governments signed the treaties demarcating the territory between the upper Benue and Lake Chad and the Germans gave the name 'Kamerun' to their entire 'Protectorate' from the Atlantic Ocean in the south to Lake Chad in the north. In this study the term 'northern Cameroon' has been used for convenience sake and not to refer to a geographical or precise legal entity. 'Fombina' or the 'Emirate of Adamawa' were the names which were used before the European partition. They, however, covered more territory than that covered in this study. It should be stated that this study has not been approached from the perspective of the individual lamidates, which were about 50 in number by the close of the century. Rather, the emphasis is on major historical developments, and on how they affected the region as a whole. In a region where much evidence has been unearthed within the past couple of decades, even though it is still far from being digested, the risk this essay faces is that many local events will not get extended treatment. Likewise, the essay might fall short of expectations from a centrist point of view. Scholars who have been accustomed to treating Yola (the political and cultural capital of the region) as the centre *par excellence* for the diffusion of new ideas and the Islamic traditions would not entirely understand how the history of Yola can be separated from its districts, even when the districts were eventually amputated from Yola and constituted into separate entities under different colonial regimes.

Modern northern Cameroon, the limits of this study, refers to the territory which stretches from the Adamawa plateau (*lesdi hosere*) in the south (5°50′N latitude) to Lake Chad in the north (12°N latitude), within the savannah region of West Africa. For several centuries since the second millenium AD this region has been a refuge zone peopled by successive waves of migrants called Sao from the empires of Kanem and Borno in the north, and by Jukun-speaking peoples from the Kwararafa empire on the mid-Benue river in the South. In the process of dispersal and regrouping of splinter groups over the centuries, most peoples lost their tribal (ethnic) names and languages, and ceased to practise their ancestral customs, which, hitherto, had been the hall-marks of their ethnic identity and group solidarity. Peoples like the Fulbe, Mbum, Laka, Duru, and Batta, whose ethnicity has survived destruction, have all moved into their present habitats within the last three centuries. Others, for example the Kotoko, Matakam, Mandara, Nyam-Nyam, Toupouri, Massa, Mofu, Tikar and Fali, although their names pass for ethnonyms, are recent regroupings of people due either to widespread Fulbe invasions or to colonial resettlements.[1]

Thus, in the past, strong ethnic ties were the exception rather than the rule in the region. In many places settlements were dispersed, areas thinly peopled, and the inhabitants too poor materially to support a strong government. However the exception was that by the end of the eighteenth century, around the Lake Chad basin, the rulers of Borno, Mandara and Baghirmi exercised varying degrees of authority over the peoples in the region north of the Benue. They had developed centralised systems of government and their ruling dynasties practised Islam and ruled by grafting Muslim law, the *Sharia*, on local customary law.

The Fulbe, like most of the other ethnic groups which lived in northern Cameroon, were immigrants. But their settlement differed from those of the other peoples. Firstly, Fulbe immigrations spread over a long period dating from the seventeenth century. Secondly, the Fulbe did not occupy a single homogeneous territory; instead, as they arrived, each migrating band formed its own independent settlement without joining earlier Fulbe immigrants. Thus by the second half of the eighteenth century, if one could have cast a searchlight over northern Cameroon (Fombina)[2], one would have seen that Fulbe settlements were dotted all along the course of the Benue and its tributaries and in the vast territory between the Gongola-Hawal-Yedseram axis in the west and the Logone and Shari in the east. Though individual clan loyalties were strong and created a basis for social and political organisation, the Fulbe as a whole shared many common characteristics and attitudes. They spoke the same language (*Fulfulde*) and, even when they abandoned a nomadic life and became sedentary, they were first and foremost herdsmen. Their ambitions centred around improving or augmenting their stock of cattle.³ When Islam came to West Africa, the Tukulor and many Fulbe groups were among the first peoples to convert to Islam and in turn to start to pass on the religion to others. Thus by the end of the eighteenth century, some of the best Muslim scholars (*modibbe*) in West Africa were Fulbe.

From 1804, the Fulbe revolt or, as it was popularly known, the *jihad* of Uthman dan Fodio, challenged the *status quo* and began a new historical process. In this chapter we focus on the nature of the *jihad* and its broader consequences, and then on how European competition for economic and political dominance led to the laying down of colonial frontiers.

The purpose of the *jihad* in northern Cameroon was to achieve both religious and political ends. Politically, the *jihad* aimed at setting up governments run by Muslim leaders in accordance with Islamic practices, because under the rule of the 'infidels', the human rights of the Muslims were unduly violated. Where Islam already existed, for example in Mandara and among Fulbe families, the *jihad* aimed at enforcing orthodoxy by improving and increasing the people's knowledge of and commitment to Islam; in other words, the task was 'to strengthen the tradition of the Messenger of God and wake up the people from slumber'.⁴ This is why at the outbreak of the *jihad* there was a preference for entrusting leadership to Muslim scholars.

With regard to the non-Muslim population, there was ambiguity, even uncertainty, about the objectives of the *jihad*. Local conditions were a strong factor in determining the goals the *jihadists* set before themselves. For example, where the non-Muslim population had an organised political system through which the Muslims could communicate to reach the entire group, as was the case with the Musgum, Batta, Mbum, Wute and Tikar, the objective was to attempt a dialogue with the view of either converting them to Islam at once or allowing them to remain non-Muslim but pay tribute to the Fulbe. On the contrary, where the non-Muslims lived in small scattered settlements without centralised authority, as was the case with the Fali, Duru and Baya, the *jihad* sought to enslave such peoples. In any case, it was obvious to the *jihad* leaders that they would not gain power over their opponents without resistance. Thus the overall policy of the *jihad* was to convert the non-Muslims by the use or threat of force and later to undertake conversion to Islam through what could be described as benevolent enslavement. As Uthman himself put it:

... Whenever you gain victory in the Holy War, you should give good treatment to the slaves you capture, make them Moslems, do not force them to any task that is beyond their powers, treat them as well as you possibly can .... If you teach them how to read and they complete the Koran and they acquire understanding of the Moslem religion, you may inter-marry with them and liberate those who have had the opportunity of becoming true Moslems as it is written in the Holy Koran.[5]

Such aspirations upset the *status quo*. The result was a series of armed confrontations between the old established forces, which re-jected domination, and the Muslim culture and the newly constituted Muslim forces operating under Fulbe authority.

From the foregoing, it is clear that the theoretical basis of the *jihad* and much of the early initiatives for the *jihad* came from Uthman dan Fodio. His reforming movement reached the Borno-Mandara region around 1806. In the first shock, the Borno empire was split and new Fulbe emirates were formed at Hadejia, Katagum, Jemaare and Misau. Borno's capital was temporarily occupied by the Fulbe under Ibrahim Zaki who forced the old and blind Mai Ahmad Alimi (1793–1810) to abandon the town with all his courtiers and later to abdicate in favour of his son, Mai Dunama (1810–1845).[6] Although El-Kanemi emerged as the strong man in a situation in which the Sefawa dynasty had virtually collapsed, and though he succeeded in liberating Ngazargamu from the Fulbe, yet the once extensive empire of Borno shrank to its heartland around Ngazargamu and Kukawa.

The invasions of Borno had serious snow-ball effects in the region south of Lake Chad. Many people, especially Shuwa Arabs and Fulbe, migrated out of the war-torn regions. The Fulbe became *persona non grata* in Borno. This caused many of them to emigrate with their cattle to Gombe and Fombina. These refugees championed Uthman's *jihad* with military zeal in northern Cameroon and were joined in a spirit of ethnic solidarity by the local Fulbe elements. However, the Muslim communities of Mandara and the Kotoko principalities refused to join Uthman's *jihadists* perhaps for the same reasons that the Borno leaders, Mai Ahmad and El-Kanemi, had rejected the appeals of the Sokoto scholars to make *jihad*. They claimed the *jihad* was inappropriate and had been motivated by personal and ethnocentric considerations.[7] Thus the *jihad* never became a pan-Islamic movement combining the strength of the Kanuri, Kotoko, Mandara and Fulbe Muslims.

But being desirous of pursuing the *jihad*, the Fulbe set up their own government and demanded submission from Mandara's vassal states on the Diamare. After a series of hit and run battles Modibbo Damraka emerged as the successful Fulbe leader on the Diamare, with his residence at Marua. This was in 1808.

A year later, the *jihad* also spread rapidly to the Fulbe population in the Benue region. In 1808 they had received the news of Uthman's *jihad* through messengers and itinerant Muslims, but the reactions of the *ardo'en* were full of misgivings. For one thing, the personal qualities of Uthman were not widely known, and his objectives had not been made clear. The Muslims wondered whether he was a reformer (*Mujaddid*) or the *Mahdi*, a special messenger of God sent to fill the earth with goodness even as it had been filled with evil. For another, though the Fulbe had settlements in many parts of the territory, they could not claim any military superiority over most of the communities they were called upon to subdue. Again, with the exception of the Batta who, in the Gurin, Yola and Song districts, had subjected Fulbe to their custom of *jus primae noctis*, on the whole the Fulbe were not an oppressed people.[8] They had enough means to defend themselves. In some areas, either through inter-marriage, or through the use of force, they had succeeded in creating states inhabited by Fulbe and non-Fulbe populations. Finally, there were no reports about religious persecution which could easily have provoked hostilities between the Muslims and non-Muslims. On the contrary, there was much religious accommodation and syncretism among the various religious beliefs. All these considerations made the minds of the Fulbe unprepared for widespread fighting, particularly since the outcome was uncertain. Thus Strumpel's view that on the eve of the *jihad* the relation between the Fulbe and non-Fulbe populations were at daggers drawn and only a slight wind was required to start war, was probably true of the Batta and Fulbe in the Yola-Song area, but not in other areas.

The actual transformation of the Fulbe from peaceful herdsmen to warriors and conquerors came from two principal sources. Firstly, as we have seen, from the influence of the Borno refugees; and secondly from Uthman's appointment of Modibbo Adama (1809–47) of Yola as leader of the *jihad* for Fombina within the context of a fairly defined structure of administrative hierarchy, thus:

> ... I instruct you to tell them that it is you to whom I have given this *jihad* flag, and tell them that whoever obeys you obeys me, and whoever swears fealty to you it is exactly as if he had sworn fealty to me. You should meet and come to terms with these Fulani leaders, since they have all been chiefs under

the rule of the infidels since we want them to spread God's religion; you should allocate to them districts that each can hold appropriate to his rank. They should carry on the Holy War for the sake of God.[10]

These instructions clarified many doubts about the *jihad*, provided a legal framework, and structured the activities of the Muslims. The willingness among the Muslims to carry out the *jihad* was total, especially when they saw that their war capabilities were increased by Hausa warrior-immigrants who had accompanied Adama from Hausaland. These men not only convinced the Fulbe of a successful outcome, but were also a guarantee of a repetition of the rather miraculous successes which Uthman's followers had had in Hausaland and in some of the states bordering on Fombina.

In 1810, Adama hastened to join forces with Damraka and the other Fulbe leaders in the Diamare since the enthusiasm for the *jihad* was highest in this region. The purpose was to conquer Mandara. Several reasons dictated the wisdom of this move. Politically and geographically, Mandara held a strategic position between Borno and Baghirmi, the other two super-powers of the Lake Chad basin. If Mandara fell to the *jihadists*, it would facilitate the conquest of Borno and Baghirmi by reason of its proximity to both states. Adama had spent several years schooling and teaching in Borno and was apparently anxious about establishing Fulbe rule there. He would bring relief to the Fulbe who were then desperately fighting to seize power from the Sefawa rulers. Besides, in the Mandara heartland (centred on Krewa, Mora and Dulo), by a rigid system of administration, the *Tlixe* or Mais of Mandara commanded vast populations which were locally organised much as in a European feudal state.[11] The Mandara bred some of the best horses which were great military assets. These peoples, their resources, and experiences in warfare would bring considerable advantage to the *jihad* movement. Already, in 1808, the prestige of Mandara among the vassal states inhabiting the region south of Meme on the Mangave river had been injured by Mai Boukar Adjama's (1789–1845) inability to promptly aid his vassals when they were attacked by Ngara and Mbewe Fulbe led by Modibbo Damraka.

From the religious point of view, the Fulbe desired the co-operation of all the Muslim forces in Fombina. Mandara and the Kotoko principalities were important Islamic centres by the beginning of the nineteenth century. Mandara Islam presumably shared the general tendency to syncretism and accommodation between Islamic and pre-Islamic forms of worship. But the Yola chroniclers do not indicate whether or not the Fulbe criticised Mandara Islam in the same manner as, say, Uthman and Bello had been critical of Hausa and Borno Islam.[12] However, given the double objectives of the *jihad* to reform and to spread Islam, the submission of Mandara would have greatly increased the general credibility of the *jihad* by quickly broadening the ethnic base of its protagonists. When Mai Boukar would not submit to the Fulbe forces, the Fulbe invaded Dulo, the capital of Mandara, and forced the Mai to flee to Mora. But the Fulbe could not set up a Fulbe administration at Dulo because there were no Fulbe in residence there, and so the Mandara Muslims stayed out of the *jihad*.

The failure to turn Mandara into a Fulbe state constituted a great set-back for the Fulbe who had aimed at a complete conquest of Mandara and its dependent population. Henceforth, the burden of subduing the population – the Marghi, Mofu, Mada, Meri, Muktele, Mafa, Potokwo, Kapsiki, Guiziga, Musgum, Massa, Toupouri and many others both on the Mandara chain of mountains and on the plains (Yaerée and Diamare) became difficult for the small local Fulbe populations. Nevertheless, the Fulbe were strongly motivated by the thought that a new era had dawned for them, calling on them to become rulers, and by the lessons they had learnt from the 1810 Mandara invasion. Besides, the campaigns had revealed the inability of the Mais of Mandara to protect their dependent peoples. They were left to rely on their own resources, while from time to time the local Fulbe received military assistance and reinforcements from the Benue Fulbe. Thus were founded the lamidates of Marua, Mindif, Bogo, Pette, Guider, Uba, Madagali, Mitchika, and Magba out of a population which once formed a part of the kingdom of Mandara. At the same time the Fulbe forces were defeated in the Yaerée districts by the Massa, Toupouri and Musgum with whom they had several skirmishes throughout the nineteenth century. Knowledge of the terrain and the fact that for nearly one half of the year the region was hardly accessible to Fulbe cavalry worked in favour of these non-Muslim populations.

As the years advanced, the Fulbe were more successful in the region bordering on the river Benue and its tributaries. Except for some Batta and Nyam-Nyam populations, Muslim victory in the Benue districts and over the Adamawa plateau was relatively rapid and complete. One piece of evidence for this is that the surface area of the average lamidate was larger than in the north (*Waila*). This success could be explained in several ways. The bulk of Fulbe lived along the Benue and its tributaries because the conditions for pasture for cattle were favourable. The groups were cohesive and showed much solidarity due to good organisation under powerful *ardo'en*. Some of the *ardo'en*, like Hamman of Gurin, Buba Njidda of Rai, Njobdi of Turua, Hamman of Song, Njundi of Garua, Sambo of Chamba and Sabena of Zummo for example, were so powerful that they had carved out specific territories over which they ruled mixed populations of Fulbe and non-Fulbe, presumably according to Muslim Law. Though these *ardo'en* were angry that Uthman had appointed Adama ruler (*Lamido*) over them,[13] they nevertheless joined in the *jihad*. But they did so by simply expanding their existing territories independently of Adama hoping thereby to create several new emirates which would by-pass Adama and establish direct links with the 'Caliph' in Sokoto. This tendency towards fragmentation militated against early administrative unity, but it brought rivalry among the *ardo'en* and thus fostered interest in the wars since all the Fulbe felt committed to succeed in their various localities.

Furthermore, the ethnic groups like the Fali, Verre, Namchi, Chamba, Kutin, Mono, Dama and Duru, lived in small, scattered, and often isolated homesteads which could hardly be defended collectively against external invaders. The sense of group solidarity and the concentration of political power in the hands of one or a few persons was absent. As interviews by Eldridge Mohamadou with local informants indicate, these peoples were not accustomed to organised, let alone sustained, warfare. They relied on natural features for defence against potential invaders and when these were surmounted, they became an easy prey to the Fulbe forces. The Mbum and the Wute who had larger settlements and respectable administrations, negotiated with the Fulbe and a protectorate was established over their settlements. The strategy of 'domino' seemed evidently in force as one victory added more fighters to the side of the Fulbe. The defeated peoples were rapidly incorporated into the Fulbe fighting forces. In this region, there were no serious obstacles to the movement of horses, whose widespread use gave the Fulbe much mobility and consequently a great advantage over the rest of the population. Training in cavalry warfare was part of élite education and considered resources were invested in the purchase of horses and their equipment.[14] Borno and Mandara, whose armies also fought on horse-back, were aware of the power of the cavalry and soon after the *jihad* broke out, they banned the sale of horses to Fulbe. Nevertheless, imports of horses and an efficient armament, such as chainmail, daggers, swords, and barbed spears, reached Fulbe hands through Hausa traders coming from Katsina and Kano. The traders exchanged them for slaves who became useful as porters before they were disposed of at the end of the traders' destination.

Before we examine the consequences of the *jihad*, let us pause for a while and review the reasons which stopped the Muslim advance to the coast and the extent to which the *jihad* was a 'Holy' War. It is estimated that by the end of the nineteenth century, the territory which fell under Fulbe control either directly or indirectly amounted to nearly 40 000 square miles with a population of around 1 500 000 inhabitants.[15] As the Fulbe approached the forest region, it became logistically harder for them to form new lamidates. Good pasture grounds became scarce, while heavier rains and the existence of tsetse flies proved fatal to cattle which constituted the basis of Fulbe economic prosperity. The expeditions to subdue distant peoples to Fulbe rule became expensive to support far away from the Fulbe bases. They required much time and endurance to carry out, especially when the region began to be visited by Europeans who used guns to oppose the southward military expansion of Islam. As a consequence two types of expeditions became distinguishable: those that turned out to be mere raiding bands, for slaves and booty, and those which opened up tributary relations between their lamidates and distant towns. Towards the end of the nineteenth century towns such as Kunde, Babua and Gaza in the Baya country, and Yoko and Ditam in the Tikar country, were ruled by their own local chiefs and the Hausa and Fulbe who later settled in these towns did so principally to facilitate tribute and trade relations. Equally the Fulbe failed to establish lamidates among the western Tikar, including the Bamenda Grassfields, because they met with organised and sustained opposition.[16] The Bamum, for instance, dug a trench round their capital town, Foumban, during the reign of Mbuombuo (c. 1817–55), the eleventh monarch, and this protected them against subsequent Fulbe raids.

The Fulbe themselves argued on the basis of their undertakings since 1809, that every step they took in the *jihad* was for Islam 'to acquire and spread understanding of Islam as it is written in the Holy Koran'. They point to the fact that in accordance with Islamic tradition they sought initial authorisation from the reformer, Uthman dan Fodio, before beginning war. In the course of the *jihad* efforts were made to act within the laws governing the conduct of *jihads*. For example, villages were not attacked without prior notice. They were given the option to accept Islam or recognise the authority of the Muslims by paying tribute (*jizya*). Those that accepted conversion to Islam were given teachers (*Malams*) who taught them how to pray and live like Muslims. The *jihad* chroniclers claim that 'the faith (Islam) was purified and exalted and none said nay'.[17]

There is little doubt that the Fulbe viewpoint idealises the situation with many theoretical elements. With a central leadership that was initially very weak militarily, and with activities ranging over such a large expanse of territory and involving peoples and leadership with such diverse backgrounds, uniformity in the actions of the *jihadists* was an exception rather than the rule. Some concrete evidence shows the extent to which the ideals were negated.

The Mandara campaigns were a classic example. Exhilarated by their swift victory, the Fulbe armies became 'puffed up and difficult to manage; and in the enjoyment of their pleasures, they neglected the duties of their Faith'.[18] Their attitude to booty confirmed that no fixed pattern prevailed on how booty was shared despite the clear directives in the Koran on the subject. Errors and omissions that characterised the application of the legal precepts were sometimes due to ignorance. At other times, the rules were difficult to enforce since the motives of the principal leaders were often mixed and uncoordinated.

The *jihad* became a complex matter as some leaders projected their personal ambitions and started competing with each other for recognition by the Caliph in Sokoto. For example in the wars against the Namchi (situated near present-day Poli), Buba Njidda (1798–1866) of Rai refused to help Modibbo Adama of Yola, and so Adama was defeated. Later Njidda invaded the Namchi alone, defeated them and sent the captives to Adama as a present.[19] Lamidates like Rai, Garua, Tibati and Banyo considered the unsubdued regions in their neighbourhood as a sort of 'private reserve' which they raided in times of need. Interference in each others so-called 'private reserve' was a source of constant friction among the Fulbe leaders. There is the case of Hamidu Nyambula (1848–1878), son and successor of Hamman Sambo, who fought Ngaoundéré, Banyo and Tignere because they invaded Duru and Tikar settlements he considered belonged to Tibati. Likewise when Lamdo Bibemi, Hamman Joda, as ally of the non-Muslim chief, Peve of Dari, attacked the Laka, Buba Njidda joined the Laka, whom he considered his protégés, though this involved Muslims fighting against Muslims.

Finally, the Muslims had the spiritual duty to train the people they conquered to become fully fledged Muslims and to integrate them as full citizens of the new Islamic community. But the Fulbe often refrained from this obligation because systematic conversion before enslavement would have brought about legal equality and consequently a loss in slaves. Lacroix appropriately talks of '*une sort de confiscation de l'Islam à leur profit qui explique pour une part leur peu d'inclination à faire du proselytisme*'.[20]

All of these grossly limited the *jihad's* effectiveness as an instrument for the propagation and spread of Islam. By the end of the period, it is true, the *jihad* had brought the Muslims into the territory of many non-Muslims, but it is also true that the *jihad* worked no miracles on the religious attitudes of the Fulbe. Conversion was a slow process whose progress depended a good deal on peoples' proximity to the Fulbe administration, which served as a back-up for religious aspirations.

The effects of the *jihad* over the region were multiform. It is customary for Fulbe traditions to ascribe major changes in the northern Cameroon society after 1809 to the *jihad*. This is normal though open to dispute. What cannot be gainsaid is that many current attitudes about Islam and politics date from the *jihad*. The most dramatic of all the changes were the political innovations. Suddenly, from simple herdsmen, many Fulbe became rulers.

Several features of government were introduced for the first time in the region in order to legitimise and consolidate the authority of the Muslim Fulbe. Towns like Marua, Bindir, Garua, Rai Buba and others became capitals of a centralised political system called a lamidate or sub-emirate. By 1860 there were over forty such lamidates headed by Muslim leaders. Yola was the headquarters of the Emirate, and from Yola, the Lamido (*Emir*) exercised paramountcy over the administration of the lamidates by representing them in the caliphal government located at Sokoto.[21] Uthman dan Fodio had set the ground rules in his instructions to Adama so that the creation of lamidates could be achieved in an orderly way. He ordered Adama to give to each of the Fulbe *ardo'en* a flag, as he had given one to Adama, allocating to them districts which each could hold in accordance with their respective ranks.[22]

In practice this worked out as follows: the old *ardo* leadership apparatus was used to serve the new system. Each *ardo* with a non-Muslim population as target for submission, sought investiture from Yola. He was then authorised to constitute a lamidate provided his population(s) was not already claimed by another *ardo*. In the region north of the Benue there was no evidence of serious friction in the formation of lamidates. But in the already established pre-*jihad* lamidates, the story was different. In Rai for instance, where before the *jihad* several *ardo'en* like those of Bibemi, Mayo Wuro and Jarendi fell under the authority of Lamdo Rai, granting of an independent status created friction between Yola and Rai and hostilities between Buba Njidda and the neighbouring *ardo'en* for a long time. Also, during the time of Hamman Sambo (1808–48), Tibati was the most important lamidate in the south. And by virtue of being the first Fulbe *ardo* to install a government on the Adamawa plateau he had insisted that all subsequent *ardo'en* who settled on the plateau were under him. But under Ardo Njobdi (1821–49), the lamidate of Ngaoundéré developed so fast that it eclipsed Tibati, and the newly created lamidates of Tignere and Banyo looked to Ngaoundéré instead of Tibati for leadership. This, as we have observed, led to armed conflict between the successors of Njobdi and Sambo, Ardo Issa and Nyambula respectively, over the question of seniority in the region.

A new political position resulting directly from the *jihad* was the office of Lamdo (*pl.* Lambbe).[23] The office was one of the principal institutions for ensuring political integration among the diverse peoples in the respective sub-emirates. Although the Fulbe were a simple egalitarian-minded people, following Islamic respect for leadership and authority, the Lamdo easily assumed all the trappings of a medieval Muslim Caliph. The structure of government was modelled after the Fulbe-Hausa emirate system in Hausaland.[24] In this system, the Lamdo or governor was head of an administration. The Lamdo, unlike an *ardo* who was a leader of people, was first and foremost an administrator of a territory with fairly well defined frontiers. The Lamdo appointed his close collaborators and they were answerable to him.

They were expected to show considerable personal loyalty to him. Loyalty here meant the prompt execution of all instructions from the Lamdo, and leading the chorus in singing the Lamdo's praises to others at all times. In theory the Lamdo was also expected to be the spiritual leader (Commander of the Believers) of the community, thus combining political, religious and judicial headship in his person. In practice this was not always so, since a certain degree of technical knowledge was required to perform successfully such functions as those of Imam and Alkali. These functions were often entrusted to persons who had undertaken special studies and had won respect in the local communities and could thus be trusted for their uprightness and impartiality. In one of Uthman's instructions he put it as follows:

> Address your chief emir as 'Commander of the Believers', and the emir of each province as 'Emir of such and such a province' and the emir of each place as 'Emir of such and such a village', and he who has charge of God's statutory punishment as 'Emir of the statutory punishment'.[25]

As the first generation of leaders started dying, succession to the office of Lamdo passed from father to son. Thus it was, for example, that when Sambo of Tibati died, he handed over power to his eldest son, Nyambula, and similarly Njobdi of Ngaoundéré handed over to Isa, Njundi of Garua to Bakari and Buba Njidda of Rai to Jirum. This form of succession had no legal basis in either the Islamic or Fulbe systems, but it seemed to have been in keeping with the tradition which Uthman started in the Sokoto caliphate when he appointed his son Bello to succeed him.

The Lambbe held a unique position because they were personally responsible for making all important appointments and for enforcing Koranic law with the assistance of an Alkali. The administration revolved around the person of the Lambbe. Indeed, to a large extent, the administration often reflected the character of the Lambbe. As Passarge observed: 'the type of government is despotic; a Sultan is at the head of each state and the state and districts belong to him directly'.[26] They controlled the arms in their respective lamidates by organising their fabrication locally, or their purchase from abroad or from visiting traders. Only the Lambbe could summon the people to war. Their palaces were often sited at the centre of the town near the mosque and market place, so that they never lived in isolation from the people. Towards the end of the nineteenth century the prosperity of a Lamdo could be measured by the size of his palace. The palace consisted of several huts surrounded by a huge wall often constructed with dried mud bricks. The architectural designs imitated Borno and Hausa styles or oriental patterns.

The lamidate system made room for the appointment of councillors who were charged with specific functions in the administration. The number of councillors varied from one lamidate to the other depending on the population and valuable resources of the lamidate. Appointments as councillor took into account the diverse ethnic origins of the people in such a way that all important ethnic groups were represented at court. In lamidates such as Marua, Rai, Chebowa, Ngaoundéré, Tibati and Garua, to name only a few, the various ethnic groups were represented at court either in a single hierarchy of councillors of mixed Fulbe and non-Fulbe, or there were two separate hierarchies of councillors, one made up exclusively of Fulbe (*majalisa herobe*) and the other of the non-Fulbe (*majalisa machube*).[26] The fundamental purpose was to make government accessible to all and sundry, but unless the functions of each of the two hierarchies were well defined and adhered to, this arrangement could, as in the case of Rai and Ngaoundéré, lead to competition between the two hierarchies of officials for control of the office of Lamdo.

The councillors assumed either Borno or Hausa titles since the administrative machinery was structured after the Borno and Hausa systems. The titles for the northern Lambbe were much influenced by the Borno system, while those on the Benue and Adamawa plateau region were influenced by the Hausa system. Thus the principal councillor in Marua and Kalfu had the Borno title, *Kaigama* or *Galadima*, while in Garua and Ngaoundéré he bore the Hausa title *Waziri*. The councillors were selected from among the élite of the lamidate, that is from among those Muslims who had distinguished themselves in war or in Koranic education or who were successful traders or herdsmen. They were the intermediaries between the Lambbe and the population. They ensured that the people's complaints reached the Lambbe and also that the orders of the Lambbe were executed. There was no salary, but as part of their patronage, and as the occasion offered itself, the Lambbe bought and distributed expensive gifts such as arms, horses, richly embroidered dresses, red caps, carpets and religious books, to their collaborators. This custom increased their dependency on the Lambbe. The councillors in turn gave presents to those in their service. Such patronage reinforced the personal character of government. In this kind of set up, Fulbe and other Muslim élites, principally from Hausaland, benefited the most and consequently stayed in the upper echelons of the political and social pyramid.

A principal function of the administration was to maintain law and order. In the rural areas (villages), where the Muslim population was small or non-existent, local traditional ways of settling disputes continued to operate. In the lamidate towns, however, despite their mixed population, *Alkali* courts were introduced to enforce the *Sharia* in civil and criminal cases.[27] In each of the lamidates, cases were tried at three levels, first at the level of the families involved without recourse to outside intervention; second, at the level of the quarter head (*Lamdo fatude*) or in the presence of an elderly and respected councillor acting as arbitrator; and finally at the level of an Alkali court. An essential feature was that those who adjudicated at each level were conscious of their legal and administrative limitations and took into account the importance of each case which was brought before them.

There are no records of which cases went to which courts; what probably mattered were the issues at stake, the importance of the person or persons who were involved in a litigation, and the possible effects of the court decision on the well-being of the community. The Lamdo and his councillors had a collective responsibility to enforce the law and general discipline; for this reason, they kept themselves well informed about the activities and ambitions of the inhabitants in the lamidate. The knowledge that nothing that one did was hidden from the authorities in many ways restrained conduct that was likely to disrupt the peace.

Developing simultaneously with the creation of new political institutions and idealogy were several economic changes. These changes involved, in particular, mobilisation of the region's inhabitants and rechannelling of the resources into the hands of the new rulers. Industrial and commercial activities developed around the new centres of political power. As the Islamic traditions were consolidated in the lamidate system, long-distance traders took advantage of the new peace (*amana*). They traded along the newly opened inter-lamidate communication links. This way they integrated the region's economy into the older established commercial network of the rest of the Sokoto caliphate, Borno and the trans-Saharan system.

The *jihad* caused considerable displacement of peoples from their ancestral homes because the conquered peoples and those captured during raids were carried off and resettled in new urban centres, the capitals of the lamidates. Such movements, sometimes referred to as 'enslavement' in European sources, were greater in northern Cameroon than in Borno or Hausaland since the opponents of the *jihad* were all non-Muslims and it was permissible (*sunna*) to enslave them. Another reason was that the Lambbe of Fombina had no political and geographical limits to the area they could exploit in the east and south of the latitude of Garua. Their forces could therefore raid several kilometres from their bases uninterruptedly. The degree of 'enslavement' however differed, judged from the way the displaced persons were treated by their captors. Some of them became important citizens in their new milieu on conversion to Islam or at least on accepting to live their lives in conformity with Muslim culture. Others were gainfully employed in public construction and various domestic works.

In lamidates, such as Marua, Ngaoundéré and Garua, where the displaced populations were large, the Fulbe and some Hausa aristocrats acquired tracts of unoccupied land not too far from the towns and turned these into resettlement villages called *rumde* (or sometimes, *dumde*). Although Barth observed that 'many private individuals owned more than 1000 slaves'[28], the average size of *rumde* seldom exceeded 100–200 adult slaves. The *rumde* functioned as both economic and political entities. Thus they were the foci for intensive economic activities including plantation-type cultivation and various forms of craftsmanship such as tanning, weaving, and pottery. The inhabitants cultivated such crops as maize, sorghum, millet, rice, sweet potatoes, groundnuts, yams, beans, onions and various other kinds of vegetables. Smelting iron and dyeing cloth were rather specialised occupations and the participation of 'slaves' in the production processes was marginal. Their major occupations were farming and raising animals for the profit of the *rumde* owner (*baba*).[29] The inhabitants of *rumde* were a readily available work force for their owners or for whomsoever their owners directed them. They usually constructed or repaired *baba's* residence, the town wall, mosque or other public buildings. Many European visitors of the latter half of the nineteenth century saw the *rumde* as the lynch-pin of an extensive slavery system as well as a means of accumulating and storing wealth. In other words, the size of the *rumde* was an index of an individual's wealth and influence in the society. It also indicated nobility and high status.

Politically, the *rumde* was an effective way of subjecting slaves, who were brought from distant expeditions, to Fulbe rule. The *rumde* had their own officials who enforced martial discipline and taught the people about the Muslim way of life, for example, how to pray, dress and behave like Muslims, and speak *Fulfulde*. During the lull from farm work, after the harvest season, the *rumde* workers joined in military or long distance expeditions serving as porters and bodyguards. They lived an ordinary village life, owning homes, maintaining families and subsisting on their own labour. Their handicap, in one sense, was the knowledge that they were not free to move about as they pleased, but this handicap was compensated for by the satisfaction that they were protected by, and indeed that they belonged to, the extended family of an important person.

Development of communication links between the various parts of the territory is among some of the lasting results of the *jihad*. Before the *jihad* pathways were kept open for farming, hunting and transhumance purposes.[30] But the founding of lamidates under Muslim leaders automatically created pockets of population centres sharing many common interests, and the need to transfer tribute to and from these towns as well as visit relatives kept the pathways constantly open. Military expeditions and raids led the Muslim forces to penetrate isolated territories, which of course, led in turn to the opening of new routes. As the wars abated, especially after 1870, and 'legitimate' commerce increased in volume, the *jihad* routes became the highways for long and short distance trade. Such new trade patterns were inspired by the changes in the status of a number of persons following the creation of the lamidates. The requirements of the new aristocracy for special provisions and exotic prestige goods were high, and so were the profit margins and the prices paid. Accordingly, traders linked the lamidates to Borno and Kano (the two most important southern termini in the trans-Saharan trade), to European trading posts in the Congo, to the western grassfields of the Bamenda and Bamileke highlands, to Yorubaland and to the West African Atlantic coast. The professional traders were mostly Arabs, Kanuri, and especially Hausa who were encouraged to conduct long-distance trade by the fact that Hausa and Arabic were two widely spoken languages throughout the Western Sudan.

Among the professional traders, the Hausa were the chief agents in bringing about economic change. They formed self-sustaining settlements (Hausa quarters) in the lamidates to facilitate production and trade.[31] There is no evidence to indicate precisely when Hausa started settling and carrying out business in the region. It is unlikely that this was much before the *jihad*.[32] After 1809 many Hausa came to the lamidates as volunteers or mercenaries to participate in the *jihad*; others came as malams to settle permanently; and still others came to trade in the needs of the local aristocracy. Barth provides the earliest certain reference to the presence of Hausa traders in the region and from his account one could conclude that the Hausa traders were already quite active before 1851. A large number of Hausa settled in the lamidates in the 1870s and 1880s when they came in the company of important visitors like Malam Maunde, the 'Kofa' or man in charge of supervising the affairs of the Eastern Emirates in the Sokoto administration. It was the custom for such visitors to be accompanied by caravans of traders who wished to trade in the regions they visited. The Mahdist expectations, which reached their climax with the migration of Hayatu (great-grandson of Uthman dan Fodio) and his followers from Sokoto to Balda in the Bogo-Marua district, brought many Hausa settlers into the region. Because the Hausa were very enterprising and hardworking, their settlements within the lamidates grew as intermediate centres for the collection, purchase and reselling of goods. As a consequence, the local populations were encouraged to produce more in order to meet the demands in the Hausa settlements.

Another source of stimulus to production and distribution of goods was the tribute system. Tribute was not a form of Muslim taxation like *Zakat* or *Jizya*.[33] It therefore had no legal basis in Muslim law. Tribute grew as a social and political custom whereby subordinate rulers or persons sent presents to their hierarchical superiors as a mark of honour and friendship. In the early days of the *jihad*, tribute was an index of a Lamdo's success since there was often a correlation between the size of the tribute and success at wars. Socially, tribute payment was a way of openly showing collective respect for authority. Its religious significance was that the proceeds from tribute were used to finance the *jihad* and to enable the leaders at the various levels to meet their Koranic obligations of gift-giving and charitable redistribution of incomes, especially to the needy. Muslims and non-Muslims alike contributed to the tribute package. Levies for military purposes were sometimes considered a form of tribute, but they belonged more to the obligatory assistance incumbent on every free man to fight when called upon to do so by the 'Commander of the Faithful' or his lieutenant. By the middle of the nineteenth century the amount of resources that changed hands as tribute was considerable. In 1851 Barth estimated that in slaves alone the Lamido of Yola received 5000 from the lamidates annually.[34] Although payment of tribute was voluntary and no fixed amounts were imposed, non-payment reflected bad relations. The lamidates of Rai, Tibati and Bindir used non-payment of tribute to indicate dissatisfaction with, even disregard for, the Yola administration. On such occasions, they sent tribute directly to the caliphal government in Sokoto, thus hoping in return to obtain direct political linkage with the Caliph.

The cultural transformation of the communities was also evident, though the rate of involvement of all the people in the innovations was slower than in the political and economic fields. As the gains of the *jihad* were consolidated, the application of Islamic culture, as it was known in Borno and Hausaland, was a principal preoccupation of the Muslims in all the lamidates. This was done with a certain degree of messianic zeal and impulsion because the Muslims considered this to be the way of progress and of putting into practice the new spirit of religious revival. External manifestations of the new culture were to be seen in the observance of the routine aspects of the 'Five Pillars' of Islam, for example prayer, the fast of Ramadan, and gift-giving. Also to be seen, were physical structures like mosques or communal prayer places and *sare* or fenced dwellings.[35] Other introduced culture features included new architectural designs for dwellings, and new forms of dress and diet for the multitude of non-Fulbe who became a part of the 'Islamic abode'. Good sites for gauging the depth and range of the popular culture were around the palaces of the Lambbe, the mosques and market places. As a matter of daily routine all sorts of people (drummers, musicians, tricksters, animal charmers, medicine men making and bearing charms (*laya*), and fortune tellers) congregated in these places.[36] Their activities constituted important ingredients in the new culture.

As we observed earlier, the *jihad* had stimulated much enthusiasm among the Muslim élite for a better understanding of Islam and thus created a willingness among the élite to live according to its precepts.

In this regard, Koranic education became the chief mark of the success of the cultural transformation. Local scholars even predicted that the *jihad* would last for one hundred years. Half of the time would be devoted to wars and the other half to acquisition of Islamic knowledge through concentration on learning.[37] As more people accepted Islam, so it was necessary to teach them how to pray by making them memorise the liturgical verses of the Koran. It was also necessary to produce specialists in the various branches of Islamic studies, such as theology and law, so that the universal traditions and values of Islam could prevail. Several persons took up this challenge, prominent among whom were scholars like Modibbe Abdullahi and Hassan, both of whom held senior positions, Waziri and Alkali respectively, in the administrations of Adama (1809–47) and Lawal (1847–72).[38] Alkali Hassan joined Adama from Wadai and became the first officially appointed Alkali at Yola in the 1840s. He opened a school for training members of the royal family including the sons of Lambbe from the lamidates. The scholastic reputation of Ibn Hajj Emir, another celebrity from Wadai, earned him the appointment of a special envoy of Adama to the south of Wadai and Darfur to recognise the Mahdi when he appeared and to pledge the loyalty of the Sokoto regime to the Mahdi.[39] Muhammad Raji ibn Ali, Muhammad Nakashiri, Mo Allahyidi, Alkali Bilkijo and Hayatu ibn Said were each accompanied by a following of students who came from various parts of Hausaland to settle in northern Cameroon. These men also made a great impact on the scholastic and cultural life of Yola and the lamidates. From Yola they visited the lamidates and held seminars with local scholars.[40] Modibbe Raji, for example, preached and sought converts among the Muslims to the Tijaniya brotherhood (*tariqa*). The Tijaniya doctrine frightened Lawal of Yola[41] because it pointed to new leadership in Islam. He therefore proceeded to make a list of all the influential scholars residing in the lamidates and requested them to transfer their residence from the lamidates to Yola. Modibbo Adama Gana of Turua and Ngaoundéré, a specialist in medicine, was also obliged to leave Ngaoundéré where he had been ruling as regent, to reside in Yola.[42] While these transfers enabled Lawal to control the scholastic and cultural activities of the *modibbe*, they favoured the intellectual growth of Yola at the expense of the lamidates since students of worth followed their masters to live permanently in Yola. This is why, for instance, Alkali Ahmed Joda, though a native of Ngaoundéré, studied under Modibbo Raji in Yola before proceeding to study law at the al-Azhar University in Cairo. On his return in 1886, he set up his practice in Yola.[43]

The activities of the scholar-prince, Hayatu ibn Said, involved many more people religiously and politically.[44] Hayatu came to Yola as a teacher and prince of the Sokoto dynasty in about 1878 during the reign of Umaru Sanda (1872−90). He preached the doctrine of Mahdism and after 1882 he allied himself to Muhammad Ahmad, the Mahdi of the Anglo-Egyptian Sudan. Through persuasion and *jihad* he carved a Mahdist state in the Balda-Bogo-Marua region. Many young men from the neighbouring lamidates, as well as immigrants from Hausaland and the Sudan, joined Hayatu. But Abdulrahman (1891−1902) could not be convinced that Muhammad Ahmad was the true Mahdi, and that Hayatu was not motivated by personal ambition to become Sultan of the Sokoto Caliphate. War became inevitable between Zubeiru (1890−1902) of Yola and Hayatu when the latter could not be persuaded to abandon the Mahdist cause and return to Yola. At the end of the Hayatu-Zubeiru war (1892), Balda was burnt down and Hayatu was thus forced to leave Balda. He immediately joined forces with Rabeh, another adherent of the Mahdi, whose headquarters were then in Baghirmi. Many of Hayatu's followers, who could not go with him to Rabeh, migrated to various parts of northern Cameroon and individually continued to encourage fellow Muslims to increase their knowledge of Islam and take an active part in politics. The attempt of Hayatu to encourage Muslim scholars to play leadership roles in the politics of the lamidates and Caliphate as a whole, failed, but the general effect was that many Muslims took the opportunity of Mahdism to improve their religious knowledge and to acquire literacy in the Arabic script.

While the cultural transformation was real, it covered principally the urban and cosmopolitan centres like Ngaoundéré, Garua, Marua, and Yola. The rural areas continued to live by their old customs. The result was that even after a century of Fulbe hegemony, cultural differentiation was still very much a characteristic feature of northern Cameroon society. Cultural differentiation continued to follow ethnic and linguistic lines chiefly because the Fulbe could not subdue all the ethnic groups politically. Also, the Fulbe permitted some ethnic groups such as the Mbum, Wute and Musgum to live under 'indirect rule', which consisted of accepting Fulbe overlordship by paying tribute, while the Fulbe refrained from interfering in their political and religious life. This meant that there were practically no political pressures upon these populations to abandon their ancestral culture for the new one. Thus though the non-Fulbe learnt and spoke Fulfulde as a *lingua franca* for trade and social intercourse, and though they would imitate Fulbe mannerisms in their daily style of life, outside the urban centres cultural differences continued to prevail, based on ethnicity and the observance of some ancestral customs. Everywhere proficiency in Fulfulde, rather than conversion to Islam, was responsible for social solidarity and unity in the region.

The history of northern Cameroon in the second half of the nineteenth century, particularly in the last quarter of the century, is marked by the intervention of Europeans in the commercial and political affairs of the region. Such contacts between Cameroonians and Europeans had already been common on the coastal region since the sixteenth century. The need to penetrate into the interior of Africa arose when some European countries resolved to cut off the supply of slaves coming from the interior of Africa to furnish either dealers on the coast or dealers who transported slaves across the Sahara desert to north Africa. For this reason, the British government led the way and undertook exploring missions to northern Cameroon from the Atlantic coast and from across the Sahara desert. The visits of Major Denham in 1823 and Barth in 1849–51 respectively were projected to study the conditions of fluvial communications in the region with the view of using them to abolish the slave trade and opening up the territory to 'legitimate' commercial relations. However, it required too much effort to interfere with and abolish the existing institutions of slavery. The British therefore abandoned the original intention of fighting against slavery and the overland slave trade and instead put all their efforts into exploiting the commercial potential of the region. Consequently, the presence of the Europeans did not have any impact at all on the cultural patterns of life in the territory though it gave rise to new trends and pressures on the commercial and political life.

All British trade in the region was carried out through a chartered company, the Royal Niger Company. The company established itself in the early 1880s and in less than a decade its influence was felt in all the lamidates. It had an important factory at the town of Ibi for buying and selling produce since the river Benue was navigable up to this point all the year round. During the rainy season (July to September) company steamers traded further up the river to Yola and beyond. However at Garua and Bibemi near Rai, though not at Yola, the company was granted permission to build on land. On the whole the company's activities did not disrupt the traditional ways of trading which, we have seen, were dominated by Hausa merchants. In addition to its own agents who were brought from the Atlantic coast, the company used Hausa traders because they had extensive knowledge of the interior market situation. The company agents, indeed all the foreign traders, used the existing political structures to carry out business successfully. They also subjected themselves to traders' customs like giving periodic presents to the Lambbe. There was therefore co-operation rather than competition between the old and the new traders. In the course of this interaction, the Hausa were among the first interior people to learn English, which gradually spread in the form of pidgin English as an additional language of commerce.

The buying facilities of the company, especially the one which permitted traders' goods to be bought in large quantities and paid for immediately at the company's depots or warehouses greatly encouraged inter-regional trade and increased activities in the European-oriented sector of the economy. The company linked up the Benue trade with such distant markets as the ivory and cattle markets of Banyo, Tibati and Ngaoundéré, and the kola nut markets at Bamum and the Bamenda Grasslands either via Yola, Kontcha and Gashaka, via Jebu, Bakundi and Gashaka, or via Ibi, Wukari and Donga.[45] The popular trade items on all the routes were gum, benniseed, rubber, natron, meat, raw hides and skins, kola nuts and ivory. The company exchanged these commodities for salt, beads, English and Indian cotton cloth, and for many British manufactured products. Firearms were not a common item of trade. Their use had never been popular among either the Hausa or the Fulbe. Moreover, Europeans were convinced that it was in their long-term interest to keep these weapons away from the Africans unless they were in European service. In 1890 the Brussels Act formally forbade Europeans to sell or cede firearms to Africans. Nevertheless there were enough trade items to sustain a mutually beneficial commercial relationship between Europeans and the local inhabitants.

Until 1890, the company's involvement remained restricted to trade. As long as the company was the only European enterprise in the region, it felt secure enough to limit itself to trade and trade alone. But the situation changed dramatically in 1890 when, for political reasons, the Germans and the French also became interested in Borno and the region south of Lake Chad. Accordingly the subsequent history of the region became dominated by foreign colonial problems. The Lambbe found themselves in the midst of a series of diplomatic wrangles initiated by visiting Europeans.

In this regard the British made the first move. The 1886 Treaty between the Royal Niger Company and the Sultan of Sokoto by which the lamidates of northern Cameroon fell under British 'protection' was revived and[46] reconfirmed in 1890 by Umar Ali, Sultan of Sokoto, despite protests from Yola. In 1890, the Germans followed suit. They felt the time had come for them to take bolder initiatives to secure the Cameroon protectorate. One such initiative was 'effectively to occupy' the Muslim regions of northern Cameroon. Firstly, the Germans thought of resuming the negotiations with Britain on colonial frontiers which had been suspended in 1887 and of asking that the Anglo-German boundary be extended from the Benue river to Lake Chad. Secondly, they dispatched German explorers such as Zintgraff and Morgen on political business to conclude treaties and make the German presence felt among the Lambbe. The Germans based their action on the nebulous legal claim that their sovereignty over Cameroon since 1884 was not limited to the coastal regions, but extended uninterruptedly to as far north as Lake Chad.

By 1890, unlike the British and Germans, the French had no vested interests in northern Cameroon, either through the discoveries of French explorers and traders or through diplomatic settlements. Indeed, the frontier Agreement of 1885 between France and Germany[47] excluded any French action west of 15° East longitude and the Anglo-French Convention of 5 August, 1890[48] shut-off the French from the kingdoms of Borno, Kotoko and Mandara, and from the lamidates of northern Cameroon. But in 1890 the French were interested in the upper Benue and Chad regions because of an ambitious colonial project to unite France's already existing colonies in the Congo with those in West and North Africa. This would be achieved, it was hoped, by constructing an extensive trans-African railway system. The Chad region was looked upon as an important junction for the railway network. For this reason its colonisation by France was imperative. In order to underline the seriousness of the French colonial strategists, in the year 1890 alone, three separate missions, led by experienced African explorers, Crampel, Monteil and Mizon, left France with the aim of converging on Lake Chad through the Congo, the Western Sudan and the Niger-Benue respectively.

Of these three missions, that of Mizon had the greatest political repercussions in northern Cameroon. In the summer of 1892 it turned Yola, the political and spiritual capital of the lamidates, into a stage for serious competition involving British, French and German delegations which wished to sign a political treaty with Lamido Zubeiru. The uncompromising attitude of Zubeiru to the European requests also added political dynamite to an already charged situation. At first Zubeiru made up his mind not to grant concessions to any European power, justifying his action on the religious dogma that between Muslims and heathens there is no compromise.[49] But later he showed willingness to ally himself only with the power that would give him military aid in order to solve the internal problems of his regime. These problems included the divisive activities of Hayatu's Mahdism in the Balda-Bogo-Marua region and the manoeouvres of the Sandites, his political opponents, who sought a suitable opportunity to replace Zubeiru by Sanda's son, malam Iya. What frightened the Europeans the most was that, because of Zubeiru's strong personality and command over the lamidates, whoever signed a treaty with him would gain his support to drive away rival powers from the entire northern Cameroon region, including Yola and its vicinities. Mizon, the French representative, showed willingness to support Zubeiru militarily. He assured Zubeiru he would furnish him with arms and train an army for him, officered by Frenchmen, to make it possible for him to dominate the neighbouring peoples and stabilise his regime internally.

> ... *au Sultan Zoubir, j'expliqais l'importance qu'il y avait pour un souverain, à posseder une garde armée et exercée à l'européenne, et que dans toutes les guerres, qui donnerait la supériorité sur ses voisins, les mettrait au-dessus de ses grands vassaux et, chose qu'il comprenait trés bien, les mettrait à l'abri des revolutions de palais.*[50]

Furthermore, since his arrival, Mizon and his Arab companions from north Africa had remained close to the Arab merchants. Mizon promised them that he would divert north Cameroon trade to Borno and across the Sahara desert to north Africa in such a way that the Arab merchants would be the greatest beneficiaries. On its part, the Royal Niger Company refused to support Zubeiru militarily, preferring to stick to its man, malam Iya, or alternatively to interest Fadel-Allah, Rabeh's son, in becoming ruler at Yola. The German delegation, led by Uechtritz, was in total despair. It neither had the means to satisfy Zubeiru nor even to win indigenous supporters to its cause. In these circumstances, Zubeiru started favouring the French and even signed a treaty of mutual assistance with Mizon.[51]

The British were furious and chagrined by Mizon's apparent successes. They decided to topple Zubeiru's government, but since the Royal Niger Company was not sure it had enough means to do so, and what the long term effects would be, it decided to negotiate with the Germans through European diplomatic channels, firstly to expel the French from Yola and secondly to partition the Adamawa Emirate between Nigeria and Cameroon. Indeed the German Colonial Society, led by its President Vohsen, made the first diplomatic move.

The Society was afraid that in case of war against the Fulbe rulers, the German government was not ready to provide troops to fight for German interests. Under Chancellor von Caprivi German colonial policy was quietist, trusting more to negotiations than relying on direct confrontations with rival colonial powers. Consequently, both the British and Germans developed common strategies and combined their efforts. Their foreign ministries put pressure on the French government to recall Mizon who in the dry season of 1893 had proclaimed 'the French Protectorate of Central Sudan' which included the states of Baghirmi, Wadai and the Emirate of Adamawa, and set up an administration at Koana with himself as supreme commander.[52] In France, the investors in the Mizon mission were worried about the losses they would incur should the Mizon mission be involved in a war in a region where his enemies had more fighting power. In these circumstances, the French Minister of Foreign Affairs, M. Deville, decided to recall Mizon in order to avoid what he described as *'les graves incidents que faisaient prévoir les menaces violentes de la compagnie anglaise et pour discuter ses revendications'*.[53]

The Anglo-German negotiations, which officially began in July 1893 for the purpose of demarcating British and German spheres, ended in November 1893 with an Agreement which made Yola and one-quarter of the Emirate a part of Nigeria and the remaining three-quarters a part of German northern Cameroon. The French government protested vehemently against the Treaty, and demanded its suspension because, by it, Germany recognised the existence of British interest to the south and west of Lake Chad, areas over which France claimed she had treaties which Monteil had made with the Mai of Borno. Moreover, it was felt that in such negotiations where more than the interests of Britain and Germany were involved, it was essential to have included France in the negotiations. Both the German and French governments wanted to settle the northern Cameroon question quickly in view of pending general elections in their respective countries. By 1894 agreement was reached between France and Germany over the eastern frontiers of northern Cameroon. In return, France was allowed the possession of Bifara, an important ivory town at the head of the navigable portion of the river Kebbi (the so-called duck's beak on the Logone river), and also a part of the southern shores of Lake Chad.[54]

Though the treaties were exclusively of European making, they constituted both the legal and moral framework for the subsequent intervention of European powers in the politics of the region. Thus, for example, in 1900 the British government bought out the interests of the Royal Niger Company and set up an army to impose colonial rule over the Sokoto Caliphate. Yola fell under the artillery of Colonel Morland in 1901. Lamido Zubeiru was forced to take refuge among the lamidates of northern Cameroon in Beka, Chebowa, Garua, and Marua. Colonel Morland's victory affected not only the government in Yola, but also dealt a death-blow to the entire Fulbe organisation in the region. It unseated the central authority which had the political and moral power to organise the lamidates to resist collectively both the British and Germans. It left the Lambbe confused and powerless, particularly when the news reached them that even the Sokoto administration had capitulated to the rule of the Europeans.

The Germans were quick to cash in on the general confusion which the fall of Yola had created in the lamidates. They organised two series of invasions as a prelude to the establishment of German administration among the communities of northern Cameroon. In 1899 von Kamptz led a ferocious military expedition which reduced the southern lamidates to German rule after looting and much destruction to life and property. The second expedition was led by 'Kommandant' Dominik who waged wars against Mandara and the important lamidates of Garua and Marua between 1901 and 1903. As a consequence of these German victories over the Muslim rulers, the Germans set up military and administrative posts at Dikowa, Kousseri, Mora, Marua, Garua, Ngaoundéré, Tibati and Banyo. These stations were instructed to facilitate trade and to recruit labourers for various German enterprises. Above all, they were to bring German authority, won first by diplomacy and then by war, closer to the Muslim rulers.

Thus at the end of the period under review, Muslim Fulbe and then European influences were plainly visible in the economic and political spheres. Economically, markets multiplied themselves. More people than ever were involved in pastoral and agricultural production for both the subsistence and external markets. Large-scale production was organised in *rumde* and in the extended family set-up. The Hausa handled most of the external trade, the volume of which considerably increased with the advent of Europeans on the rivers Niger and Benue during the last two decades of the nineteenth century. Little happened either to reduce or abolish slavery as a social system, but the slave trade was abolished as a form of business. Politically, the rule of the Fulbe did not immediately suffer since the Europeans were too few to make an effective presence all over the territory, and since it was in the interest of the Europeans to support existing Fulbe administrative machinery to maintain law and order and collect taxes. Even after the German conquest, it took more than two decades before European rule began to be felt directly by the population as a whole. One thing was certain however, that European conquest brought the *jihad* to an end and started a new process in which both Muslims and non-Muslims would be called upon to adjust their ways of life to the exigencies of modernisation.

Notes

1   This point was evident in the essays presented at the C.N.R.S. colloquium held in Paris in September 1973. See C. Tadits, (ed.) *Contribution de la recherche ethnologique à l'histoire des civilisations du Cameroun*, CNRS, Paris, 1981, Vol. 1, pp. 101–273.

2   'Fombina' is a Fulfulde word which means 'South'. The word was probably used by the Borno Fulbe before the nineteenth century to designate the territories south of Borno, part of which became northern Cameroon during the colonial days. For more on this term and its use, see Saad Abubakar, *The Emirate of Fombina, 1809–1903*, Zaria, 1977; A.H. Kirk-Greene, *Adamawa Past and Present: an historical approach to the development of a northern Cameroon Province*, London, 1958, p. 15.

3   There are many scholarly works which have studied the Fulbe of the region. See for example, D.J. Stenning, *Savannah Nomads*, London, 1959; C.E. Hopen, *The Pastoral Fulbe Family in Gwandu*, London, 1958; and M. Dupire, *Peuls nomades: les Wodaabe du Sahel Nigerien*, Paris, 1962.

4   M.Z. Njeuma, 'Uthman dan Fodio and the Origins of Fulani Jihad in Cameroon Hinterland, 1809–47', *AFRIKA ZAMANI, revue d'histoire Africaine*, no. 3, 1974. It analyses a document (Uthman dan Fodio to Adama, March 5, 1809) entitled 'Memorandum on the *jihad* in Adamawa', translated from Hausa to English by Professor D.W. Arnott.

5   *Ibid.*, p. 51

6   L. Brenner, *The Shehus of Kukawa: A History of the Al-Kanemi Dynasty of Bornu*, Oxford, 1973, pp. 25–33.

7   M. Last, *The Sokoto Caliphate*, Ibadan, 1967, p. 58; Brenner, p. 28. For the English translation of the official correspondence on the Borno criticism of the *jihad*, see J.C. Arnett, *The Rise of the Sokoto Fulani*, Kano, 1922, p. 100ff.

8   This argument which is contrary to one expressed by E. Mohamadou 'Histoire des lamidates Foulbé de Tchamba et Tibati', *Abbia*, 6, (1964) and Sa'ad Abubakar (1977) has been developed in M.Z. Njeuma, *Fulani Hegemony in Yola (Old Adamawa) 1809–1902*, Yaoundé, 1978, pp. 12–14, 'the relation between the Fulani and non-Fulani differed from one locality to the other; it seems that the Fulani were free, whenever they wished, to leave the territory of a chief they did not like'.

9   'Lamidate' has been coined from the *Fulfulde* word 'lama' meaning 'to rule', Lamido or Lamdo means 'ruler' and consequently Lamidate is a territory ruled by a Lamdo. The title Lamido was reserved for the Emir of Yola, while the rulers of the sub-emirates bore the title Lamdo (pl. Lambbe). For a more detailed explanation of the word see Njeuma (1978) pp. 68–70.

10   Njeuma, 1974, Uthman to Adama: 'Memorandum on the *jihad* in Adamawa'.

11   E. Mohamadou, *Le Royaume du Wandala ou Mandara au XIXe Siécle*, Bamenda, 1975; Rodinson and J.P. Lebeuf, 'L'origine et les Souverains du Mandara', *BIFAN*, XVIII, 1956, pp. 227–255.

12   This opinion perhaps reflects only a weakness in the sources because it is highly improbable that if indeed Adama had criticised Mandara Islam, this fact would have been completely ignored by the Fulbe chroniclers (see R.M. East, *Stories of Old Adamawa*, Zaria, 1936, pp. 19–25) when this would have provided the only real legal basis for Adama's attack on the Muslims of Mandara. See A.D.H. Bivar, 'The Wathiqat ahlal-sudan: A Manifesto of the Fulani Jihad', *Journal of African History*, 1961, pp. 240–41, where Uthman gives eight instances when *jihad* is considered legal by consensus; see particularly, XIV-XVI; M. Khadduri, *The Law of War and Peace in Islam*, London, 1940, pp. 36–37, for an even stricter view which makes *jihad* a duty only when the enemies of Islam are the aggressors.

13   Njeuma, 1978, pp. 30–31.

14   At Rai and Ngaoundéré horse owners estimated that the cost of buying equipment (saddle, bridle, protective charms, face and leg covers, etc.) was sometimes more than what one paid for the animal. For examples of horses in their full war apparel see H. Labouret, 'Les sultans peuls de l'Adamaoua', *Togo Cameroon*, Paris, 1935, pp. 88–93 (mainly pictorial).

15   G.N. Barclay, 'History of Yola Province', 1906, (JJ. encl. 3, National Archives, Kaduna); Kirk-Greene, *Adamawa Past and Present*, 1958, p. 15. It was probably on the basis of people raided by the Fulbe that E. Mohamadou in *L'Histoire des Peuls Ferobe du Diamare Maroua et Pette*, Yaoundé 1970, pp. 29, 477 describes the territorial limits as extending from 'Mandara and Kotoko in the North to the Sanaga in the South; from the frontier of Borno in the West to that of Baghirmi in the East'.

16   No single explanation can cover all the complexities of the subject. This must await more comprehensive studies on the peoples immediately bordering on the Fulbe lamidates so that the non-Fulbe perspective should also prevail. Already studies by C. Tardits, *Le Royaume Bamun*, Paris, 1980; P. Burnham, *Opportunity and Constraint in a Savannah Society: the Gbaya of Meiganga, Cameroon*, London, 1980; and N. Awasom, 'The Hausa and Fulani in the Bamenda Grasslands, 1903–1960', Doctorat de 3e cycle thesis (History), Yaoundé, 1985, are providing new insights into Fulbe failures beyond the stereotype explanations based on unsuitable climatic and ecological conditions for Fulbe cattle as one leaves the savannah region.

17   East, p. 19.

18   *Ibid.*, p. 23.

19   P.F. Lacroix, 'Materiaux pour servir à l'histoire des Peuls de l'Adamaoua', *Etudes Camerounaises*, no. 37/38, 1952, p. 30. For more examples of rivalry among the Fulbe leaders see East, pp. 51–58; Strumpell, pp. 52–53.

20   P.F. Lacroix, 'L'Islam Peul de l'Adamawa', in I.M. Lewis, (ed.) *Islam in Tropical Africa*, London, 1966, pp. 402–403.

21   Several allusions have already been made to the relations between Yola and the lamidates of northern Cameroon. For more in-depth studies see Njeuma (1978), pp. 98ff. Yola seldom interfered in the internal affairs of the lamidates unless invited to do so. Each lamidate had its own electoral college which was solely responsible for selecting its governor. Whoever was selected went to Yola to be ceremonially turbaned and confirmed in his position. For the relation between

Yola and Sokoto see also M.Z. Njeuma, 'Sokoto and her Provinces: some reflections on the case of Adamawa', in Y.B. Usman, (ed.). *Studies in the History of the Sokoto Caliphate (the Sokoto Seminar Papers)*, A.B.U. Zaria, 1979, pp. 320—335.

22   Uthman to Adama: 'Memorandum on the *Jihad* in Adamawa'.

23   See footnote 9, *supra*.

24   Sa'ad Abubakar, 1977, and M.Z. Njeuma, 'The Foundations of Pre-European Administration in Adamawa: Historical considerations', *Journal of the Historical Society of Nigeria*, Vol. VII, no. 1, 1973, provides detailed descriptions of the systems with some attempts at comparison.

25   M. Hiskett, 'Kitab al-Farq: A work on the Habe Kingdoms attributed to Uthman dan Fodio', *Bulletin of the School of Oriental and African Studies* (S.O.A.S.), XXIII, 1960, p. 570.

26   'Machube' is the *Fulfulde* word for slaves. The notion of slave here is different from the conception of slaves in a European context. Their functions varied considerably from one lamidate to the other; but often they featured prominently in public administration and their status had nothing to do with civil liberties. For most of the time the 'slaves' were distinguished by the simple form of dressing and lack of headgear. The Fulbe councillors relied on the Lambbe to curb any excessive influence of the 'slaves' in public affairs. For details on the situation in Ngaoundéré, see, J.C. Froélich, 'Le Commandement et L'Organisation Sociale Chez les Foulbe de l'Adamawa', *Etudes Camerounaises*, 1954, pp. 5—91. D. Abwa, 'Le Lamidate de Nagoundéré, 1915—1945', thesis for the Master's Degree, University of Yaoundé, 1980.

27   Njeuma, 1978, pp. 102—104. I owe much of the information on the judiciary from Ahmadu Marafa, Yola (1966). From the records, the most frequent cases were robbery and failure to repay debts. See S. Passarge, *Adamawa*, Berlin, 1895, pp. 165, 305—06.

28   H. Barth, *Travels and Discoveries in North and Central Africa, 1849—55*, London, 1857—58, vol. 11, p. 478.

29   *Ibid.*, p. 478. Mockler-Ferryman who also visited the region in the late 1880s made several remarks on the *rumde* system. See for example A.F. Mockler-Ferryman, *Up the Niger*, London, 1892, p.52, where he observed that the *rumde* 'bred indolence among the Fulani ruling class as they left everything to their head slaves in order that they themselves may live at ease'.

30   Njeuma, 1978, pp. 141ff; Sa'ad Abubakar, 'A Survey of the Economy of the Eastern Emirates of the Sokoto Caliphate in the 19th century', in Y.B. Usuman (ed.) *Studies in the History of the Sokoto Caliphate* (*The Sokoto Seminar Papers*) A.B.U., Zaria, 1979, pp. 105—24.

31   See Passarge, 1895, p. 300: Hausa established bases for the ivory trade on the Kontcha-Faro axis; E. Zintgraff, *Nord Kamerun*, Berlin, 1895, p. 256 makes the same point but uses the town of Ngilla, south of Tibati, as his example. The role of the Hausa in general, and the traders in particular, in the lamidates requires closer attention by scholars. The European sources since Barth (1851) contain many scattered references. Two contemporary sources by local Hausa traders are: (a) E.R. Flegel, *Löse Blätter aus dem Tagebuche meiner Hausa Freunde und Reisegefahrten*, Hamburg, 1885. The authors, Madugu Mai Gassin Baki and Madugu Dan Tambari, were professional caravan guides; (b) Abdullah al-Kanawi, *Nubdha Min Dhikr Awsaf al-Bilal Adamawa*, I.A.S. acc. no. AR/128, Institute of African Studies, University of Ghana. It is a 14-page document and was obtained from the library of al-Hajj Umar ibn Abubakar of Kete Krakye,

Ghana. From internal evidence it was likely to have been written in 1917 when Njoya re-established Islam at Fumban.

32 Interviews (1966) with Hausa men in Yola, Garua, Ngaoundéré. They explained that before the *jihad* no one 'invited' them to the region.

33 F.M. Ruxton, *Maliki Law*, London, 1916, pp. 73—74, lists various obligatory taxes. See also H.A. Gibb and H. Bowen, *Islamic Society and the West*, Oxford, 1957, Vol. 1, part 11, pp. 17ff., make the distinction that *zakat* and *jizya* were standard impositions. Informants in the various lamidates insisted on the non-compulsory nature of tribute.

34 Barth, 11, p. 478.

35 The construction of the *sare* took into account the polygamous nature of the households and the Muslim custom of keeping women in seclusion (*purdah*).

36 The principal purpose of these gatherings, besides occasional attendance on specific business, was to keep abreast with news in and outside the lamidate. Another feature of the culture which required frequent meetings was exchanging greetings. Greetings are exchanged every morning and evening and this is a social obligation (see Barth, 11, pp. 425—26, 'The Fulbe of Adamawa are especially rich in compliments, which, however, have not yet lost their real and true meaning .... They vary greatly from that usual in other countries occupied by the Fulbe, and, of course, all depends on the time of the day when friends meet.')

37 Njeuma, 1978, p. 120.

38 Barth, 11, p. 449.

39 Adama prof, GOK, Box 2, no. 94 Bello to Adama (National Archives, Kaduna).

40 See Barth, 11, pp. 287, 283, 'they endeavour to obtain from them (Lambbe) all they can by begging and by the parading of learning'.

41 This was probably due to the fact that divination and foretelling the future were most prevalent among the Tijanis. See D.M. Last, *The Sokoto Caliphate*, Ibadan, 1967, pp. 215ff, for the case against a Tijaniya affiliation for the rulers of the Sokoto caliphate.

42 C. Vicars-Boyle, 'Notes on Yola Fulani', *Journal of the African Society*, X, 1910—11, p. 86.

43 Njeuma, 1978, pp. 136ff.

44 *Ibid.*, pp. 182ff.

45 Contemporary reports and correspondence on the activities of the Niger Company are found in the Public Record Office (PRO) Archives, London, in the FO84 series, 'Slave Trade Papers (Domestic Various, France, Germany).' See J.E. Flint, *Sir George Goldie and the Making of Nigeria*, London, 1960.

46 E. Hertslet, *The Map of Africa by Treaties*, 3rd ed., London, 1909, vol. 1, pp. 129—30. According to the wording of the 1885 treaty, the Sultan of Sokoto granted and transferred to the National African Company or others with whom they may arrange, 'the entire rights to the country on both sides of the River Benue and rivers flowing into it throughout my dominions for such distance from its and their banks as they may desire'.

47 Hertslet, *Map of Africa*, Vol. 11, pp. 635—56.

48 *Ibid.*, pp. 738—39.

49 Vicars-Boyle, 1910, p. 87. See also Kirk-Greene, 1958, p. 143. 'Zubeiru was a fine type of the Fulani ruler, well educated but possessed with a religious fanaticism which rendered him extremely intolerant of European infidels'.

50 L. Mizon, *Une Question Africaine*, Paris, 1895, p. 34.

51   Efforts to locate the Treaty have been in vain. Both Company and French
     sources however agree that Mizon signed a treaty with Zubeiru. See e.g., the
     arbitration verdict of Baron Lambermont on the Mizon affair reproduced in
     Njeuma, 1978, pp. 254–61; Flint, p. 179; R.A. Adeleye, *Power and diplomacy
     in Northern Nigeria, 1804–1906: the Sokoto Caliphate and its enemies*, London,
     1971, p. 146.
52   Mizon, *Une Question Africaine*, pp. 39–46.
53   Afrique III, 17, Dévélle to Mizon 28.6.93 (Archives d' Oûtremer, Paris). Another
     telegram (Delcassé to Mizon 4.7.93) which apparently did not reach Mizon,
     explained that he had been recalled because of his intervention in Muri.
54   Hertslet, *Map of Africa*, Vol. II, pp. 657–58.

Chapter Two

Trade and diplomacy on the Cameroon coast in the nineteenth century, 1833–1879: the case of Bimbia

Lovett Z. Elango

Introduction

As early as the eighteenth century, perhaps earlier,[1] the Isuwu chieftaincy of Bimbia was known to Europeans as a minor trading centre on the Guinea Coast of West Africa. Located on the western spur of Mount Cameroon, otherwise known as Bimbia promontory, Bimbia developed from these humble beginnings to become one of two[2] mercantile hegemonies which, in the nineteenth century, dominated the Cameroon coast, that is the region between Rio del Rey in the northwest and Campo to the southeast. At the height of its power Bimbia comprised three villages – Dikolo, Wonyangomba, and Wonyabile. The latter, better known to whitemen as Williamstown, was the most important of the three. These villages were basically autonomous sublineages, each ruled by a merchant prince who was the head of the sublineage. The three villages however co-operated in war and peace as their rulers deemed necessary. To these three villages, which may conveniently be called Central Bimbia, must be added what may be called 'Greater Bimbia', territories to the northwest and in the hinterland, which formed Bimbia's sphere of influence and which she variously dominated or tried to dominate.

Bimbia's ruler in the first half of the nineteenth century was Bile, of Williamstown, known to Englishmen as King William. Under William, Bimbia became a centralised state. Although he had some traditional claim to the Bimbia kingship, in the nineteenth century William was essentially the *primus inter pares* of Bimbia's ruling mercantile élite whose co-operation, competition, and conflicts dominated the internal politics of the state. He owed this primacy to his popularity with Europeans, especially the British. When Britain formally abolished the slave trade early in the nineteenth century and began her efforts to establish trade in commodities other than slaves, the principal task which faced William and his colleagues was the abolition of what remained of the slave trade within their domains and the development of legitimate commerce – trade in palm oil, palm kernels, ivory, and rubber, to name only the most important.

This difficult economic adjustment, sometimes brief, sometimes prolonged, was not peculiar to Bimbia: its social and political consequences were common to virtually all West African coastal societies, and had an enormous and fateful impact on their internal affairs and external relations. Like many of these coastal states, Bimbia undertook this adjustment with the encouragement of, and under considerable pressure from, Britain, then the leading European power on the Cameroon coast. The new Anglo-Bimbian commercial partnership which developed out of this effort was increasingly buttressed by Anglo-Bimbian diplomatic relations. Those relations passed through two overlapping phases: a preconsular phase which lasted from 1833 to 1850, and a consular phase which lasted from 1850 to 1878. The preconsular phase was marked by the attempts of British naval officers and other agents to establish formal diplomatic relations with Bimbia. Although these attempts were largely abortive, we shall argue that the resulting contacts were crucial for the prestige, power and influence of Bimbia's nascent monarchy. The consular phase, on the other hand, was characterised by increasing consular intervention in Bimbian internal affairs, and this study attempts to show how William tried to exploit British diplomatic support to achieve his personal ambitions.

Britain's formal abolition of the slave trade on 1 January 1807, necessitated practical steps to destroy what remained of the traffic. The anti-slavery squadron of the Royal Navy accordingly became the main instrument for achieving this goal.[3] To ensure its effectiveness, the British government acquired the island of Fernando Po from the Spanish government as a base for the squadron. Aside from its location close to the centre of legitimate trade in the Niger Delta, the island was chosen because it was in the centre of what was then considered the most active slave trading area in West Africa,[4] and because it was generally regarded as the healthiest spot on the Guinea coast. Naval officers could therefore retire to the island to recuperate from the fevers and other associated medical problems which gave West Africa a reputation as the whiteman's grave in the nineteenth century.[5] As is well known, many officers died from these fevers or had to be invalided from the service of the squadron because of these medical problems.[6]

Nevertheless, for much of the period between 1833 and 1850, the officers of the squadron, particularly those based on Fernando Po, were the only official link between Britain and Bimbia and her Guinea coast neighbours. They were, however, essentially 'birds of passage' − to use Dike's phrase − and their knowledge of African realities, though better than that of their countrymen at large, was often based on information given to them by Liverpool and other English supercargoes resident in the Oil Rivers,[7] and was therefore often distorted by the commercial interests and contacts of the traders. From Fernando Po the squadron patrolled the high seas and coastal waters in search of slavers. Captured vessels and their cargoes were usually taken to Freetown, Sierra Leone, where the Court of Mixed Commissions had been established, to try the crews of captured slavers.

In 1827 a settlement for liberated slaves was founded by the British government at Fernando Po and named Clarence. Clarence was to have ultimately replaced Freetown as the seat of the Mixed Commissions Court, and as the centre of British authority in West Africa. Perhaps because of the propaganda of persons who did not want the court transferred from Freetown to Fernando Po[8], by 1830 the island had lost its reputation as the healthiest place in West Africa.[9] Even so, however, it remained the most convenient place from the point of view of naval patrols in search of slavers or in defence of British legitimate trade. Not surprisingly, when it was rumoured in 1832 that Spain would cede the island to England for £100000 sterling, Colonel Edward Nicolls, Governor of Clarence, urged the British government to pay the sum and acquire it.[10] But the opposition of the African Institution and the humanitarians forced the government to abandon the scheme.[11] It is against this background that Nicolls' subsequent attempts to formalise Anglo-Bimbian relations must be examined.

Frustrated and disappointed, Nicolls stubbornly remained at Fernando Po in 1833 despite instructions that he abandon the settlement.[12] In the interim, he concluded a treaty with Bile at Williamstown. The terms of the treaty were as follows:

Know all men by these presents, that I, Belley, sovereign Prince of Bimbia in Western Africa, do hereby voluntarily make over to his Majesty King William the 4th of Great Britain and Ireland, the sovereignty of my country, reserving to myself all of my property at present held by me in the said principality, and I do herein swear allegiance to King William the 4th as his subject, in return for which I am to receive all the protection and care due to a British subject, and have leave to hoist the British colours.[13]

Bile's 'principality' over which Nicolls' protectorate was proclaimed by the terms of this treaty included all the coastal territory between Bimbia and Rio del Rey[14], but its inland boundary was undefined.

This treaty was the first attempt to establish formal Anglo-Bimbian diplomatic relations. Its wording was most certainly European, but it was clearly mutually advantageous in spirit and in letter. From Bile's point of view it achieved two things. First, in return for the voluntary cession of his principality, Bile was formally invested with the title of 'King' of Bimbia. Henceforth, he became King William of Bimbia to the Europeans and to his people, even if only by the grace of King William IV of Great Britain. This was probably uppermost in his mind, for his accession to the chiefship had not been entirely regular. His recognition as King by a European power therefore gave whatever legitimacy he lacked or thought he lacked. At the same time, it enhanced his primacy in Bimbian affairs. In his new role, he claimed the sovereignty not only of Central Bimbia, but also of the coastal littoral between Bimbia and Rio del Rey, territories which his predecessors presumably once claimed. In 1862 Consul Burton[15] described these territories as Bimbia's 'dependencies', thus confirming the terms of Nicolls' treaty. Second, King William and his people became British subjects and were therefore entitled to British protection.

In pursuing these two goals, one personal and one political, King William was carrying one step further a tradition of European involvement, direct or indirect, in Bimbian internal affairs. This European involvement was an important factor and was partly responsible for the elevation of Bile from the status of a mere chief to that of a monarch. One result of this development was the beginning of a trend which cast the monarchy in the role of a centralising institution within the Bimbian political system. Bile did not thereby abandon the traditional basis of his power. Indeed, his acknowledgement of *Jengu* as the equivalent of God, and his participation in a *Jengu* ceremony in 1845,[16] clearly evidenced his sensitivity to the importance of these traditions.

By the same token, however, he was very proud of his standing with Englishmen, and was anxious not only to retain their esteem, but particularly to please English agents. In 1840, for example, Allen reported that the King 'prided himself on his connection with whitemen, and of the many good things he possessed from their country.'[17] William was particularly proud of a portrait of Queen

Victoria which John Clarke presented to him in 1845, and even turned it to some financial profit. When Bakweri from the interior visited him, he habitually showed it to them and made them pay him the value of two yards of cloth in palm oil or palm nuts.[18] Because of this pride in his English connection, and because he was anxious to strengthen that connection, William and fifty of his men visited Governor Lynslager at Fernando Po in 1845 to protest against his threat to nominate another King for Bimbia.[19] This was clear evidence that King William recognised his dependence on English support for the retention of his status in Bimbia.

The treaty of 1833 may in fact have been Nicolls' idea in the first place, and from his point of view it had several practical advantages. To Nicolls the acquisition of Bimbian territory promised to solve the problem of a new naval base, a problem which became more urgent as the reputation of Fernando Po declined. Even more critical was the problem of transporting liberated slaves from the Niger Delta and other points further south to Freetown. In 1833, for example, he reported to the Colonial Office that 78 out of 278 liberated slaves had died en route while being transported to Sierra Leone from the Niger Delta.[20] In the same dispatch he announced King William's voluntary cession of his territory which he recommended as a site for a settlement for liberated slaves. He argued that the death of liberated slaves en route to Freetown was a common occurrence and that casualties could be reduced if the slaves could be landed at Fernando Po or a 'convenient settlement on the opposite coast such as Amboises Bay or Bimbia'. The establishment of such a settlement, he concluded, would soon give rise to a 'flourishing colony that would amply repay the money laid out'.[21]

In broaching the subject of King William's cession of his territory, Nicolls was careful to emphasise that it had been 'voluntary on the part of the chief neither asked or hinted at by me or anyone from me'. He also pointed out that he had accepted the cession provisionally while awaiting 'the pleasure of His Majesty' on the transaction.[22] Despite his caution, there can be little doubt that Nicolls wanted the transaction ratified. Indeed, there is little doubt that he expected it to be ratified. As Dike has pointed out with regard to Nicolls' motives:

> At the back of Nicolls' mind no doubt lurked the thought that the government who refused to pay one hundred thousand pounds (sterling) for the purchase of the island of Fernando Po would not object to a free grant of land on the Delta coast [23] . . .

As indicated earlier, the idea of a treaty with Bimbia might have originated with Nicolls, for as Dike has pointed out, he had a 'passion for treaty-making'.[24] This passion stemmed from his belief that the most effective way of exterminating the slave trade was not the suppression movement led by the Navy, but the negotiation of alliances with the Delta and other states which through treaty obligations, would become Britain's partners in the suppression of the slave trade and the development of legitimate trade.[25] He clearly had this kind of alliance in mind when he invited King William and the Kings of Old Calabar, Cameroons, Malimba and Bonny to Fernando Po to discuss the formation of a grand alliance against pirates and slavers on the Guinea coast.[26] Knowing the reluctance of the British government, he again emphasised that the scheme involved no expense to the government, that he had merely appealed to the 'good sense and experience' of the chiefs, and that he had taken care 'in no wise to commit any interests of our own'.[27]

So far as the establishment of a settlement on Bimbian territory was concerned, Nicolls was especially impressed by the suitability of the coast of Ambas Bay. To the Colonial Office he described its prospects thus:

> The harbour is more secure than the River Thames, capacious enough to contain 50 sail of the line and merchant vessels perfectly secured by a long point of land from tornadoes and quite open to the sea breeze which always blows moderate and fresh right into the Bay. In short, it has every good quality that this place has, except the whole of it may not be an island...[28]

Nicolls' ideas and schemes complemented the ambitions of African rulers like King William, but his persuasive arguments failed to win a reluctant British government. Only in 1838 did the British government become convinced of the soundness of his idea of treaty alliances with African chiefs as an effective means of suppressing the slave trade.[29] There seems to be no record of the British government's response to Nicolls' treaty with Bile and Nicolls' protectorate, but there can be no doubt that had a response been forthcoming, Nicolls would have been told, as Captain Close was told in 1864 when he tried to annex Ambas Bay and the Cameroons, 'to confine himself to the suppression of the slave trade and not attempt acquisition of colonies'.[30]

Nicolls' protectorate died a premature death, but it nevertheless had important short-and-long-term consequences for subsequent Anglo-Bimbian relations. In the short term, it had helped to focus attention on Bimbia, and especially on Ambas Bay, as a possible location for a settlement of one kind or another. Because of the somewhat temperate climate at the foot of Mount Cameroon, behind the coast of Ambas Bay, the area gained a reputation as the healthiest spot on the Guinea coast. It mattered little that this reputation was exaggerated and that, as Hutchinson later pointed out, Ambas Bay was only the least unhealthy spot in West Africa.[31] Its reputation as the healthiest place on the Guinea coast held fast. As late as 1862 Consul Burton lent his considerable reputation as a widely travelled explorer to this myth when he wrote that:

> There are few spots on the earth's surface where more grace and grandeur of beauty and sublimity, are found blended in one noble panorama than that at the equatorial approach on the West Coast of Africa. The voyager's eye, fatigued by the low flat melancholy shores of Benin and Upper Biafra, rests with inexhaustible delight upon a 'Gate' compared with which Bab-el-mandeb and the Pillars of Hercules are indeed tame.[32]

Like Nicolls, Burton was convinced of the suitability of Ambas Bay and the adjacent coast for a sanatorium,[33] but like Nicolls before him, his eloquent and distinguished testimony was unavailing.

In the long term, Nicolls' ideas proved even more enduring and beneficial for Bimbia. In the 1840s his ideas and schemes were revived and recast by leading humanitarians who, like him, desired the extinction of the slave trade and African slavery on which it fed. Thomas Fowell Buxton, the humanitarian leader upon whom the mantle of Wilberforce had fallen, called for the mobilisation of all 'civilising' forces at Britain's disposal for a final and decisive onslaught on the slave trade.[34] Under the leadership of Buxton and his colleagues, various schemes for the moral, material and spiritual regeneration of Africa were elaborated and canvassed. Among these was Buxton's own scheme for founding agricultural settlements along the banks of the Niger. In the last analysis, the scheme not only called for treaty relations with African chiefs, but also for territorial expansion in one form or another.[35] Buxton's and other schemes eventually culminated in the disastrous Niger Expedition of 1841,[36] sponsored by Buxton and his colleague. The expedition did not achieve its objectives, and the significance of its failure for the humanitarian movement and for subsequent Anglo-African relations have been fully discussed[37] and need not detain us here.

Despite the failure of the expedition of 1841, it had an important side effect. Once again it focused attention on the geographical, climatic and strategic merits of Ambas Bay as a suitable site for a

British settlement and sanatorium. Captain Allen, who was a member of the expedition, commented on these merits in the following terms:

> During our frequent visits to the Bay of Amboises we had ample reason to be satisfied with having selected it as our principal station while we were obliged to remain in this part for orders, as the continued health of the crews of *Wilberforce* and *Soudan* justified the opinion that had been formed of its comparative salubrity.[38]

This was good, if indirect, publicity for Bimbia too and this opinion endured for a long time. Among others, it was propagated by men like McGregor Laird who, like Nicolls and Burton, wanted a settlement and sanatorium built there.[39] In the meantime, Allen suggested that because of Bimbia'a growing importance as a trade centre, Anglo-Bimbian relations should be regularised. In a dispatch to Lord Stanley on 18 May 1842, he wrote:

> In a position so advantageous for commerce, it is very desirable that it should be on a better footing by the interference of our government by establishing some authority to enforce simple regulations as without throwing an impediment in the way of trade, might afford protection to the merchants against the extortion of the natives, and enable them to recover their just debts; while on the other hand, it should secure the natives against the arbitrary proceedings on the part of the whites by preventing the necessity of having recourse to them.[40]

Allen's call for the regularisation of Anglo-Bimbian relations in the interest of trade went unheeded, but the popularity which Bimbia evidently enjoyed as a result of the importunings of men like himself and McGregor Laird could not have been more welcome from the point of view of King William and the chiefs of Bimbia. For as Bimbia's trade during the pre-consular phase profited indirectly from Bimbia's proximity to the Niger Delta, so the prospects of formal Anglo-Bimbian diplomatic relations were improved by the abortive humanitarian schemes which led to the Niger expedition of 1841.

Another seven years were to elapse before formal Anglo-Bimbian diplomatic relations were established. But in the meantime, King William and the chiefs of Bimbia showed that they were alive to the significance of this growing British activity and interest in their territory. That they were anxious to turn this interest to their advantage is evident from the two treaties which they concluded with Britain during this period. The first treaty was the Anglo-Bimbian anti-slavery treaty of 1844. It was the first formal Anglo-Bimbian treaty, and it illustrated the extent to which Britain had been won over to Nicolls' view that treaty relations with African rulers were a better means of ending the slave trade than mere naval blockades. It was also a model for other treaties with African rulers,[41] as well as the first substantial step in the direction of a more forward looking British policy towards West Africa. In particular, the treaty sought to make Bimbia the instrument of British policy, and therefore essentially a client state, roughly three decades before that policy was formally adopted in 1870.[42]

The first article of the treaty accordingly proclaimed the formal abolition of the slave trade and committed King William and the chiefs of Bimbia to make laws to punish offenders who either exported slaves or helped their export.[43] The second article pledged the chiefs to forbid the residence of any European slave traders within the territory of Bimbia, or the erection of any buildings or structures for the purpose of slave trading.[44] The third clause promised the chiefs an annual subsidy of twelve hundred dollars in British goods,[45] and was obviously an attempt to compensate them for the loss of revenues which they once derived from slave trading.

Articles IV and V were perhaps the most crucial clauses of the treaty for they foreshadowed the possibility of British involvement in Bimbia's internal affairs, despite the fact that the treaty recognised Bimbia as a sovereign state. Article IV provided that:

> If at any time it shall appear that the Slave Trade has been carried on through or from the territory of the chiefs of Bimbia, the Slave Trade may be put down by Great Britain by force upon that territory, the British officers may seize the boats of Bimbia found anywhere carrying on the Slave Trade, and the Chiefs of Bimbia will subject themselves to a severe act of displeasure on the part of the Queen of England.[46]

Article V further provided that:

> The subjects of the Queen of England may always trade freely with the people of Bimbia in any article they may wish to buy and sell, in all the places and ports within the territories of the Chiefs of Bimbia and throughout the whole of their dominions; and the Chiefs of Bimbia pledge themselves to show favour and to give no privilege to the ships and traders of other countries which they do not show to those of England.[47]

The initiative for this and other slaves' treaties belonged to Britain, but from the Bimbian point of view were as mutually advantageous as the Nicolls' treaty. True, unlike Nicolls' treaty, the other Bimbian chiefs were signatories of the treaty. While it did not say so, it in fact ratified King William's status. In principle, it recognised Bimbia as a 'civilised' African state and, formally at least, Britain's trade partner. By the same token, Bimbia became Britain's ideological partner in the cause of anti-slavery. From an economic point of view it was of considerable importance too since it granted them subsidies. But it was the British trade which it assured Bimbia which perhaps constituted its greatest achievement from the Bimbian point of view, for it was a culmination of their efforts to attract English traders and trade to Bimbia.

As if they had not done enough by gambling away their sovereignty, the chiefs of Bimbia concluded another treaty with Britain in 1848 by which they promised to abolish all Bimbian 'superstitions'. Signed on 31 March, 1848 at Williamstown, the agreement read:

> I, King William, and the chiefs of Bimbia, do solemnly promise to do away with the abominable, inhuman, and unchristian-like custom of sacrificing human lives on account of the death of any of their chiefs, or on account of any of their superstitious practices.[48]

The conclusion of the treaty coincided with the beginning of the campaign of mass evangelism launched by the Baptist missionaries. Missionary influence cannot, therefore, be ruled out either in its conception or in its wording. Unlike the anti-slavery treaty, this one seems to have been directed mainly at the chiefs. As the treaty suggests, it was the custom for slaves to be sacrificed at the deaths of Bimbian chiefs. From the point of view of the chiefs, therefore, this seems to have been one more concession which they were willing to make in order to ingratiate themselves with Europeans. Together with the anti-slavery treaty, it indicated the lengths to which King William and his chiefs were willing to go in their efforts to win European approval of themselves as a civilised, ruling élite. Ultimately, directly or indirectly, it was also an indication of King William's willingness to abandon formally the traditional basis of his power in favour of European support, for the wording of the agreement, unlike that of the anti-slavery treaty, implied, if not recognised, his pre-eminence at Bimbia. It is of course entirely possible that this was an empty gesture on William's part. But it is equally possible that it was a hasty and short-sighted action whose fullest implications William only belatedly recognised.

True, as we pointed out earlier, William did not totally ignore or minimise the traditional basis of his power, and as late as 1846 he still affirmed the importance of *Jengu* in Bimbian society and engaged in *Jengu* festivities and ritual. But he was equally cognisant of his need for, and dependence upon, European support and to this end he was willing, formally at least, to pledge himself to work for the abolition of traditional usages. These were huge concessions to the spirit and demands of British secular and religious humanitarianism. Whether William understood their fullest implications any more than his successors understood their treaties with the Germans must, unfortunately, remain a matter of conjecture. In terms of Anglo-Bimbian relations, the only quid pro quo for such concessions was the unspoken assurance of increased Anglo-Bimbian trade, and the resulting Bimbian prosperity. This prosperity was ultimately shared, to one degree or another, by all Bimbians. Nevertheless, it seems to have been largely synonymous with the prosperity of the ruling élite. This was the crux of William's policy, a policy which can best be described as monarchical. It was on such a policy that he staked his and the nascent monarchy's prestige and success. How wise − or unwise − this policy was in the long run will, hopefully, become clear in subsequent discussion.

In 1849, partly in response to the cogent arguments of men like Allen, and partly because of the growing British commercial interest and activity in West Africa, the Foreign Office appointed John Beecroft to be the first British Consul for the Bights of Benin and Biafra. As Consul, he had jurisdiction over the territory between Cape St Paul in the west and Cape St John in the east. Bimbia fell within Beecroft's consular jurisdiction, whose headquarters were at Fernando Po. Henceforth, therefore, Bimbia and her Guinea coast neighbours became, from the point of view of British interests in, and relations with, West Africa, a single diplomatic sphere rather than isolated enclaves, and Anglo-Bimbian relations accordingly became an integral part of those relations. This was the beginning of a formal or consular phase of Anglo-Bimbian relations and, among other things, this phase witnessed the increasing involvement of British Consuls in Bimbian − and also African − internal affairs.

Significantly, Beecroft's appointment had been contemplated, but postponed, as early as 1844 at about the same time that the Anglo-Bimbian anti-slavery treaty was concluded. At any rate the consular system which his subsequent appointment inaugurated was an improvement on the pre-consular system which depended on the squadron and naval officers. Stilliard has succinctly stated this improvement thus:

> The Consular system was an improvement of the rise of the squadron as a protection of trade. The influence of the latter was exercised solely from the sea, whereas the consul was able to establish personal contacts with the natives of the different rivers by going on shore, while at the same time making use of the sea for purposes of communication.[49]

In the circumstances of the 1850s, the job obviously required the appointment of someone with more intimate knowledge of African realities than the naval officers seem to have possessed, and it is no accident that, with the notable exception of Consul Burton, all British West African Consuls of the time were appointed from among traders with long experience in West Africa.[50] Little wonder, then, that in his letter of appointment to Beecroft, Viscount Palmerston informed him that he has been chosen:

> ... in consideration of your personal knowledge of African affairs and the habits of the black, and because of the influence which you appear to have acquired over the native chiefs of the places to which your consular jurisdiction will extend.[51]

This knowledge and experience was crucial and, as we shall see, Beecroft had acquired his during a long, distinguished career as a trader, explorer and administrator in West Africa[52] (which, unfortunately, still awaits its biographer). Among other things, he rose to be the unsalaried Governor of Fernando Po,[53] and established a factory at Bimbia in 1832. As diplomats, Beecroft and his successors were the most immediate link between British commercial interest in West Africa and government action. Like Lord Palmerston, their original sponsor, they had wide ranging visions of British commercial interests and development in West Africa. Thus, although they were mostly traders, they represented the 'official' rather than the commercial mind.[54] Theoretically, their duties were limited to the promotion and protection of legitimate trade within the terms of Foreign Office dispatches, their own knowledge of local conditions, and their vaguely defined powers. In practice, the promotion and protection of trade involved more.[55] It certainly ultimately involved them in local politics to a degree not anticipated in their instructions. Their impact on Anglo-African relations cannot therefore be overestimated and has been aptly assessed by, among other authorities, Sir Alan Burns.[56] How well Beecroft was chosen for the job will become clear in subsequent discussion. But even before he formally assumed the duties of Consul, he had revealed his understanding of African realities and of what it required to promote and protect trade in the agreement abolishing Bimbian superstitions which he was largely instrumental in concluding.[57]

In trying to promote and protect trade, Beecroft and his successors often had to perform a number of associated functions which can be described as diplomatic, magisterial and arbitrative. In the last analysis these functions were interrelated, and so far as they became accepted aspects of consular duties, Beecroft helped to establish the precedents. It was only in 1852,[58] for example, that the Foreign Office formally acknowledged the practice of fining African and European traders as within the Consuls' competence. Even before he officially began his duties as Consul, Beecroft had already visited Bimbia twice: in 1846 to secure the ratification of the anti-slavery treaty of 1844, and in 1848 to conclude the agreement abolishing Bimbian superstitions. What actually transpired between him and the Bimbian chiefs on both occasions is, unfortunately, unknown. But there can be no doubt that he took these opportunities to remind them that these concessions were the price they had to pay if they wanted British trade and favour. This is precisely what he had implied in 1841 when William asked him why no big ships had visited Bimbia for several months.[59] In 1850 he visited Bimbia again in his capacity as Consul to pay William and his chiefs the second of five annual instalments of the 1200 dollar subsidy stipulated in the anti-slavery treaty.[60]

But his first test as a Consul came on 30 December 1850, when he paid a routine visit to Bimbia and was obliged to perform his magisterial and arbitrative functions simultaneously. His actions on this occasion illustrated Beecroft's 'official' cast of mind, his understanding of local customs, and therefore the aptness of his choice as Consul. He had been invited there to settle a dispute outstanding between Bimbians and British traders at Bimbia.[61] In his report to the Foreign Office, he told Palmerston that he and his party had been kept waiting by William for fifteen minutes after arrival. When William did finally appear, Beecroft read his commission to him 'to instil into his weak and disordered mind by whose authority I was acting'. He then informed William that 'we merely waited on him today to pay our respects' in the hope that he would see the necessity of returning our visit on board the *Jackal*.[62]

Beecroft was obviously anxious to establish proper protocol because this was his first official visit and he did not want William to treat him as the ordinary trader with whom he had traded previously. No doubt, he also wanted to impress William with the enormous power of his new ally the Queen of England and to remind him of how much he, William, was obliged to the Queen for his status in Bimbia. In this effort, Beecroft's attitude was nothing short of bullying. Not surprisingly, his reaction to William's refusal to visit him on board the *Jackal* was to tell him that 'I considered it a duty imperative upon him to visit the said vessel'. Initially, William seemed willing to do so, but after 'more mature reflection', begged to decline, stating that he had never before been on a Man O'War.[63] But Beecroft reminded him that he had previously been on board the steamer *Ethiope*, adding:

I then told him that it wasn't my desire to use any coercive measures to oblige him to do his duty and show that respect due to me as he had already acknowledged that I was one of the parties that had placed him on the seat and called me his father, I must acknowledge that it very ill became him to treat Her Majesty the Queen of England's representative with disrespect whose subject he professed to be.[64]

Clearly, what Beecroft had in mind in making this statement was not the terms of the anti-slavery treaty of 1844, but Nicolls' treaty of 1833. As indicated earlier, the British Government never ratified that treaty, despite William's voluntary cession of his territory. Beecroft's action was therefore both unfair and in clear violation of William's and Bimbia's sovereignty. But it was not the first time William had been bullied by an English official and reminded of his dependence on the Queen of England for his Kingship. Allen had done similarly in 1841 by reminding William that it was Nicolls who had made him King, and William had been forced to apologise.[65]

The confrontation with Beecroft did not end nearly as easily or pleasantly as the one with Allen. Among other things, Beecroft told William that he had become a 'childish and unfit' ruler, to which William weakly replied that he could not help it and that Beecroft was at 'liberty to do as I pleased with him'.[66] Considering further discussion futile, Beecroft broke off the interview. But William did try to make peace with Beecroft by sending him a gift of two 'Egbo' goats which the latter rejected.[67] The following morning William again refused to visit the *Jackal*. Beecroft accordingly fined him a bullock and two 'good Egbo goats', and summoned him to a conference with other Bimbia chiefs at the home of the agent of James Lynslager on Nicoll Island.

This episode was scarcely less humiliating for William. The conference began after considerable delay, with Beecroft presiding. Its purpose was to settle a dispute between William and his arch rival Dick Merchant, the chief of Dikolo. Apparently, there had been a fight between Dick Merchant's people and William's, in which one of William's men had been killed. William naturally fined Dick Merchant. Although Merchant initially agreed to pay the fine, he later reneged on his promise, claiming that the fine had been arbitrary.[68] As frequently happened in such cases, the quarrel seems to have embroiled the people of the two villages and led to suspension of trade. Beecroft was therefore obliged to settle the dispute with a view to removing its root cause and restoring trade. But even more important, he was obliged, at the request of the chiefs, to draw up a code of regulations for their guidance,[69] in the interest of enduring peace and stability without which trade was difficult if not impossible. The regulations which Beecroft drew up were embodied in an eleven clause treaty known as the Nicoll Island treaty adopted 'unanimously' and ratified on 19 December 1850.[70] It naturally dealt with a wide range of problems between European traders and Bimbians, among them the payment of African pilots and compensation of Europeans for any damage done to their factories or 'cask houses'. But the critical clause dealt with the payment of comey or trade tax to Bimbian chiefs. This was no small problem. Apparently, in their competition for European trade, some chiefs or their subordinates not infrequently tried to extort comey from the traders after the latter had presumably already paid it to the chief of the village where the Europeans established their factories. When the Europeans refused to yield to such extortionate demands, such chiefs or their agents proceeded to foment difficulties for the European traders, and thus for the chief of the rival village. The third clause of the Nicoll Island treaty accordingly stipulated that once a trader had paid his comey to the chief of the village where his factory was located, no other chief, headman or trader could thereafter demand further comey from him. The clause did not remove the internal rivalries and jealousy engendered by growing trade at Bimbia, but it did at least provide a framework for peaceful competition and settlement of disputes.

Having disposed of the quarrel between the Europeans and Bimbians, Beecroft next turned his attention to the quarrel between King William and Dick Merchant, a quarrel which was no less detrimental to trade because it stemmed from a fundamental problem of Bimbian society. The problem concerned the ownership and custody of escaped slaves. Apparently, a slave girl had escaped from Dick Merchant's town, Dikolo, to Williamstown — an indication that she wanted to change masters. Her escape led to a fight between two war canoes from Dikolo and Williamstown respectively, during which one of King William's men was killed. In addition, there were two other slave girls who apparently wanted to change masters, and who had therefore aggravated the problem.[71] Both chiefs, with the consent of the girls, wanted Beecroft to settle the dispute and it is against this background that he proposed his solution.

He wrote:

> I would impress it upon them that whenever a male or female ran from each other's towns and went to the headman, his clapping his hands on the head of the party, there and then, confining him or her as his slave, at the same time killing a goat and inviting the party to partake of some of it, so as there can be no doubt as to the slave changing masters, I told them that I should certainly make the laws astringent ... particularly on that point which had been the cause of all your squabbles and broils so as to prohibit in future if possible all such abominable practices ...[72]

Beecroft's comments were well taken. As a trader with long experience of, and association with, Bimbia, he must have known that the status and custody of slaves was one of the most sensitive socio-political problems of Bimbian society because slaves often found it difficult to get justice under Bimbia's judicial system and their status and rights – such as they were – were often subject to abuse. This was even more so in times of crisis such as famine or epidemic. In such circumstances, a slave's personal security and wellbeing depended on his escaping from an ungenerous master who abused him, or who could not protect him, to a new master whom he considered more generous, powerful and influential. Such a patron naturally benefited in terms of enhanced prestige and influence. The slave master who lost his slave in this way correspondingly lost prestige and influence, and could therefore not be expected to take kindly to his rival. But the least he could do was to demand compensation for the loss of his slave from the new master.

That such escapes were common and that they might in fact have been encouraged by Bimbia's ruling élite is not difficult to understand. It seems to have been a natural outcome of the differential wealth and influence among the ruling élite. In 1844, for example, Clarke reported that a young slave girl and a canoe load of other Bimbian slaves had fled to Fernando Po from Bimbia to seek employment with Mrs Merrick.[73] The dispute between King William and Dick

Merchant was more serious, however, because it seems to have been part of a more fundamental conflict between them. On 18 September 1846, Clarke reported an incident which casts some light on the rivalry, perhaps even a power struggle, between the two men.

According to Clarke, a young trader named Nako had visited one of Bimbia's slave villages and while there contracted to buy a bullock for which another prominent trader, John King, had already paid one instalment of the price, in the Bimbia fashion. A dispute naturally arose as to who owned the bullock. As a result, two women from Nako's village were seized as hostages by the villagers and taken to the inland village of Bwenga. In protest, Nako decided to move his people from his village to neighbouring Dikolo, Dick Merchant's village. Bimbia's other chiefs began to take sides in the dispute until it embroiled all of Bimbia. King William took sides with John King, while Dick Merchant and his brother, Duke, sided with Nako.

Clarke's comment on this otherwise trivial incident is significant. The Merchant brothers, he reported, had invited Nako to move to their village in an effort to undermine the influence of King William while correspondingly increasing theirs.[74] In other circumstances, the confrontation might have remained a mere incident. But in the context of Bimbian society it was more than an incident: it was a major episode in the rivalry between the monarchy and the chiefs for power and influence. As Clarke's comment implies, it threatened to upset the tremulous balance of power between the monarchy and the chiefs. William's determination to prevent this from happening was therefore understandable. The contest with the chiefs is one reason why William so sedulously courted English and European favour. In the light of this fact, his first encounter with Consul Beecroft must have been particularly painful and humiliating for him, for it must have shown him that his new friendship and alliance with the Queen of England did not necessarily secure him against his potential and actual rivals. As things stood, he could not sustain his fine against Dick Merchant, and he was in turn fined by Beecroft after the latter had rejected his traditional peace overture.

William's behaviour throughout his confrontation with Beecroft was puzzlingly peevish — like that of a person who could not help himself. It therefore contrasted markedly with his cocky, ebullient attitude when he encountered Allen in 1841. On that occasion he was at least self-confident enough to threaten to attack Clarence because the agents of the West African Company failed to pay his indentured men.[75] Perhaps he was still fresh from being invested as

King by Nicolls and did not yet realise that the monarchical policy which he inaugurated was fraught with danger including the kind of humiliation which he had just experienced at the hands of Beecroft. But whatever may have been the cause of peevishness, his own status as King had come to depend so much on English support that it would be foolish and fatal to have abandoned his friendship with the Queen of England.

Beecroft's intervention in the internal affairs of Bimbia and the Cameroons was part of a pattern that was to be repeated with even more dramatic consequences in the Niger Delta and at Lagos during the 1850s, and by his successors between the 1860s and 1880s.[76] Such intervention was not, however, without precedent elsewhere in West Africa, especially on the Gold Coast, where George McClean's forceful but skilful intervention in the Fanti-Ashanti disputes and conflicts in the 1830s and 1840s[77] not only helped to establish British influence there, but also had epoch-making consequences for British colonial policy towards West Africa at large. Nor, for that matter, was such intervention without its analogues in East Africa, where John Kirk and his successors laid the foundation of British influence, short of actual territorial expansion.[78] As more than one scholar has shown, especially since the publication of Robinson and Gallagher's much debated article in 1953,[79] such intervention was consistent with mid-Victorian – especially Palmerstonian – commitment to informal empire and free trade.[80] Yet, as Newbury has pointed out,[81] only in 1852 did the British government formally approve such intervention. Until that was done, the British government theoretically continued to adhere to the fiction of informal control.

The rivalry between William and Dick Merchant continued into the 1860s. In his 1864 report on the state of trade and politics at Bimbia, Burton indicated that William's 'rapacity' and the 'villainy' of his people had ruined Bimbia's trade. More significantly, he reported that the people of Dikolo and Williamstown were on bad terms with each other. He added, however, that the people of Dikolo 'drive a small trade with the Cameroons'.[82] One possible explanation for the latter comment was, perhaps, Burton's attempt to show that while the trade of Williamstown was declining that of Dikolo was relatively prosperous. King William thus had reason to be jealous and suspicious of Dick Merchant, while Dick Merchant and his people might have seen no compelling reason for continuing to be subordinate to King William. This was natural enough since relative wealth had become the single most important criterion by which power and prestige were measured at Bimbia.

Despite vigorous consular intervention and missionary mediation, internal strife continued and the enduring peace and stability which Beecroft and his successors sought, continued to elude Bimbia. In this connection, 1873 seems to have been a particularly bad year. Quoting Robert Smith, the Baptist Missionary Society's Annual Report for 1873 indicated that:

> The year closes with war, bloodshed, and cruelty; not only are the Duala people at war, but the Isubu people also. Mr Pinnock and I have made special visits to the latter, at their request. On the first occasion, we found them fighting in a narrow bay or creek; we passed between their fire and succeeded in persuading each party to retire to their towns. We visited them again, but their animosity was so great, they would not meet each other then. Since then, several of their number have been killed.[83]

Unfortunately, Smith did not indicate the cause of the war or which villages were involved. In view of the endemic tensions between King William and Dick Merchant, Williamstown and Dick Merchant's Town were probably the two antagonists. In that event, the war would have been a civil war and eventually almost certainly embroiled all of Bimbia. The usual instability followed, leading to 'cruel and blood-thirsty practices' which stopped trade and communications. So intense were the resulting animosities that the Bimbians rejected the normally effective missionary mediation which they had requested in the first place. That the resulting turmoil was particularly intense and widespread, is perhaps best evidenced by the fact that both John Holt and George Thomson, as well as the Baptist missionaries, were forced simultaneously to close their respective operations at Bimbia in 1873.

In 1855 Bimbia was ravaged by war and famine. This double crisis engendered widespread social dislocation.[84] In the midst of this social upheaval, William again seized the diplomatic initiative and persuaded Acting Consul Lynslager, who had succeeded Beecroft, to bombard the Bubi Islands. These islands were claimed as Bimbian territory, and its people were considered Bimbian subjects. Yellow Nako in fact claimed sovereignty over two of these islands, Mondoleh and Ndami, which he presumably inherited from his father Old Nako, William's immediate predecessor. Indeed, when Allen visited the islands in 1841 with Yellow Nako as his guide, he reported that the latter still raised livestock there, some of which he sold to Allen.[85] It was also in 1841 that William first complained to Allen about the 'sauciness' of the native islanders, the Bubi. After having drunk 'fetiche water', that is an oath, declaring the islands to be his, they had nevertheless shot at some of his people, kidnapped some of his wives, and killed his son. He also pointed out that they invariably attacked canoes which they thought not strong enough to resist them. For all these crimes, according to Allen, William had broadly intimated the 'propriety of Her Majesty's steam-vessel, *Wilberforce* declaring war upon the refractory subjects of our firm ally, and that we should at once proceed to burn their town as a lesson to them'.[86]

These were the same complaints, with minor variations, with which he persuaded Lynslager to bombard the islands.[87] To make his case more convincing this time, William complained not only of the rebelliousness of his Bubi subjects, but also that the islands were potential slave trading haunts. Should the slave trade be revived there, he pointed out, he would in the circumstances be unable to stop it. Because he was afraid of incurring the censure of Her Majesty's government as provided in the anti-slavery treaty,[88] he wanted Lynslager to help him to fulfil his treaty obligations. In other words, having conferred the title of 'King' on William, the British government was now being called upon to give effect to William's status as a monarch.

It was a clever diplomatic ruse and it worked to the extent that Lynslager was persuaded to take such drastic action. After failing to recover the Bimbian slaves and canoes seized by the Bubi, Lynslager ordered Commander Young to open fire on the village. The Bubi submitted and the Foreign Office approved Lynslager's action.[89] In one quick stroke, William had secured formal and effective British recognition of his sovereignty over the territories once included in Nicolls' protectorate. This was territory in which his predecessors had enjoyed suzerain authority, and he proved that his alliance with the Queen of England could work. What is more, perhaps it helped to divert the attention of Central Bimbians from the social dislocation and misery resulting from the famine and war during this same period. In such desperate circumstances, the need to control the flow of trade along the creek route, which included the islands, must have been even more imperative. This was a high point of the success of monarchical policy especially as Bimbia was simultaneously engaged in war with inland tribes. But it was also the last time British power was to be so employed.

The sequel to this episode was the signing of two Bimbia-Bubi treaties in which the Bubi promised never to rebel against their lawful sovereign,[90] while the Bimbians promised that in future 'we will in no way or manner whatever molest the inhabitants of the islands of Boobee adjacent to Amboise islands'.[91] In 1856 Consul

Hutchinson visited Bimbia and reported to the Foreign Office that the terms of the treaty were being observed.[92]

From William's point of view the reservation against Bimbians 'molesting' the Bubi made his victory an ambiguous one. Not only was the term 'molest' imprecise in the context of Bimbia-Bubi relations, but it meant in the ultimate analysis that William could not assert his authority over the Bubi without running the risk of being faulted for 'molesting' them. Only with British supervision, then, could he expect to exercise any authority over the Bubi. The resulting arrangement made Bimbia and Britain co-suzerains and a serious check was thus imposed on what seems to have been the expansionist ambitions and the sovereign authority of Bimbia. Nevertheless the Bimbia-Bubi war seems to have been only the first of a series of conflicts between Bimbia and her nominal subjects in the period between 1855 and 1879. Between 12 January and 30 June 1875, for example, a virtual state of war existed between Bimbia and the Batoke and Bota people to her west. Unfortunately, the Reverend Robert Smith's rather cryptic diary entries, to which we owe our knowledge of these events, gives us only their barest outlines. On 12 January when he visited Batoke, he found the people arming themselves. On the 13th he reported 'sorrowful tales of oppression and fear from Bimbia and Cameroons people' which had forced the Batoke to relocate their village further from the coast.[93]

About the same time the Bimbians were at war with the people of Bota, one of the Bubi islands. On 31 March 1875, Smith's diary indicated that Money, a Bimbia Chief, and his people had left 'to make war on the Bota people'. It added that Bimbians had been followed by several canoes of Cameroons people.[94]

A second entry on 1 April indicated that Smith had visited Bota to care for the wounded Duala and Bimbia people, but his offer had been rejected.[95] On 30 June he again reported that the Bota people had seized several Bimbia women and that Bimbians had seized two Bota women in retaliation.[96] The conflict, in other words, had resumed. Other wars with other villages occurred during the same period, but these will be discussed subsequently. Here it will suffice to say that partly as a result of these wars, the Batoke and no doubt other coastal people were long afterwards fearful of the Bimbians.[97]

No immediate cause is given for these extended hostilities but as Consul Burton reported in 1863, such incidents were not uncommon at these coastal markets and they often embroiled whole districts for long periods during which trade or any kind of intercourse was suspended.[98]

Although these conflicts arose from relatively trivial incidents, they must be viewed against the background of the recurrent tensions between Bimbians and their nominal subjects, and as a continuation of these desperate efforts, discussed earlier, to control inland and coastal resources. These resources, normally so vital to Bimbia's commercial prosperity, became even more desperately so following the widespread social dislocation and instability induced by the famine and war of 1855. For despite evidence that the situation within Bimbia was returning to normal by 1856, Bimbia never seems to have fully recovered from that double crisis economically, demo-graphically or otherwise. Robert Smith's description of Bimbia in 1869 as a 'rocky wilderness' was an indication that Bimbia's econ-omy, if it was not declining, was perhaps stagnating. Politically, the situation within Bimbia does not seem to have been much better. The frequency with which Bimbian chiefs apparently acted indepen-dently in these raids and other matters suggests, among other things, a decline in monarchical initiatives and influence which in turn suggests a serious breakdown of authority and leadership. In other words there seems to have been a failure in monarchical policy and the monarchical experiment.

To a great extent, Bimbia's changing circumstances were somewhat reflected in a discernible change in William's personal material cir-cumstances during these years. In 1841 Allen described William as a 'fine specimen of a savage potentate ... tall and with a good forehead, though somewhat ferocious features ...'[99] Then, he lived in a 'very good-looking wooden house', whose principal floor, Allen added,

> ... is raised from the ground, and surrounded by a verandah; it contains some good rooms. Around the *grand salon* were ranged about a dozen large chests, containing cloth of European fabric. The walls were adorned with looking glasses of diverse sizes, and abundance of crockery-ware, for no other purpose than show and some of it in very curious juxtaposition; a backroom had chairs and tables, with presses around the walls, the depositories of his wealth, and various articles for trade with the natives of the interior.[100]

Beneath this floor, Allen continued, were other apartments or 'magazines'. Behind the palace were two long lines of huts occupied by his numerous wives, children, slaves and cattle. The palace and another house of smaller dimensions, were constructed by a Mr Scott, agent of the West African Company at Fernando Po, and cost one hundred dollars. It was distinguished by its 'commanding position, size and European form, and the splendour of its whitewash from the numerous other huts, scattered *en amphitheatre*' along the banks of the Bimbia River.[101] Such were William's material circumstances in better times, and they made the monarchy the best symbol of the wisdom and success of Anglo-Bimbian trade and diplomatic partnership.

In 1869 William still commanded enough respect to be given a ceremonial gun salute when he visited European vessels in the harbour[102] or a European factory.[103] As in the 1840s he still occasionally dined and socialised with traders and missionaries at their homes.[104] Much later, he was described by Grenfell as 'an ostentatious and boastful monarch who resembles a parish beadle in his attire ... [105] But these outward manifestations of power and prestige belied his changing fortunes and influence. As early as 1869, Robert Smith described him as a 'suspicious recluse'. His once beautiful mansion was now so dilapidated that Smith had to 'tread very carefully lest I should be landed ten feet below'.[106] Though still in relatively good health, he seldom left his home. His relations with his subjects had obviously deteriorated, and anyone seeking an interview with him was compelled to 'sit in the street while he converses with them from an elevated window'. Everyone approaching him was regarded as an enemy, and he would allow only one of his wives to attend him.[107]

With Bimbia's economy stagnating or perhaps declining, and perhaps because of his disappointment with British friendship and support of his policy, William turned elsewhere for help to bolster his declining commercial and political fortunes. In 1862 he signed a treaty with the Spanish Governor of Fernando Po in which he promised, *inter alia*, to 'prefer' Spanish ships and traders in trade to those of any other nation. This was clearly in violation of Article 4 of the anti-slavery treaty of 1844. When Consul Burton reported the existence of the treaty to the Foreign Office, Lord Russell reacted vigorously. He instructed Burton to:

> ... take the opportunity of making known to the chief that the British government cannot allow British ships and traders to be at a disadvantage within this district as compared with ships and traders of Spain. The British government had no desire to obtain from the chief commercial advantages from which other nations were excluded, but rejoices to share in commercial advantages conceded by the chief to any other nations.[108]

British commitment to free trade at Bimbia and elsewhere was thus formally reaffirmed only two years before Burton was to report that

Bimbia had ceased to be an important trade centre.[109]

Although King William's death was officially reported by Acting Consul Hopkins in December, 1878, the precise date of his death is unknown. He may, in fact, have died earlier. He was succeeded by his son, Ngombe, known to Europeans as young King William, but only after a succession dispute with another of his father's rivals, Yellow Money, which Hopkins was invited to settle.[110] Hopkins wisely postponed intervention in the dispute until he could more fully ascertain the issues involved, but there is no indication that he did so subsequently. Nevertheless, with or without British Consular support, young William seems to have won the succession dispute.

Young William also inherited his father's problems. How far the situation inside Bimbia had deteriorated by this time is best illustrated by a confrontation which took place in 1877 between the Bimbians and the Baptist missionary, Quintin Thomson. Thomson, who had just returned from vacation in England, was still waiting on board ship before proceeding to his station at Bonjongo, when he was informed of the opposition which awaited him. The incident is best recounted in his own words:

> On arrival at Victoria, while still on the mail, a report came to me that I was not to be allowed to go up to Bonjongo – that the Bimbia people were determined to stop me. After landing, I was told, on all sides, of the expressed determination of the Bimbia people to make me bring my house down from Bonjongo ... A number of people came from Bimbia; young King William came to me and told me they had met and had a big palaver about my being among the Bakweris. A great many wanted to come and take me away to Bimbia and make me live there; but he had quieted them, and now he wanted to warn me not to trade with them, and not to spoil their prices. He said he wanted a whiteman at Bimbia, and I was to see about it.[111]

In the last analysis, this confrontation with Thomson was, however indirectly, clearly a confrontation between the Bimbians and Bakweri. It shows that Bimbian chiefs were capable of uniting when their vital common interests were threatened, in this case by the disloyalty of inland people. But such unity was occasional and ephemeral, and it did not prevent quarrels among them which contributed greatly to the chronic instability which plagued Bimbia during the 1860s and 1870s. Clearly, the main concern of the Bimbians which led to this confrontation were two. First, they did not want Thomson to engage in trade with their Bakweri suppliers, for fear that this could undercut their middleman role and profits.

This is the implication of the phrase 'spoil their prices'. Second, they wanted a whiteman at Bimbia, for the presence of a whiteman was a guarantee of continued European interest in Bimbia, and of trade. But it was also a matter of prestige. As Mr S.I. Ekema put it, Bimbia was respected by inland people because Bimbians were the first to see the whiteman.[112]

Monarchical authority seems to have been a major casualty of the deteriorating situation within Bimbia. Sometime between 1878 and 1879, for example, young William was asked by Thomas Comber, a Baptist missionary doctor stationed at Victoria (Limbe), to intercede on behalf of a Bimbia man who was going to be hanged on a witchcraft charge. Although young William admitted the injustice of the sentence and was personally inclined to intercede, he was nevertheless afraid even to summon the other chiefs to a Council palaver at Williamstown to discuss the matter, as his father might have done.

According to Comber, young William confessed that although he was King, there were several other men as powerful as himself whom Comber had to persuade. Without their consent, William implied, he could do nothing.[113] This was some indication not only of the growing powerlessness of the monarchy, but also of the growing strength and influence of its rivals. This development was predictable. Since commercial wealth rather than royal pedigree had become the single most important criterion for determining political leadership and influence at Bimbia, theoretically anyone who was a successful trader could become a 'gentleman' or chief. With wealth and a little charisma, then, anyone, except perhaps a slave, could soon muster a following or increase his following and influence by a careful distribution of 'gentlemanly' largesse. Consequently, Bimbia's ruling élite had come to consist of equals or near equals, and the rivalries and tensions among them and their respective villages increased and intensified correspondingly.

In such circumstances, there was no reason why any one of Bimbia's 'gentlemen' could not challenge the monarchy and aspire to the Kingship, especially if the King's wealth had discernibly declined or his policy had failed. From the point of view of these 'gentlemen' there was no reason why they should continue to be subordinate to a King who was less successful than his subordinates. The challenge to monarchical authority and influence was easier because traditional modes of securing and retaining power and influence, those Bimbian customs and superstitions which consuls and missionaries helped to destroy, were increasingly of secondary importance. During the time of William (Bile), limited consular support had tipped the scales of power in favour of the monarchy. But after his death, even this grudging support was virtually nonexistent. The monarchy therefore became more vulnerable to its rivals.

The available evidence suggests that after King William's death, individual Bimbian chiefs and villages began to act even more independently than previously. The consequent absence of a central and unifying authority, especially after the murder of young William in 1882, was a clear indication that the policy of consolidating monarchical primacy through a skilful exploitation of British consular support, had failed. On the other hand, the very fact that young King William had managed to hold on to the kingship despite the fierce opposition of his father's rivals, meant that William's policy had been partly successful in establishing the monarchy in his family. Ironically and significantly, it was an achievement which far outlasted the existence of Bimbia as an independent African state.[114]

Conclusion

This study has examined Anglo-Bimbian diplomatic relations between 1833 and 1878. It has tried to show that these relations were primarily a result of mutual Anglo-Bimbian interest in developing and expanding legitimate trade. For Britain, this was an end in itself, but it was also a means to an end, namely, the abolition of the slave trade. Central to Bimbian interests was the desire of Bimbia's ruling élite to attract British trade and traders to Bimbia and thus to ensure Bimbia's commercial prosperity and theirs. Even more important, it was in King William's interest to do so, on the one hand to enhance the primacy and prestige of the monarchy inside Bimbia, and on the other to use British influence and support to reassert and expand Bimbia's influence and suzerainty over her coastal and inland neighbours in the interest of trade.

This was the crux of the monarchical policy which William pursued when he formally became King of Bimbia in 1833 with British support. This policy remained the motive force of Bimbian policy until his death, but it was only partly successful. Two main reasons account for this. First, recurrent internal crises undermined Bimbia's prosperity and frightened away the European traders who came to Bimbia, and whose presence there had helped to sustain Bimbian commercial prosperity. Naturally, it also frightened away other traders who, under better conditions, might have considered coming to Bimbia and thus helped to expand trade. These crises were unfortunate, because they occurred at a time when there was an influx of small independent traders into the smaller Oil Rivers of the

Guinea coast owing to improved communications between West Africa and England and Europe. Bimbia's commercial *floruit*, on which William's monarchical policy was predicated, was therefore relatively brief.

Second, for reasons which have partly to do with the theory and practice of informal empire, the British government rejected and ignored every initiative by its naval officers and consuls to acquire Bimbian territory, most importantly Nicolls' protectorate. We have indicated that this reluctance to acquire African territory when it would have been politically and financially costless to do so was not limited to the instance of Bimbia alone: it was a major feature of British-African policy and British-African relations. To this extent, therefore, Anglo-Bimbian relations in particular may be considered a catalogue of lost opportunities.

The decline of the Bimbian monarchy following the failure of the policy on which it had staked its prestige and influence, exposed the monarchy to its rivals, exacerbated the rivalries and quarrels among Bimbian chiefs, and created a leadership vacuum inside Bimbia. In their desire to share equally in what remained of Bimbia's declining prosperity, they acted increasingly independently, despite an occasional show of unity. Their independence was, however, at the expense of the nascent monarchy. By 1878 when William died, the prestige of the monarchy was clearly at its lowest ebb. Although William's son was able to succeed him, his hold on the monarchy was at best shaky. Unfortunately, even this shaky hold ended abruptly and prematurely when young William was murdered in 1882 at precisely the moment when it seemed that his initiatives might restore some monarchical prestige and influence, and with it some stability and prosperity. The experiment in monarchical centralisation with British support, which King William had inaugurated, thus barely outlasted him. That young William was able to succeed his father at all despite the opposition of his father's rivals represented a major, if personal, achievement for William's policy in that, however briefly, it confirmed the monarchy in his line. But because of young William's death in 1882, even this personal achievement was too brief to resolve the crisis of the monarchy, to sustain monarchical policy, or to save the Bimbian state from eventual collapse.

Notes

1   See E.W. Ardener, 'Documentary and Linguistic Evidence for the Rise of the Trading Polities between Rio del Rey and Cameroons, 1500–1650', in I.M. Lewis, (ed.) *History and Social Anthropology*, London, 1968, pp. 108–109.

2   The other comprised the Duala Polities of the Wouri River Estuary, the 'Cameroons River' of nineteenth century Englishmen.

3   R.A. Austen and W.D. Smith, 'Images of Africa and the British Slave Trade Abolition: The Transition to an Imperialist Ideology, 1787—1807', *African Historical Studies*, vol. II, No. 1, 1969, p. 82.

4   P.D. Curtin and Jan Vansina, 'Sources of the Nineteenth Century Atlantic Slave Trade', *Journal of African History*, vol. V, 1964, p. 82.

5   P.D. Curtin, *The Image of Africa: British Ideas and Action 1780—1850*, Madison, 1964, p. 177; L. Berthell, 'The Mixed Commission for the Suppression of the Transatlantic Slave Trade in the Nineteenth Century', *Journal of African History*, vol. II, 1966, p. 81.

6   C. Lloyd, *The Navy and the Slave Trade*, London and New York, 1969, p. 183.

7   K.O. Dike, *Trade and Politics in the Niger Delta 1830—1885*, London, 1956, p. 86.

8   T.J. Hutchinson, *Impressions of Western Africa*, London, 1967, p. 176.

9   Curtin, *Image of Africa*, p. 353.

10 Dike, p. 57.

11 *Ibid.*, pp. 58—59.

12 *Ibid.*, p. 59.

13 C.O. 82/6, p. 105 Enclosure, Nicolls to Hay, 24 July 1833.

14 C.O. 82/6, Nicolls section, Nicolls to Hay, 10 December 1833.

15 F.O. 2/45. Confidential, Burton to Foreign Office, August, 1864.

16 Clarke, *The African Journal*, vol. 3, pp. 61—63 MS at BMS Archives. See note 73.

17 Allen and T.R.H. Thomson, p. 295.

18 J. Clarke, *The African Journal*, vol. 3, p. 139.

19 *Ibid.*, p. 281.

20 C.O. 82/6 p. 99, Nicolls to Hay, 10 December 1833.

21 *Ibid.*

22 *Ibid.*

23 Dike, pp. 65—66.

24 *Ibid.*

25 C.O. 82/6, p. 80, Nicolls to Hay, 14 September 1833.

26 *Ibid.*

27 *Ibid.*

28 C.O. 82/6, p. 80, Nicolls to Hay, 14 September 1833.

29 Dike, pp. 65—66.

30 Quoted in A.F. Mockler-Ferryman, *British Nigeria*, London, 1902, pp. 213—214.

31 T.J. Hutchinson, *Ten Years' Wanderings Among the Ethiopians*, London, 1967, p. 317.

32 R.F. Burton, *Abeokuta and the Cameroons Mountain*, vol. II, London, 1863, p. 25.

33 *Ibid.*, p. 44.

34 T.F. Buxton, *The African Slave Trade and Its Remedy*, London, 1840, p. 41.

35 C.C. Ifemesia, 'The "Civilizing" Mission of 1841: Aspects of an Episode in Anglo-Nigerian Relations', *Journal of the Historical Society of Nigeria*, vol. II, No. 3, December, 1962, p. 291.

36 P.D. Curtin, *The Image of Africa: British Ideas and Action, 1780—1850*, Madison, 1964, p. 291.

37 *Ibid.*

38 Allen and T.R.H. Thomson, p.320.

39 F.O. 84/1061, p. 320. Enclosure, Thomas Hutchinson to Seymour Fitzgerald, August, 1858.

40 Quoted in Allen and T.R.H. Thomson, p. 270.

41 See Admiralty Instructions to Senior Officers for Negotiating with African Chiefs, June 12, 1844, in *Parliamentary Papers*, 1844, pp. 15–17.

42 Curtin, p. 465; J.D. Hargreaves, *Prelude to the Partition of West Africa*, New York, 1966, p. 244.

43 Great Britain, Foreign Office, *British and Foreign State Papers, 1846–1847*, 'Sierraleone; Treaty between Her Majesty the Queen of England and King William of Bimbia, for the Abolition of Slave Trade, agreed upon between King William and Lieutenant Earle, of Her Britannic Majesty's Brig Rapid, 17 February 1844', vol. 35, Enclosure 6, pp. 320–321.

44 *Ibid.*

45 *Ibid.*

46 *Ibid.*

47 *Ibid.*

48 Great Britain, Foreign Office, *British and Foreign State Papers, 1847–1848*, 'Africa: Promise made by the King and Chiefs of Bimbia-Williamstown, 31 March 1848', vol. 36, p. 866.

49 N.H. Stilliard, 'The Rise of Legitimate Trade in Palm Oil with West Africa', Unpublished M.A. thesis, The University of Birmingham, October 1938, pp. 240–241.

50 R.A. Austen, 'The Abolition of the Overseas Slave Trade, A distorted theme in West African History', *Journal of the Historical Society of Nigeria*, vol. 5, No. 2, June, 1970, p. 261.

51 F.O. 84/775., Cancelled Passage, Palmerston to Beecroft, No. 1, June 1849.

52 H.H. Johnston, *The Colonization of Africa by Alien Races*, Cambridge, 1913, p. 183; A.F. Mockler-Ferryman, *British Nigeria*, London, 1902, p. 36; K.O. Dike, 'John Beecroft, 1790–1854: Her Britannic Majesty's Consul to the Bights of Benin and Biafra, 1849–1854', *Journal of the Historical Society of Nigeria*, vol. 1, December 1956, pp. 7–9.

53 A. Burns, *History of Nigeria*, 7th ed., London, 1969, pp. 95–96 ff.

54 R.A. Austen, p. 261.

55 K.K. Nair, 'Politics and Society in Old Calabar, 1841–1906: A Study of Political and Social Development in a Southern Nigerian Trading State', Unpublished Ph. D. Dissertation, University of Ibadan, November 1967, p. 159.

56 A. Burns, 'Her Britannic Majesty's First Consul to Nigeria', *West African Review*, June 1949, p. 609.

57 P.A. Talbot, *The Peoples of Southern Nigeria*, 7th ed., London, 1965, p. 376.

58 C.W. Newbury, *British Policy Towards West Africa, Select Documents*, Oxford, 1965, p. 376.

59 J. Clarke, *The African Journal*, vol. 1, pp. 17–18.

60 F.O. 84/816, p. 140, Palmerston to Admiralty, 16 October 1850.

61 F.O. 84/816, p. 140, Beecroft to Admiralty, 16 October 1850.

62 *Ibid.*

63 *Ibid.*

64 F.O. 84/816, p. 318 Beecroft to Palmerston, 30 December 1850.

65 M. Allen and T.R.H. Thomson, p. 291.

66 *Ibid.* p. 291.

67 *Ibid.*, p. 230.

68 Beecroft to Palmerston, p. 321.

69 Beecroft to Palmerston, p. 321.

70 Great Britain, Foreign Office, *British and Foreign State Papers, 1849–1850*,

'Africa: Treaty with the King and Chiefs of Bimbia, Nicoll Island, 19 December 1850', vol. 39, pp. 1052–1054.

71 F.O. 84/816, p. 320, Beecroft to Palmerston, 30 December 1850.

72 *Ibid.*, p. 321.

73 J. Clarke, *The African Journal of John Clarke. August 1843–November 1844*, Second Journey, vol. 1, Box A/2, London, Baptist Missionary Archives, p. 300.

74 *Ibid.*, pp. 301–302.

75 Allen and T.R.H. Thomson. p. 230.

76 J.D. Hargreaves, *Prelude to the Partition of West Africa*, New York, 1966, pp. 54–78.

77 G.J. Moutafakis, 'The British Colonial Policy and Administration of the British West Africa Settlements, 1886–1888', Unpublished Ph.D. dissertation, New York University, Duxe University, 1965, pp. 20, 22 and passim.

79 J. Gallagher and R. Robinson, 'The Imperialism of Trade', *Economic History Review*, Second Series, vol. 64, 1953, p. 134.

80 See D.C.M. Blatt, 'The Imperialism of "Free Trade": Some Reservations', *Economic History Review*; Robinson and J. Gallagher, *Africa and the Victorians*, New York, 1961, p. 35 ff.

81 C.W. Newbury, *British Policy Towards West Africa, Select Documents, 1786–1874*, Oxford, 1965, p. 375.

82 F.O. 84/1221, p. 197, Burton to Foreign Office, 15 April 1864.

83 *Annual Report*, 1873, p. 79.

84 See *The Missionary Herald*, April 1885, p. 58, *The Missionary Herald*, May 1855, p. 88; *Annual Report of the Committee of the Baptist Missionary Society for the Year Ending March 31*, 1855, p. 8.

85 Allen and T.R.H. Thomson, p. 235.

86 *Ibid.*

87 F.O. 84/975, p. 83. (Enclosure), Lynslager to Commander Young.

88 F.O. 84/975, p. 83, Lynslager to Commander Young.

89 F.O. 84/975, 10 May 1855, p. 11.

90 Great Britain, Foreign Office, *Britain and Foreign State Papers, 1856–1857*, 'Africa: Engagement of the Chiefs of Boobee, 7 February 1855', vol. 47, pp. 546–547.

91 Great Britain, Foreign Office, *British and Foreign State Papers, 1856–1857*, 'Africa: Engagement of King and Chiefs of Bimbia, 7 February 1855', vol. 47, p. 547.

92 F.O. 84/1001, p. 122, Hutchinson to Clarendon, January 1856.

93 Robert Smith, *Reverend Robert Smith's Diary*, Box A/4, London, Baptist Missionary Society Archives.

94 *Ibid.*

95 *Ibid.*

96 *Ibid.*

97 As late as August 28, 1884, when Lieutenant Furlonger of the *H.M.S. Forward* visited Bibundi to conclude a treaty, the Chief was afraid to do so because of the presence of Bimbians in the village. Only after considerable delay did the Chief finally come on board the *Forward* and even then he would not accept the gift which was offered him because he feared the Bimbians might seize it from him. See Furlonger to Admiralty, 3 September 1884, Adm. 123/87, 1882–1885, p. 190.

98 Burton, *Abeokuta and the Cameroons Mountain*, pp. 35–36.

99 Allen and T.R.H. Thomson, p. 233.

100 *Ibid.*

101 *Ibid.*

102 *Annual Report*, 31 March, 1869, pp. 68–69.

103 Cecil Holt (ed.), *The Diary of John Holt and the Voyage of the "Maria"*, London and Prescott, 1948, p. 765.

104 J. Clarke, *The African Journal*, vol. 3, pp. 281, 301, 304 ff.

105 Quoted in G. Hawker, *The Life of George Grenfell, Congo Missionary and Explorer*, London, 1909, p. 70.

106 *Annual Report*, 31 March 1869, pp. 68–69.

107 *Ibid.*

108 F.O. 84/1176, p. 11, Russell to Burton, 20 April 1862.

109 F.O. 84/1221, p. 195, Burton to Foreign Office, 5 April 1864.

110 F.O. 84/1508, pp. 421–422, Hopkins to Foreign Office, 3 December 1878.

111 *Annual Report*, 31 March 1877, p. 102.

112 Interview with Mr S.I. Ekema, New Town, Victoria, 10 December 1971.

113 John B. Myers, *Thomas J. Comber, Missionary Pioneer to the Congo*, 10th ed., New York and Chicago, n.d., p. 55.

114 William would certainly have felt gratified that one of his descendants, *Manga ma Nambeke*, better known as Chief John Manga Williams, was appointed the District Head or Paramount Chief of Victoria Division in 1908. In this capacity, he became the leading traditional ruler of the districts defined as Great Bimbia in this study. He subsequently rose to prominence in Cameroon politics both as a member of the Eastern Nigerian House of Representatives, and of various Cameroon delegations to pre-independence constitutional conferences in London. He was also a member of the then Southern Cameroons House of Chiefs and was decorated by Queen Elizabeth II. He died at a ripe old age in 1959, one year after a centennial of the founding of Victoria, when this writer was a tenant in his compound at Victoria. See E. Ardener, *Coastal Bantu*, p. 29.

Chapter Three
Trade and supremacy on the Cameroon coast, 1879–1887

Verkijika G. Fanso

This is an account of the economic and political rivalries between European traders and imperial officials on the Cameroon seacoast from 1879, when the kings of Douala began earnestly to request British protection from Queen Victoria and the British Government, to 1887, when the Victoria enclave was officially and effectively transferred from Britain to Germany to make the latter the supreme power in the area. The study is both complementary and supplementary to an earlier study published in the review *Abbia.** It is divided into four parts: commercial and political developments before 1879; commercial activities from 1879 on; the struggle for imperial supremacy; and the consolidation of the German protectorate.

Commercial and political developments before 1879

Trade and political contacts between the coastal Cameroonians and visiting European supercargoes and officials became increasingly friendly and more trustworthy from the 1840s following a series of treaties between the Cameroon chiefs and the British who wanted to abolish the slave trade and human sacrifices, and to encourage legitimate commerce. These contacts became even closer when missionaries of the English Baptist Missionary Society (BMS) led the way in setting up European settlements in the suburbs of the township of Douala in 1845 and in the Ambas Bay enclave in 1858. European settlements began to grow as more missionaries were sent to Cameroon, more liberated slaves were brought and resettled by the British naval squadrons, and more white traders were assured of their security and peaceful trade as they began to open trading stations and build factories and stores.

In January 1856, a major commercial treaty was signed between, on the one hand, British officials and supercargoes led by Her

Britannic Majesty's Consul for the Bights of Benin and Biafra and Fernando Po, and on the other hand, kings, chiefs, and traders of Cameroon.[1] This treaty established by-laws for the better regulation of trading activities and related matters between Cameroon and European traders, and also set up a Court of Equity to settle all disputes that threatened trade and trading relations between local traders and the supercargoes. Following this treaty, white business-men began to flood the Cameroon coast. Indeed, it was estimated in the early 1860s that between 150 and 200 white traders could be found at any time in the Douala township alone, and that the number usually more than doubled during the export season along the length of the Cameroon shoreline.[2]

Until the end of the 1860s, the import and export trade of the Cameroon coast was dominated by the British. The Cameroon coast then already formed part of the British sphere of influence in the Bights of Benin and Biafra. There were at that time, five English firms permanently established and operating in Douala and other Cameroon coastal townships. In 1868, a German firm, the Firma C. Woermann, from Hamburg, established and began business in Cameroon. The second German firm to establish and enter the Cameroon trade was the Jantzen and Thormählen firm, also from Hamburg, in 1875. French firms also joined the Cameroon trade in the 1870s, and opened their trading stations south of the Douala enclave at Malimba, Big Batanga and Campo.[3] No other European country, excepting England, Germany, and France, had business firms or traders and supercargoes in any significant numbers operating in Cameroon before the German annexation in 1884. While the English and German firms and agents traded co-operatively under the Union Jack in the Douala and Victoria townships and westward to Rio del Rey and beyond, the French operated alone in the districts from Batanga towards their Gabonese enclave.

Euro-Cameroon trade before the annexation was confined to the Cameroon coast and strictly controlled by the Africans of the different coastal townships. It was often trade by barter in which the coastal traders, who were principally middlemen in the trade, monopolised the exchange of goods between the European traders and the Cameroonian producers who lived in the interior. The important Cameroon items for exchange, following the abolition of the slave trade, included palm oil, palm kernels, and ivory. These products were bartered for such European merchandise as cloth, arms, gun-powder, liquor, trinkets, shoes, mirrors and clocks. Each exchange transaction between a European and a Cameroonian trader was accomplished in the 'African way' namely, in the course of a drink, usually offered by the foreign trader, and after a great deal of haggling. Rudin noted that 'because the white man had a stronger demand for African products than the black man had for most European manufactured goods, liquor and arms played a large role in early trade'.[4] Although the major centres of this trade were Victoria in the Ambas Bay enclave, Douala in the Wouri River estuary, and the Batanga and Campo districts, it was the Douala centre that attracted the Europeans the most and thus the Duala middlemen who dominated the Cameroon trade.

In the arena of politics, the ground for imperial rivalry for supremacy on the Cameroon coast in the 1880s was prepared during the decades of the implementation of legitimate trade. As in the case of the abolition of the slave trade, the implementation of legitimate commerce was accomplished through treaties some of whose clauses had political implications. Such clauses often allowed the British officials to intervene directly in the internal affairs of the coastal chiefdoms on the pretext of offering protection both to foreign and Cameroonian traders against all kinds of arbitrary proceedings in commercial transactions. In 1844, for example, the king and chiefs of Bimbia and of the neighbourhood entered into a treaty of legitimate commerce with the British, accepting to 'subject themselves to a severe act of displeasure' on the part of Her Majesty's Government, if they did not respect the terms of the treaty.[5] Again, in 1855, 'under the penalty of incurring the displeasure of Her Britannic Majesty's Government', they engaged themselves before the British Consul to respect King William of Bimbia as their rightful king, and to refer all disputes which could not be settled amicably to the Consul at Fernando Po.[6]

Another example to cite is the Anglo-Cameroon commercial treaty of 1856 which set up the Court of Equity on the Cameroon coast at Douala. This treaty, which outlined by-laws for the better regulation of trading matters in Douala and its environs, prepared the way for the imperial struggle for annexation of that commercially coveted township. The kings and chiefs of Douala agreed in the treaty that: the Court of Equity house would be British property under the protection of the British Consul; the report of each Court meeting would be forwarded to the Consul; all appeals from the Court would be made to and heard by the Consul; the case of those Cameroonians evading the penalties of the Court would be decided in the presence of the Consul; all parties would abide by the decision of the Consul; kings and chiefs attempting to detain or maltreat any British subject would incur the displeasure of Great Britain and be declared her enemies; and 'the men-of-war will, upon such complaints being made to them, immediately come ... to protect British subjects'. This treaty, no doubt, made Great Britain the political suzerain of the Cameroon coast. Later, in 1861, the kings and chiefs agreed that they or their subjects caught practising what the British regarded as barbarous and inhuman customs would be subjected to confinement on board a British ship or to deportation to Fernando Po.[8] The Duala kings and chiefs had, by this act, informally lost their independence and sovereignty to Great Britain.

The British dominance in trade and politics of the major trading areas of the Cameroon coast during the greater part of the nineteenth century could only be challenged if merchants (and officials) of other imperial nations joined in and competed in increasing numbers in the Cameroon trade. During the 1870s only a few such merchants and officials were active on the coast, virtually all of them from France and Germany. 'Although only a few German traders were engaged in this ... trade, their loyal co-operation with the British as well as their acceptance of the measure of British control ... gave English traders no reason for fearing the Germans'.[9a] The French, whom the British and the Germans feared, were still a long way south of Douala and their treaties of trade and friendship with the local chieftains were only at the initial stages. But the Duala kings, who probably feared a possible French encroachment upon their territory, began in the late 1870s to solicit formal British protection.[9b] In 1877 they wrote offering to surrender their territory to Britain. In 1879 they wrote again asking that an 'English Government' be established in Cameroon, and that 'every' law and custom be altered, presumably, to English law.[10]

The reason given by the chiefs for their application for formal British protection was that rivalry between European and indigenous traders in their townships was causing instability and making it difficult for them to rule their people. Indeed, according to the English Baptist missionaries in Cameroon, every dispute, particularly between the chiefs or indigenous traders in Douala, led to war and to great loss of life.[11] The crises were not limited to the chiefdoms of Douala but were spreading to other coastal villages including Tiko and Bimbia.[12] The kings and chiefs were therefore seeking the protection of a stronger power which would hold local passions in leash and control both the white and indigenous communities.

Commercial rivalry from 1879 on

Trade and commerce on the Cameroon coast continued to prosper in spite of reports of frequent political disturbances in the major townships. There were three groups of people who were actively engaged in the various transactions, namely, the inland producers of primary products, the local intermediaries along the coast, and the European traders and supercargoes. As already said, these overseas traders and supercargoes were chiefly from Britain, France and Germany. They brought in European manufactured goods for exchange or barter for raw materials. The greater share of their trade was in the hands of British merchants, although by 1880 the two German firms were fast closing the gap between the Germans and the British. All the coastal transactions between Cameroonian and European traders took place in European house-boats, factories or stores where the exchanges were made in bits of products, or in bulk to middlemen who traded them inland for raw materials.

Perhaps the most active and most controversial participants in the Euro-Cameroon trade were the intermediaries of the coastal townships. Their chief services were bulk buying, transporting goods to and from the interior, and extending credit. In return for these services they seized every opportunity to benefit from whatever the Europeans brought to or exported from Cameroon. In order to do this they erected two boundaries as it were, between them and the interior producers of export products on the one hand and between them and the European merchants on the other, and resisted every attempt by the whites to by-pass them and trade directly with the inland people. Among the leading intermediaries were the Duala, the Bimbians and the Malimbas who, as the missionary George Grenfell observed, monopolised for themselves the right of trading with the Europeans. They were very suspicious of every whiteman – missionary or explorer – who ventured into the interior, and warned such men not to engage in any trade whatsoever with the inland people. 'So determined are [these intermediaries] to preserve these boundaries', wrote Grenfell, 'that I was brought back by a party of eight armed men from a point 20 miles from the Mungo towns past which I managed to creep in the darkness of night'.[13] The coastal middlemen had two markets – one at the coast where they traded with the foreigners and the other in the interior where they traded with inland peoples.

Transactions differed in the coastal and interior markets. In the 'white' market these go-betweens received goods from European trading houses on credit and bartered them in the interior for local products. These they brought to their creditors and exchanged them for new goods, the original credit being paid only slowly in the course of many months or years. Carl Scholl, a German trader, explained in a letter to his family that there were fixed market days for these transactions. He said the indigenous traders knew very well how to conduct their business and were not stupid; they knew the value of all goods 'and cannot be duped by us'. Carl Scholl explained that every Cameroon trader knew what he was entitled to and became hostile if he got 'only a little less'. He explained to his family that local goods from the interior passed through several intermediaries before reaching them at the coast. 'These local products ... mostly pass, not just through two, but often through many hands until they reach the coast, and thus increase in price as everyone takes a share of it'.[14]

George Grenfell, who observed the interior trade between the coastal intermediaries and the interior people, also reported that the immediate interior people acted as middlemen between coastal markets and those further inland and also profited from the trade. He noted that the Bimbian intermediaries gathered local products mostly from the mountain markets, the Bell people from the Mungo and Abo markets, and the Akwa people from the whole Wouri and Dibamba towns. Bakoko country was common ground for the Malimba, Akwa and Bell peoples. Grenfell observed that trade was the chief occupation of the coastal people, their chief source of income and that they either did it profitably or spent their lives in idleness. In fact Grenfell remarked that 'idleness' was the greatest vice of the coastal inhabitants who were the opposite of the skilled men of the interior.[15] He regretted that although the coastal land was rich and suited for cultivation, the people did not make use of it. The situation, he stated, was unlike that in other parts of Africa where the people were 'blessed less bountifully and where people are compelled to work or starve'.[16] This rather exaggerated account of the coastal people only goes to emphasise the fact that the coastal intermediaries were seriously committed to their trade and worked hard for their money. Their services to both the European traders and interior producers of raw materials, not easily appreciated by the Europeans, were immense.

As has been said earlier, European trade with the coastal middlemen was regulated by the Court of Equity at Douala set up specifically for that purpose. For indigenous traders to qualify initially to obtain goods on credit from the trading houses, they had to pledge that they would always pay their debts. In fact, Clause V of the treaty setting up the Court of Equity specifically stated that 'the native kings and chiefs pledge themselves not only to pay their own debts, but to use their influence, each with his respective traders, to do the same, and that for their neglect of this they be subject to a fine, to be settled by the Court'.[17] At this time, by the end of the 1870s, membership of the Court consisted of one supercargo belonging to each trading house and four chiefs representing indigenous traders.

Between 1879 and 1884, when the Germans annexed the territory, British trade on the Cameroon coast declined drastically while German trade continued to flourish. Indeed, British domination of Cameroon trade came to an end during this time when they were overtaken by the Germans, in spite of their numerically inferior position compared with the British. Available evidence does not provide adequate explanation for this state of affairs. Consul Hewett mistakenly attributed the decline to the 'trifling quarrels between intriguing native kings, in the absence of any external authority, [which] had led to something like chaos'.[18] He failed to explain why political disturbances were affecting only British commerce. There are, however, a number of possible reasons why German trade was doing better than English trade. It may be that the Germans were buying established British and independent businesses which were closing down and therefore controlling the trade that would normally flow into the hands of the British. This possibility is based on evidence – an isolated fact though it may appear – showing that the firm of C. Woermann purchased the estate of the late George Thomson in 1881.[19] Another possible explanation might be the effect of the transition from the supercargo to the agent system of trading. Latham demonstrates, in the case of neighbouring Calabar, that the fall in prices after 1862 made it uneconomic to maintain the supercargo system; 'firms which wished to remain in business had to adopt the agent system'.[20] This may have been the case in Cameroon in the 1870s and 1880s, and the British who had more supercargoes than the Germans suffered in the transition. Although there were only two German firms, compared with six English, the Germans had factories all over the coast and were well organised.[21] Also, the fact that German merchants had always worked on friendly terms with British traders allowed them much freedom under British leadership, and so they were able to turn their maximum attention to trade. In fact when Chancellor Bismarck, about this time, instructed the Hamburg Senate to consider what measures were necessary for the protection of German commerce in Cameroon and elsewhere in Africa, he was informed that the Senate was satisfied with German commerce in Cameroon under British leadership.[22]

The last possible reason why German trade was doing much better and surpassing British trade was the heavy dependence of the Germans on the 'trust' system, a practice to which the British objected. The 'trust' system was a practice adopted by the Europeans of giving goods to Cameroonian intermediaries on credit, payment being made later after exchanging them for raw materials in the interior. The European trader who extended credit on easier terms than others, easily attracted more Cameroonian traders and won great economic advantage over his rivals. It was known that the German traders, particularly those of the firm of C. Woermann, depended greatly on the 'trust' system and extended much credit to the coastal middlemen as the only way of competing successfully with English firms in the Cameroon trade.[23] The indigenous traders saw the credit system as the right kind of trade and used it to exploit the competition among European traders to their own great advantage. The firm of C. Woermann gave out more credit from 1881 to 1884 than the English firms and the firm of Jantzen and Thormählen.[24]

British Consul Hewett's statistics comparing British and German trade in 1882 showed that the Germans exported 1317 tons of oil to the British 1283 tons; 903 tons of palm-kernels to 897 tons; 10310 lb of ivory to 7610 lb; 2000 lb of cocoa to zero; one ton of copra to 10 tons; 800 lb of ebony to zero; and 100 lb of beans to zero.[25] Hewett said that his information on exports was not very complete and that the figures were for annual exports from Douala alone. Although these statistics do not suggest any significant difference between British and German trade, they do suggest clearly that British traders were no longer the favoured group in Euro-Cameroon trade.

While commercial rivalry between British and German traders developed on a friendly footing, the relations between them and French traders continued to be hostile. The Germans were less satisfied with the treatment they received in the areas dominated by the French and, together with the British, resented them. Before the 1880s the French had established trading stations in several places north of the Campo river and, by 1883, were continuing their northward advance towards the areas dominated by the British and the Germans. What offended the British and the Germans about the French was that they were 'establishing factories, claiming territories, and introducing tariffs so high and so discriminatory as to result in the virtual exclusion of all non-French goods'.[26]

The French advance towards Douala and the decline of British enterprise led to the belief among British nationals in Cameroon that the economic situation would improve if Britain annexed the territory. These British nationals began to apply pressure on the Foreign Office, stressing the economic advantages of a British protectorate in Cameroon. George Grenfell, in an article published by the Royal Geographical Society, pointed out that the soil of the

Cameroon coast promised the most magnificent results, if only the Cameroonians could be induced to cultivate either coffee or cocoa. He argued that the expense of annexation 'would be for a few years, for the increased trade would soon produce sufficient revenue to cover it'. He said that he was patriotic enough to wish that the British would annex Cameroon, impressed as he was 'that it is the most beneficent'.[27] Messrs Jackson Fuller and Quintin Thomson also wrote from their mission stations arguing that there was something to gain from the annexation of Cameroon. Mr Fuller stressed the commercial advantages, and pointed out that the new station of Bakundu was already linked to the coast by King Bell. He had opened trading markets in the towns and on the beaches along the Mungo river.[28] Quintin Thomson wrote praising King Bell who was doing all in his power to improve the Cameroon trade. He confirmed Fuller's report that the King had opened the river the whole way to Bakundu to trade, which was twice as far as Cameroon traders had ever gone before.[29] This was possibly to enable the coastal middlemen to gain easy access to the interior markets and to bring their purchases in bulk to the coast by river, rather than to encourage Europeans to trade directly with the interior peoples.

Consul Hewett, when requested by the Foreign Office to do so, also reported on the economic advantages of British annexation. He pointed out that annexation would push the British traders into the interior and get rid of the services of the middlemen who would thus be 'forced into the cultivation of their own rich soil, and so increase the amount and variety of the exports'. As regards customs duties that would be levied after annexation, he said 'it would be difficult to levy them without also obtaining Victoria and Bimbia on the north and Malimba to the southward'. Consul Hewett stressed that the nature and fertility of the Cameroon soil appeared 'well adapted for the growth of cotton, coffee, tobacco, and other tropical productions'.[30] Earlier, in 1882, Hewett had advised the Foreign Office that all the territory commencing southward of the Cameroon coast and extending westward to Benin be taken as a protectorate, or given to a British chartered company for administration.[31] After Hewett's report, the British government became convinced that the time had come when it was 'desirable that Her Majesty's Government should decide in what way they can best protect British trade in the present, and encourage and secure it in the future, in those parts of the West Coast of Africa, which comprise the healthy regions round the Cameroons and the rich districts of the Niger and Oil rivers'.[32] Yet the Foreign Office did not see any reason for a rush, perceiving no serious threat from any quarter.

Apparently, the British had not given thought as to how their trade collaborators, the Germans, felt about the possibility of German annexation of Cameroon, or to Germany's colonial interests. Though supporting British annexation from the beginning, the German traders were slowly but firmly becoming patriotic. Secretly, they began to make plans as to what they would do in the event that Britain did not annex Cameroon but rather let the territory slip into French hands. These traders began to voice their desire to see the territories extending from the Cameroon coast to the Congo annexed by Germany. In the latter half of 1883 A. Woermann, president of the C. Woermann Trading Company in Hamburg, submitted a memorandum to the German government urging it to annex Cameroon. He requested that the government consider seriously the advantages of annexation, among which were: the expansion of German shipping lines, 'the circumnavigation' of the middleman monopoly of Douala, the assurance of a market for Germany's surplus goods, a fertile area for producing needed raw materials, the establishment of plantations, and profits from land speculation.[33] Pressure from A. Woermann, other individuals and business groups with stakes in Cameroon, no doubt convinced Chancellor Bismarck to agree in November 1883 to support the establishment of a Consular Service, a warship patrol, negotiations for a coaling station at Fernando Po, and trade treaties with the chiefs of the Cameroon coast.

Of course an explanation based on Germany's international relations sees Germany's sudden decision to obtain colonies after repeated rejections differently. It holds that Chancellor Bismarck had never really been against colonialism and used repeated rejections only to conceal his true intentions until the most propitious moment.[34] He might also have been forced to change his mind by political, economic and diplomatic considerations such as the advantage he would gain in the autumn elections of 1884; the pursuit of an anti-British move in the colonial race which would serve as a bait for an *entente* with France; mounting concern about the possible adverse consequences of continued abstention from the colonial race; the desire to carve out trading areas for Germans at a time when free trade in the areas of influence of colonial powers was fast drawing to an end; and the desire to forestall other powers which would have hoisted their flags in Germany's favoured spots, as well as concern about his own place in history.

Meanwhile German trade on the Cameroon coast continued to grow by leaps and bounds. Indeed, various assessments of British and German trade in 1883 and 1884 confirmed that the Germans had taken over the number one position from the British in both the import and export trade of Cameroon. Notoriously exaggerated as these assessments were, they had their impact in the discussions for annexation. A British newspaper calculated in 1884 that the two German firms were buying 180–200 tons of oil monthly, the six English firms were not exporting so much; the Germans up to 200 tons of palm-kernels per month, while the English bought hardly any at all. The ivory trade, about 50 000 lb per annum, was almost exclusively in the hands of the Germans.[35] The paper also provided statistics which showed that German commodities now sold better and in larger volumes than English products:

German and English trade in Cameroon 1883 and 1884

Countries	1883				1884			
	Arrived		Cleared		Arrived		Cleared	
	Ship	Tons	Ship	Tons	Ship	Tons	Ship	Tons
German steamers	15	20 035	14	19 309	27	37 791	26	37 701
English steamers	15	20 963	13	18 229	27	29 450	20	28 898
German sailing vessels	2	726	1	398	1	1 600		
English sailing vessels	6	2 052	3	1 049	7	2 005	6	1 836

With statistics like these, it was clear that Germans no longer felt content to leave their interests in Cameroon under the control of the British. Moreover, the relationships between British and German traders began to strain and English opposition to German traders generally, and especially within the Court of Equity at Douala, began to grow. The tonnage cleared from German steamers in 1884 probably included cargo from the previous year.

It is therefore clear that during the years 1879 to 1884 the situation on the Cameroon coast had provided for the economic need of each of the three imperial powers to aspire to annex the territory. The French had established themselves firmly in major towns south of Douala and stood to lose commercially (and territorially) if uprooted from the district. The Germans had surpassed the British in trade and were discriminated against by the French and opposed by the English in the Court of Equity. Consul Hewett's earlier suggestion that the Cameroon coast should be annexed and given to a British Chartered Company for administration possibly created the suspicion that foreign businesses might not be allowed the freedom they were already enjoying in the area. The British, who were the *de facto* informal masters on the Cameroon coast, saw their position threatened commercially by the Germans and territorially by the French. Their fear that French annexation might lead to the expulsion of foreign nationals and restriction of British trade in Cameroon gave rise to the urge that they should formally declare their sovereignty over the territory. By the beginning of 1884, the economic scramble for Cameroon was already under way.

The struggle for imperial supremacy

During the two or three years before 1879 and until 1885, information reaching Europe about the political situation on the Cameroon coast suggested a gloomy outlook for the future. The kings and chiefs were said to be finding it increasingly difficult to govern their people, mainly, it was claimed, because of rivalry between chiefdoms and between European and Cameroonian traders. English missionaries claimed that Cameroon rulers were seeking the protection of a stronger and firmer European power that would hold local passions in leash, and that they were making frequent overtures to British representatives to annex their country. The missionary, George Grenfell, described the terrible plight of the Duala sovereign rulers: 'The headmen in the river are anxious to be under Her Majesty's control .... They are evidently getting tired of their attempts to govern themselves. Every dispute leads to war, and often great loss of life'.[37] In a letter to a friend, Grenfell himself expressed a strong desire for British annexation. 'I have no ambition', he wrote, 'to see England take possession of Western Africa simply that she may enlarge her empire, but I must devoutly hope she may do so for the sake of the poor people who are unable to rule themselves'.[38] Other missionaries confirmed Grenfell's reports, claiming that frequent wars and unhealthy rivalry between indigenous polities were the two chief curses of the Cameroon coast which everyone would like to see eliminated. They thought that the hope of a satisfactory way of establishing law and order in the region was for England to take control of Cameroon.[39]

From 1881, the missionaries were no longer content with merely describing the political instability of Cameroon or expressing the desire to see the British annex the territory. They and the English traders and officials had now joined the Cameroon chiefs in the campaign for British annexation. Their apparent rivals in what was soon going to be a keen contest for Cameroon were the French. The British and the Germans were particularly alarmed when they learned that the French were about to annex territory just south of Douala, at Big Batanga. It appeared the French were taking advantage of British indecision over the annexation question and might themselves annex Cameroon. This thought was supported by the fact that some chiefs south of Douala were known to be enthusiastically signing away their sovereignty to the French official, Godin, who pointed out the ease with which a treaty with Malimba was signed.[40] Every missionary, trader, official and local chief in the Douala and Ambas Bay enclaves wrote to London warning about the French danger, and requesting immediate British annexation. In 1882 Consul Hewett advocated immediate British annexation of territory from Benin to Cameroon, otherwise the French would step in. In April 1883 kings Bell and Akwa, together, protested against the presence of the French anywhere on the Cameroon coast, arguing that they wanted the entire territory to be annexed by Britain, so that 'the tribes may continue to maintain the relationships that had always existed among them.'[41] A missionary, W. Collings, who had served in Cameroon launched the annexation campaign on the home front by pointing out that the Cameroon district 'is the healthiest on the whole coast, the Great Cameroon Mountain ... affording every advantage from a sanitary point of view .... On the upper slopes of the mountains all European vegetables may be grown and a home climate enjoyed'.[42] Mr Collings added that the acquisition of Cameroon would save many valuable lives in West Africa and the expense of home journeys as all would go to the sanatorium on the slopes of Mount Cameroon. He claimed that the physical characteristics of the Cameroon district were more favourable to European life than in any colony on the west coast.

In mid-1883, Consul Hewett was requested to investigate and submit a detailed report of the political, economic, social, geographical and climatological situation in Cameroon, as well as his observations on the various petitions for annexation and the feeling of kings and chiefs on the matter. In this all-positive report in favour of British annexation, Hewett argued that H.M. Government would acquire territory by annexation or by establishing a protectorate over Cameroon. In this way Britain would acquire 'the great influence in the interior now exercised by the kings and chiefs of Cameroon.'[43] As far as the kings and chiefs were concerned, he said that there would be no difficulty in governing them. Shortly after this report a treaty was signed by the Cameroon kings and chiefs and witnessed by missionaries, British and German traders affirming that everyone on the Cameroon coast would be better off were they taken under British protection.[44] It was after Hewett's report and this treaty that the official British attitude towards an early annexation began to change. But the change continued to be cautiously slow. It was because of this that the German traders in Cameroon began to campaign secretly for German, rather than British, annexation of Cameroon.

A German note on the proceedings concerning Angra Pequena in S.W. Africa in May, 1884, stated that the German Government desired to ascertain what provisions England possessed on the spot, in areas where the British Government neither possessed nor claimed sovereign rights, 'for the protection of German subjects in their commercial enterprises and lawful acquisitions; so that the German Empire might consider itself exempted from the duty of providing its subjects in that territory by direct means with the protection of which they might stand in need'.[45] All the German note appeared to say was that Germany was not yet prepared for annexation, although she had a duty to protect German trade and nationals. Earlier, in March and April, the Germans had taken steps to assert a protectorate over this same territory, 'but the ambiguity of their statements and the imperceptiveness of Gladstone's ministers ... left the British as naively ignorant as ever about where their attitude was taking them'.[46] It was definitely going to take them a long way from their goal because a German imperial commissioner already on his way to the West and South West Coast of Africa was soon to be given definite and final instructions to annex not only Angra Pequena, but also Togo and Cameroon – especially the latter, where German interests were said to lie and known to be considerable. Although it may not be accepted generally, it would appear that the Southern Africa manoeuvres were devices to obtain the West African territories.

Dr Gustav Nachtigal, a well-known African explorer, was the Commissioner appointed to undertake a mission to Cameroon to study German trade, examine the prospects of a coaling station in the Bight of Biafra, and conduct negotiations on certain specific questions. He was accompanied by Dr Buchner and Herr Moebuis.[47] The German Government informed and appealed to the British Government to give Dr Nachtigal assistance and co-operation in his work in Cameroon. The imperial commissioner reached Lisbon before definite instructions to annex Cameroon were communicated to him. He was instructed to make arrangements that would leave Germany in control of territories acquired before or after his arrival, hoist the German flag, and 'declare that the German firms had closed [sic] treaties with the chiefs'.[48] Instructions were then sent to German traders in Douala to prepare for Nachtigal's arrival. They were to obtain from the chiefs the cession of their sovereignty for the German Government, and to demonstrate to them the advantages they would have under German protection.[49] On receiving these highly confidential instructions the traders began to make secret proposals to the native kings that they sell portions of their lands to Germany and accept a German protectorate.

Meanwhile the German press began to leak out the real purpose of Nachtigal's mission. The semi-official *Nord-Deutsche Zeitung* reported that Nachtigal's mission was necessitated by the happy increase in the commercial relations of Germany with the West Coast of Africa, and the feeling that the interests of German commerce should not be left in the protection of trading consuls.[50] Similarly, the *Kölnische Zeitung* reported that Nachtigal was on a mission to establish a coaling station at Fernando Po, and hoist the German flag in the Bay of Biafra.[51] The British, not sensing any ulterior motives in these reports, sent word to their nationals — officials, traders and missionaries — to accord Nachtigal a 'proper reception'. Bismarck had also informed French authorities of the friendly nature of Nachtigal's mission. On 11 July 1884, Nachtigal and his companions arrived in Douala 'to be received with honour by all, and only their fellow countrymen suspected that there was anything in the way of a political *coup* to be enacted'.[52] The representatives of the two German firms had succeeded in concluding a number of secret treaties with the chiefs before Nachtigal could arrive. In them, the chiefs accepted to give up their sovereignty and the legislation and management of their country 'entirely' to the agents of the firms, acting as for the firms in Hamburg, and for many years trading in the Cameroon district. They, however, reserved the right of the third party, the full power of all treaties signed earlier with other foreign governments, ownership of their lands, plains and towns, respect for their traditions, and made it clear that German traders would continue to pay 'all the dash as before'.[53]

While the Germans kept their plans for the *coup* confidential, in case the British became suspicious and hastened up, the British, still suspicious of French intent, began their own moves to annex the Niger and Cameroon districts and dislodge their enemy. They allowed no room for pessimism and anticipated no contest, falsely believing that the whole of the Cameroon coast and the Oil Rivers were still generally considered as under their influence and protection. In May Consul Hewett, then on leave in England, was instructed to return to his post 'without delay' to implement arrangements for strengthening the Consular staff in the Niger and Oil River districts, express to the kings and chiefs 'the desire of Her Majesty to maintain and strengthen the relations of peace and friendship which have for a long time existed', and to inform them that the Queen is willing to extend her favour of protection over them if requested. Hewett, however, was not to accept the cession of the Cameroon river district at this time, but was to ask the chiefs 'to undertake that they would, if required, cede such portions of their territory as it may be thought desirable to acquire'.[54] He was to proclaim Ambas Bay a British protectorate and fix his residence in the neighbourhood of Douala. As Hewett approached the Oil Rivers, stopping and holding meetings with chiefs, British intelligence reported a German ship steering towards the Cameroon river, and instructions were issued to Commander Moore to communicate with Kings Bell and Akwa that Consul Hewett was coming very shortly 'with a friendly message from Her Majesty the Queen', and that they should not make any treaty with any other government until his arrival.[55] When Commander Moore reported on the situation in Douala and how time was running out, Captain Brooke sent word to Consul Hewett and himself left for Bimbia and Batanga with instructions to sign treaties with the chiefs taking their countries under British protection, subject to approval by Her Majesty's Government. He arrived too late, after the Germans had already signed annexation treaties there.

The annexation and the consolidation of the German Protectorate

Secret German campaigns and treaties of annexation had progressed as planned. On 12 July, a day after Nachtigal arrived, the chiefs of Douala presented a memorandum to the German officials which they insisted must be included in the treaty of annexation. In the memorandum they demanded that whitemen should not trade directly with the people of the interior, that their laws on marriage remain as they have always been, that their cultivated grounds remain in their possession, that no duties be levied on their livestock, and that natives should be punished only for crimes committed.[56] These hardened conditions might have been aimed at obtaining from the Germans better conditions than they probably would have received from the British. Or, perhaps, the chiefs became suspicious of Germany's eagerness to annex their lands and wanted to test their sincerity. Whatever the reasons, the Germans accepted the terms of the treaty, and on Monday, 14 July, Nachtigal officially annexed the Batanga territory, the Cameroon river district and Bimbia, and hoisted the German flag. On 15 July, Nachtigal abolished the Douala Court of Equity, and established the 'Cameroon Council' under the presidency of a German representative.

Consul Hewett arrived in Cameroon on 19 July, five days 'too late'. On being told at Victoria about the German annexation, he sailed straight to Douala to verify the story. He instructed the senior Baptist Missionary in Victoria, Thomas Lewis, to proclaim the tiny missionary settlement an integral part of Her Majesty's dominions. He also handed him a proclamation to fix on a public place.[57] The proclamation stated that Hewett was acting in compliance with the wishes of the inhabitants in notifying the public that 'the territory which has long been in the possession and occupation of certain British subjects ... constituting the settlement of Victoria, has now been taken over by Her Majesty the Queen ..., and forms an integral part of her dominions'.[58] At Douala Hewett held meetings with German officials and with the chiefs, but failed to make King Bell change his mind against the Germans. He eventually returned to Victoria to hoist the Union Jack and formalise the annexation. In August he addressed a letter to each of the kings of the German-annexed territories expressing shock and dismay that after their application for British protection they should have accepted another power: 'of Germany', he said, 'you knew nothing and she has never given any indication of interest in you ... It appears from all I hear as though you sold your country for a few chattels and guns, and that you felt no obligation to the Queen such as you formerly considered you had'.[59] King Bell replied that he signed the treaty because he and his chiefs received no definite answer to their several requests for British protection. In a letter to the Earl of Derby the king explained that after inquiring anxiously for over five years to know if the British Government would annex his country without favourable replies, he had despaired in the end, and had been 'induced to accept the offer of the German Government for annexation'.[60] The other kings explained that they had been duped by the Germans into signing a treaty whose nature and terms were not clearly explained to them.[61]

Reactions to German annexation by missionaries, British traders and officials, and some Cameroonians were unfriendly and violent. The Revs. Thomas Lewis and Samuel Silvey wrote several letters condemning the German intrigue. Lewis implored the BMS Secretary to set before the British Government, on behalf of the BMS, 'the rightful claims of England and English subjects on the River Cameroons' and put the clock back. 'We do not deem it too late', he wrote, 'to place the district and the river in the hands of the British Government, although three German flags have been hoisted here'.[62] Silvey reported in December 1884, and Lewis confirmed, that since the hoisting of the German flag the towns on the river had been 'in a very unsettled condition'. and that the Germans were unpopular with the people. He said German men-of-war were arriving and firing on the towns 'without the least warning'.[63] A Cameroonian clergyman, Pastor Joshua Tundi, reported that war had broken out between the people and the Germans, and that the Germans killed about four Cameroonians, but suffered heavy casualties themselves.[64]

British traders on their part also strongly protested against the German annexation which they said was negotiated in the dark, and constituted a violation of a treaty of 1883 which affirmed that everyone would be happy if they were taken under British protection. The BMS committee, happy with the news of the annexation of Victoria requested the Foreign Office to confirm whether the action of Consul Hewett had received sanction, and 'whether the action of the German Government with regard to Cameroons has been approved by Her Majesty's Government'.[65]

On the part of the indigenous people violence is said to have erupted between the pro- and the anti-German treaty signatories on the one hand and some Douala groups and the Germans on the other. King Bell's people rose against him, and he and his family were reported to have considered it wise to seek refuge in the bush. Several missionary letters and reports confirmed this state of affairs in Douala throughout the remaining months of 1884, although the casualty figures differed from one informant to another. In January 1885 Bismarck told the Reichstag sitting at Berlin about the war between the Cameroonians and the Germans which resulted in 'loss of many killed and wounded on the negro side and with one man killed and several wounded on the German'.[66] The German Chancellor warned the Reichstag that Germany must either give up business in Cameroon 'or make haste to establish our authority'. He said he had facts to prove that the British were fomenting hostility between the natives and the Germans. Dr Busch, Bismarck's secretary, said he found that complaints about German intrigues were based on the language of the British Consul and other officials. He said that Consul Hewett had written to the chiefs referring to them as 'great fools for selling themselves to Germany' and warning that 'they would find out later that they would have done better to accept English rather than German protection'.[67]

German authorities decided to act immediately to put an end to all anti-German activities in Cameroon. Bismarck had warned a few weeks after annexation that London was not showing the consideration to German trade to which it was entitled. He said if Germany failed to push her rights with energy, she risked 'letting them sink into oblivion, falling into a position inferior to England's and strengthening the unbounded arrogance shown by England and her colonies to us .... Seeing the want of consideration shown in British colonial policy, modesty on our part is out of place and is not the way to maintain good relations with England'.[68] German authorities denied missionary propaganda that they were unpopular with the natives, and claimed that they found Cameroonians just as anxious to become subjects of the Emperor William and averse to the English, as English accounts claimed they were 'burning' to acknowledge Queen Victoria and opposed to the Germans. The German authorities threatened, as any other power would have, to banish all foreigners – missionaries and traders – if they sided in any way with those hostile to German authorities. Missionary residences began to be screened and some mission stations were destroyed, while loaded pistols and rifles were pointed at some missionaries by German soldiers. Silvey and Lewis wrote reporting that the Germans were trying to make their position as uncomfortable as possible in the hope of driving them away from Cameroon. The Germans also began to show anxiety to obtain possession of the British settlement of Victoria, and were talking about sending German missionaries to replace the British. This attitude began to encourage the feeling among BMS circles that their days in Cameroon were numbered.

The Cameroonian reaction to the Anglo-German struggle for supremacy on the Cameroon coast was not uniform. There was a clear conflict within the indigenous society, and there is no simple explanation for the fragmentation of the community. Certainly, missionary and traders' propaganda had much to do with it. Those who had committed themselves to the treaty stayed put, perhaps as a matter of principle and those who were not were incited – a natural occurrence. Whatever the explanation, the indigenous society was divided, and only firm action by the Germans could stabilise the situation and reunite the groups. In any event, the Germans were not as unpopular, even at the beginning, as British missionaries, traders and officials tried to show they were. Young men appear to have supported them, and many entered the German army and were sent abroad for training.[69] Thomas Lewis even noted that Dr Buchner whom Dr Nachtigal left in charge of the colony 'was well liked' and quite friendly.

The German annexation of the Cameroon river enclave and the British annexation of Victoria, began a major race for other surrounding territories, which literally brought the two imperial powers near to a clash in the scramble for Cameroon. The Germans moved to annex the Cameroon Mountain region. The British began to sign treaties in territories behind German protectorates in an effort to encircle the German territories and cut them off from the interior. Prince Bismarck informed Count Münster that British agents were busy cutting German acquisitions from the mountains and the easter hinterland. He said the British were led by a Slav, named Rogozinski, and were determined to hamper the German inward extension and injure German prestige.[70] Germans in West Africa also wrote home complaining about the activities of Rogozinski.

Stephen Rogozinski, a Polish national, had come to Cameroon in 1883 on an expedition which he organised as an independent undertaking. He soon established very cordial relations with the local population, and gained tremendous respect and influence with the chiefs of the mountain region. After the Germans annexed Douala, Bimbia and Batanga, he decided to use his influence to frustrate the endeavours of Germany, a nation for which he had no sympathy. Through treaties he was able to obtain 'the Cameroon Mountain and the whole of the coast stretching from the mouth of the Niger to the German settlement on the Cameroon river', for Britain.[71] In February 1885 Vice-Consul White, acting *ultra vires*, appointed him Chief Civil Commissioner, with full powers of Governor in his (Vice-Consul's) absence. This appointment raised strong objections even among the missionaries in Cameroon and England, and was quickly terminated by the British Government.

One of the highlights of the scramble occurred on the slopes of the mountain, north of the river, wherein lay independent villages about equal distances from Bimbia, Victoria and Douala. 'Among the villages', wrote a special correspondent of the *Kölnische Zeitung*, himself a participant, 'a sort of three-cornered annexing match has been going on between certain persons from Victoria on behalf of England, the correspondent of the *Kölnische Zeitung* on behalf of Germany and the Pole Rogozinski ... on behalf of himself. And a rare scramble it seems to have been'.[72] This incident must have occurred before Rogozinski was able to convince British officials to allow him to transfer the sovereignty of the villages with which he had signed treaties to the British. It looked as though a violent clash would erupt between the British and the Germans on the Cameroon coast, but war was avoided.

The British authorities took the initiative in keeping the situation under control, once they realised they had lost Cameroon, if only for the safety of their nationals who were more numerous than citizens of other European countries put together. They had to be content that German annexation had kept the French out — a thing to be happy about. The British, however, expressed the hope that the status quo under which trade was carried out before annexation would be maintained.

In January 1885 the Foreign Office replied to King Bell's letter regretting his action, but advising him to 'remain loyal to the country under whose protectorate you have placed yourself'.[73] At Berlin Mr Meade, the British Assistant Under-Secretary for the Colonies, assured the German Government that the British would not stand in the way of Germany's endeavours to extend their territories inland, and that the BMS were ready to offer their co-operation in facilitating the establishment of German rule in Cameroon. The Colonial Under-Secretary advised his home Government to instruct the British Consul in Cameroon to use 'whatever influence he may possess with the natives to accept their new masters', and the English traders 'to keep quiet and not raise difficulties'.[74] In March the German Ambassador in London, Count Bismarck, informed the Chancellor, Prince Bismarck, that the British were ready to make liberal concessions in Cameroon 'to prove the good will of England', and that they had accepted the German position 'fully and loyally'.[75] Given the controversy over the role of Rogozinski, the British Government refused to press any territorial claims on the treaties signed by him, letting Germany have the territories in question. The British then proposed the boundary between Cameroon and their protectorate of Calabar to be on the Rio del Rey.

Rather than wait and be expelled, the BMS began to explore ways of reaching a settlement over the lands they owned in the Ambas Bay region and other parts of the Cameroon district, and to withdraw peacefully from Cameroon. This step was taken when it was known that the Germans were very anxious to obtain Victoria, and had continued to regard BMS missionaries with bitterness. The BMS therefore advised that the British and German governments should negotiate the sale of Victoria, on the understanding that the Germans would fairly compensate the BMS for the outlay they had expended upon the settlement, and for the original purchase money thereupon. The lengthy negotiations for the transfer of Victoria ended with an Exchange of Notes between England and Germany in January 1887. On 28 March the midget British colony on the Cameroon coast was effectively handed over to the German Governor in Cameroon.

The French, who had occupied territory in the districts south of Douala, had much earlier decided to withdraw from Cameroon after the German annexation. In December 1885 they reached an agreement with the Germans fixing a provisional boundary between their spheres on the Campo River, which constituted the southernmost limit of the Cameroon coast. By virtue of this Franco-German boundary, all the territories between Douala and Campo were incorporated into the German protectorate. Following the fixing of Cameroon's southern and western boundaries and the withdrawal of British and French authorities and nationals from the Cameroon coast, Germany remained the only internationally recognised imperial power supremely in possession of the entire Cameroon Coast.

Conclusion

Our account has shown how events on the Cameroon coast from the two decades or so before 1879 to 1887, catapulted the Germans into the leading position in the area. In their rise to pre-eminence in Cameroon, the Germans were able to displace commercially and politically to oust both the influential and favoured British and the isolationist French and annex the territory. The role of each of the three imperial powers and the Duala people in the annexation of Cameroon may read like an exaggeration, but the literature consulted on this subject suggests clearly that this was indeed the situation. The German success and occupation of Cameroon constituted a terrible imperial upset for British and French colonial ambitions in the Bight of Biafra.

The events on the Cameroon coast were characteristic of what happened during the European scramble for African territories in the 1880s. Indeed, the scramble for Africa was marked by conflicts of interests, disputes over territories, and oppositions to specific claims. Each power tried to prevent its rivals from claiming territories anywhere in its areas of influence by signing pre-emptive treaties with African rulers, supporting the claims of weaker and friendly nations against the interests of arch-enemies, and using territories claimed as bases for negotiating more favourable claims elsewhere. Thus, the British supported the Portuguese and Belgian occupation of the Congo territories as a means of preventing their arch-enemy, France, from occupying the area. Similarly, the French behaviour in the Congo was directed at obstructing British interests there in retaliation for the latter having ousted the French from Egypt in 1882. In South-West Africa, the Germans provoked an Anglo-German dispute over Angra Pequena in order to divert British attention from Cameroon and Togo and so occupy the two territories. In short, the scramble was a struggle to acquire and control as many portions of African territory as possible in order to deprive rivals of them. In the end, by the turn of the century, the whole continent, except Ethiopia and Liberia, was shared out among eight European nations and Turkey.

Notes

*   See V.G. Fanso, 'Background to the Annexation of Cameroon, 1875–1885; *Abbia: Cameroon Cultural Review*, nos. 20–30, 1975, pp. 231–280.

1   See copy of the 'Treaty with Kings, Chiefs, and traders of Cameroons', 14 January 1856, and renewed 'Bye-Laws' of May 19, 1862, as well as 'Additional Articles to the Treaty … of 14 January 1856', of 6 January 1869, in Shirley G. Ardener, *Eye-Witnesses to the Annexation of Cameroon 1883–1887*, Buea, Government Press, 1968, Appendix B, pp. 76–78 and 80–83.

2   F.O. 2/45, Consul Burton to Earl Russel, 15 April 1864.

3   See R. Kuczynski, *The Cameroons and Togoland*, London, 1939, p. 3; H. R. Rudin, *Germans in the Cameroons 1884–1914*, Greenwood Edition, New York, 1968, p. 157; N. Rubin, *Cameroon*, London, 1971, p. 24.

4   Rudin, p. 233.

5   S. Ardener, *Eye-Witnesses to the Annexation*, p. 63.

6   *Ibid.* pp. 66–67.

7   *Ibid.*, pp. 76–78 and 80–83.

8   *Ibid.*, p. 79.

9a Rudin, p. 19.

9b For the fear of the French, see F.O. 403/18, 403/20 and 403/32 containing letters from chiefs, missionaries and officials to this effect.

10 F.O. 403/18, Cameroon Chiefs to Her Majesty the Queen, August 7 1979.

11 George Hawker, *The Life of George Grenfell*, London, 1909, p. 86.

12 Grenfell to Rev. B. Bird, 28 February 1879 excerpts published in the *Annual Report of the Committee of the Baptist Missionary Society 1879*, p. 102.

13 G. Grenfell, 'The Cameroon District', in *Proceedings of the Royal Geographical Society*, Vol. 4 (New Series), 1882, p. 594.

14 S. Ardener, *Eye-Witnesses to the Annexation*, p. 28.

15 G. Grenfell to Rev. B. Bird, 28 February 1879, cited, p. 102.

16 *Ibid.*

17 'Treaty with the Kings, Chiefs and Traders of Cameroon, 14 January 1856'.

18 Rudin, p. 22.

19 See 'Acknowledgement receipt from the Royal Insurance Office, Glasgow to Rev. Q. W. Thomson', 3 June 1881, Box A/8, BMS, London. George Thomson was a Scottish philanthropist, trader and builder who arrived in Cameroon in 1871 with the intention of building a sanatorium for Europeans on the Cameroon Mountain. He died of malaria in 1878.

20 A. J. H. Latham, *Old Calabar 1600–1891*, Oxford, 1973, p. 63.

21 *Pall Mall Gazette*, 10 March 1885.

22 Crowe, p. 37.

23 Rudin, p. 126.

24 *Ibid.*, pp. 225–6.

25 *Command Papers*, C-4279 (1885), p. 13; also Rudin, p. 22.

26 Rudin, p. 20

27 Grenfell, 'The Cameroon District', *Proceedings of the Royal Geographical Society*, 1882, p. 594.

28 See, Grenfell, *op. cit.*, and *The Missionary Herald*

29 *Missionary Herald* 1883, p. 22.

30 FO/403/18, Consul Hewett to Earl Granville, 7 June 1883.

31 FO/403/18 Consul Hewett to Earl Granville, January 1882.

32 FO/403/18 Mr Lister to Mr Bramston, 8 October.

33 Rudin, pp. 34, and pp. 157−158 for A. Woermann's role in the German annexation procedure.

34 See, Henry Ashby Turner, Jr. 'Bismarck's Imperialist Venture: Anti-British in Origin?' in P. Gifford and W. R. Louis, *Britain and Germany in Africa*, London, 1967, pp. 47−82.

35 *Pall Mall Gazette*, 10 March 1885.

36 A leading Hamburg businessman listed increasing German trade and English opposition to German traders among the five reasons for German annexation. See, Rudin, p. 33.

37 Hawker, *The Life of George Grenfell*, p. 86.

38 Grenfell to Rev. B. Bird, 28 February 1879.

39 *Missionary Herald 1879*, p. 40.

40 R. F. Betts, *The Scramble for Africa: Causes and Dimensions of Empire*, London, 1966, p. 45.

41 FO/403/20, Bell and Akwa to Hewett, 23 April, 1883; F.O. 403/32, King William of Big Batanga later complained about the Treaty he signed with the French, 14 June 1883.

42 FO/403/32, Rev. W. Collings to the Earl of Derby, 22 August 1883; also F.O. 403/20, Rev. Collings to Mr Gladstone, 27 September, 1883.

43 F.O. 403/18, Consul Hewett to Earl Granville, 7 June 1883.

44 F.O. 403/32, British Traders to Earl Granville, 24 July 1884.

45 *German Diplomatic Documents 1871−1914*, Vol. 1, 1928, Prince Bismark to Count Munster, 25 May 1885, p. 174

46 R. Robinson and J. Gallagher, *Africa and the Victorians*, New York, 1968, p. 173.

47 Dr Buchner was described as an African traveller, and Herr Mocbius as Secretary at the German Consulate General in London. Buchner published a memoir entitled *Aurora Colonialis* in München in 1914 providing eye-witness information on what heppened in Cameroon in 1884−5.

48 S. Ardener *Eye-Witnesses to the Annexation*, p. 22; also, Rudin. pp. 37−39.

49 S. Ardener, *Eye-Witnesses to the Annexation*, Appendix C. pp. 84−86, for Instructions of A. Woermann to E. Schmidt, 6 May 1884.

50 *British Parliamentary Papers*, Colonies Africa, 51 (OUP) Lord Ampthill to Earl Granville, 23 April 1884, p. 372.

51 *British Parliamentary Papers*, Minute by Lt Col Bell, 23 April 1884, p. 373.

52 Thomas Lewis, *These Seventy Years*, London, 1930, p. 70.

53 FO/403/32 Draft Treaty Between Chiefs of Bimbia and Agents of German firms, 11 July 1884.

54 Command Papers, C-4279, pp. 16−17. Lister to Consul Hewett, 16 May 1884.

55 *Command Papers*, C-4279 Orders to Commander Moore, 10 July 1884, p. 20.

56 S. Ardener, *Eye-Witnesses to the Annexation*, note 57, p. 57.

57 Lewis, *These Seventy Years*, p. 71; also, Hertslet's *Commercial Treaties, XVII*, pp. 57−58, for the proclamations.

58 See copy of the Notification of the Assumption of British Sovereignty over Victoria in Ardener, *Eye-Witnesses to the Annexation*, p. 68.

59 Box H/23, BMS, London. Extracts from the *Cologne Gazette*.

60 FO/403/32, King Bell to the Earl of Derby, 30 September 1884.

61 *Command Papers*, C-4279, pp. 46–49. See copies of statements taken by Commander Craigie from the Head Chiefs of Dicolo Town, Money Town, and William Town, on 13 September 1884.

62 F.O. 403/32, Thomas Lewis to Mr Baynes, 3 September 1884.

63 Box A/1, BMS, London, Silvey to Baynes, December 1884.

64 Box A/5, BMS London, Pastor Joshua Tundi to Mr Fuller.

65 Command papers, C-4279, Mr Baynes to Lord Fitzmaurice, 22 September 1884, pp. 36–37.

66 *Pall Mall Gazette*, 12 January 1885. See also: Lewis, *These Seventy Years*, p. 71; Silvey's letters of December 1884 to Baynes, Box A/4 BMS for more evidence about African resistance to annexation.

67 *Command Papers*, C-4290, Memorandum by Mr Meade, 14 December 1884, Memoranda on Conversation at Berlin between Meade and Prince Bismarck and Dr Busch (1885), p. 8.

68 *German Diplomatic Documents 1871–1914*, Vol. 1, Prince Bismarck to Count Munster, 12 August 1884, p. 182.

69 Box A/3, BMS London. Miss E. Saker to Mr Baynes, 30 January 1885.

70 *German Diplomatic Documents*, Vol. 1, p. 188; and *Pall Mall Gazette*, 12 January 1885.

71 *Pall Mall Gazette*, 21 January 1885.

72 Extracts from *Cologne Gazette*, published in *Pall Mall Gazette*, 10 March 1885.

73 FO/403/32 Mr Lister to King Bell, 12 January 1885.

74 *Command Papers*, C-4290, pp. 3–7, Extracts from a private letter from Mr Meade to Earl Granville, and Enclosure 1, 'Memorandum', 13 December 1884.

75 *German Diplomatic Documents*, Vol. 1, Count Bismarck to Prince Bismarck, 7 March 1885, pp. 191–192.

Chapter Four
Rain forest encounters: the Beti meet the Germans, 1887–1916

Frederick E. Quinn

In the last chapter we saw how on 14 July 1884 Cameroon became a German colony. Several Duala traders signed treaties with Dr Gustav Nachtigal, a consul-explorer, giving the Germans access to a potentially profitable market. There was no particular reason why Cameroon should become a German colony, except that the Germans made the first move. British traders were more numerous than Germans in the Douala estuary and numerous French merchants also worked in the Cameroon coast. In fact, a British emissary, known as too late Hewitt, arrived five days after Nachtigal had secured his agreements.[1]

Economic, rather than political reasons brought the Germans to Cameroon. Traders wanted to extend their markets, and colonial societies encouraged overseas expansion through sponsored explorations, publications and lobbying. Bismarck, by contrast, did not want to sink people and monies into colonial ventures, which he believed the French were doing to their ruin. He was for minimal governmental participation overseas, believing traders should raise the revenues and govern the territories themselves.

The traders had a different view. As might be expected, they sought the maximum possible protection for the lowest possible cost. The merchants wanted gunboats and military posts, but opposed the government's efforts to collect taxes and customs, and carried on active trade in arms and contraband goods with Africans.

It was not until three years after the colony was established, in 1887, that the Germans reached Yaoundé, which would eventually become Cameroon's capital. The trek took twenty-two days through heavy rain forest and swamps, crossing the land of hostile groups, the Basa among them, who wanted to protect the inland trade for themselves.[2]

1889 – the Beti-German encounter

The Yaoundé post was established in February 1889, the first German inland station in Cameroon. It was named after the Ewondo, one of four principal Beti groups living there, but Germans misunderstood the word and transcribed it incorrectly for posterity as 'Jaunde'. The Germans sought a direct route from the coast to the interior and the ivory trade. They also hoped to siphon this commerce away from the British, and to stop the southward movement of Hausa traders toward the British in Nigeria.[3]

Without knowing it, the Germans had settled in the midst of a Bantu speaking population of some 500 000 persons, centred in the rain forest between the Nyong and Sanaga rivers. Traditional Beti government was through headmen, called *mie dzala* 'shapers of the compound'. Each compound, *nda bod*, represented an autonomous minimal lineage core segment. The land between the two rivers was filled with several thousand such units. There were no paramount chiefs, only independent headmen. A headman's compound might include the *mie dzala*, his wives, children, the headman's unmarried brothers until they raised bride price and moved off to found compounds of their own, plus clients, and household slaves.[4]

The headman owned the land about him. Such land was plentiful, for the Beti were recent migrants into the sparsely populated rain forest. Their compound chiefs also received a payment of goods by traders moving across their territory, plus a portion of anything grown or killed on it. Marriage alliances, principally through the exchange of daughters, gave headmen some stability in relations with other headmen. There were other temporary alliances for warfare and ritual action, but these units dissolved once their purpose was achieved.

There were several armed skirmishes between the Beti and the Germans between 1889 and 1900, after which Beti resistance waned. Originally some Beti believed the Germans would prevent their collecting tribute from passing trading caravans; others simply wanted to challenge the intruders, for warfare was still taught to all Beti men; still others believed the interlopers would seize their lands and women. Not all Beti resisted the German's expanding presence. Some Beti groups fought the Germans, some fought both Germans and neighbouring societies like the Basa, and some did neither.

The decade 1900–10 laid the groundwork for Beti-German interaction, for it was during these years that several hundred young Beti attended German Roman Catholic mission schools, became clerks and soldiers in the militia and key participants in the German administration.

Two central figures emerge at this time, Hans Dominik and Karl Atangana. Captain Hans Dominik was chief of the Yaoundé station for eleven years, an uncommonly long colonial posting, between 1895–8, and 1902–10. His post was made a full military district in 1910, and Dominik, now a Major, was to be named its commandant, but he died of fever while returning to Germany to complete his medical leave.[5] His early years in Cameroon were spent in bringing the region north of Yaoundé under control, building the station, and moving its caravan routes north towards the grasslands.

Dominik was an energetic personality; he was an activist whose ideas on colonisation were simple and predictable. He made a stab at learning the local Bantu dialect, Ewondo, and travelled a great deal throughout the region. The Beti spoke of him as 'the fire that burns peppers' and 'leopard-lion'. He hanged several headmen he thought had plotted against him, and once faced charges in the Reichstag that he permitted war prisoners to be mutilated.[6]

His views of colonial policy were that decisions should be made locally by the station commander about agriculture and relations with local populations. The latter he did not trust, and compared them to a wild horse that only obeyed a rider in control of the reins and spurs. Max Abé Foudda, who sometimes accompanied him as an aide-interpreter, said Dominik had a standard speech he made everywhere he visited: i.e. the Germans have come to bring peace, and prosperity, which will pass from whites to blacks, under the Kaiser's aegis. Dominik led a simple life, and received many African visitors in his quarters on a hill in Yaoundé.[7]

Karl Atangana (c.1880–1943) was the African closest to Dominik. Atangana's father, Essomba Atangana, was one of thousands of Beti headmen who lived near Yaoundé in the 1880s. Atangana was the eleventh of 12 sons, which meant that he was far removed from the line of succession to his father's title, land, and goods, as these would go to the eldest son of the first wife. Originally employed as a houseboy, in 1895 he was sent to a Roman Catholic missionary school just opened by the Pallotine Fathers in the coastal town of Kribi. While there for two years Atangana learned to read and write German and became a Roman Catholic. He was baptised in Kribi, and married an Ewondo girl, Maria Biloa, with whom he had two children.

In 1900 Atangana went to Buea, the colonial capital, as a medical assistant and interpreter. The Germans soon launched a census to establish tax collection records, and Atangana was given charge of the project. He compiled a list of 300 headmen from which the Germans selected 233 as tax collectors. Their payment was five per cent of the total collection, for which they had Atangana to thank.[8]

Dominik and Atangana worked together from 1904 to 1910. It was a close relationship. Atangana often ate with Dominik in the latter's quarters, something exceptional in that era. Atangana accompanied Dominik on many administrative tours and military patrols. Atangana was never a soldier, always an administrator; he constantly sought negotiated solutions instead of pursuing military ones.

Mayors and chiefs

During the first fifteen years of their presence in Yaoundé, the Germans named several headmen as mayors. These were usually favoured persons who had befriended German travellers, assisted a caravan or sold food to the Germans. As might be expected, sometimes the mayors were the traditional headmen of Beti society, but in other cases were headmen's brothers or clients, which was bound to create conflict in the compounds. Beti knew such persons as *Nkukuma ntanan*, 'the white man's chief', instead of *Nkukuma nnam*, 'chiefs of the country'.[9]

The 'mayors' duties were designed to bring them some profit but little favour with their people. These included tax collection, finding workers for road building, providing lodging for the administration's working porters and caravans, and keeping the administrative post, its livestock, and gardens in order.

The system of appointed mayors did not work. The tax collections were minuscule and most 'mayors' neither spoke German nor did they know how to work with the new administration. A more disciplined cadre was needed, and to this end the Germans instituted an order of chiefs with no hereditary claims to leadership positions in traditional society.

The first tax among the Beti, which Atangana helped organise, was in October 1908 and required all grown males in Cameroon to pay six marks a year or perform thirty days of labour on public works.[10]. Chiefs received an impressive red and black certificate on thick paper, with the imperial seal, and the chief's name. It noted the chief 'has supported the German flag and is placed under the special protection of the Kaiser's government'. In the following space, special conditions could be noted, like the chief agreeing to maintain roads in his district. Listed at the bottom of the certificate were the duties required of all chiefs, that is to sell food to passing caravans, and report the caravan to the nearest European if it were lost, or if its members were quarrelling.[12]

Each chief was given a tax receipt book, which was a symbol of chiefly authority and, in addition to being required to keep roads open, they were told to clear swamps, properly drain the roads, and plant palm trees or citronella along roadsides. They were supposed to build their dwellings with packed mud rather than palm thatching, the material traditionally used by the Beti.[13]

The Germans needed a police force at this time, both to assert control over the region, and to assist them in pushing inland. The original African military at the post were captives the Germans bought from a Dahomian king, who was keeping them for ritual sacrifice. The Dahomian troops were never popular among the Beti, and in 1893 they turned against the Germans over wages. The Dahomians had been freed by the Germans and originally agreed to work for five years without pay. However, they objected to the Beti, whom they had trained, receiving stipends, and to the repressive treatment they had received from the Germans. By 1895 most of the Dahomians were replaced by Beti. On the eve of World War I this force numbered 1500 African troops and 185 officers; there were also 1200 policemen with 30 German officers.[14]

The growth of inland trade

The German presence in the interior of Cameroon affected other aspects of Beti life as well; it sharply altered the power of African merchants, among them the coastal Duala, who had been trading with the Portuguese since the late eighteenth century, and the Basa, who lived between the Duala and the Beti. New trails to the interior, and the presence of German military forces, allowed the free movement of Europeans and Africans, but not always to the Germans' advantage.

In addition to expeditions supplied by German coastal firms, a proliferation of African traders leading small caravans now covered the interior. They lacked the merchandise of the larger German-sponsored caravans but many were willing to strike out into new and difficult-to-reach territory, and some had elaborate credit systems often extending payment for as long as six months or more through several intermediaries.

The African coastal traders were skilled at playing off European merchants against one another, even after terms had been agreed to by trader and supplier. The German colonial administration tried to end giving credit to African traders, but the major coastal trading house of Woermann blocked the action, arguing that no government had jurisdiction over private contracts.[15]

A German trader heading from the coast to Yaoundé in 1895, described part of the region as a free trade zone, and said the Basa had lost their intermediary role. The larger German caravans might include 120 persons and were equipped to stay longer in the field. Their competitions were a number of smaller African-led caravans of probably 30 porters, making one to two week trips about the interior for ivory and rubber.[16] The main product of the inland trade was ivory but from 1905 to 15, since elephants had been killed in great numbers throughout southern Cameroon, the trade dropped from over a million marks worth of exports to about half that figure.

The inland ivory trade usually included three or four exchanges over a long period of time before it reached the coast. First, Duala or Basa traders would pass among the Beti, encouraging them to procure ivory. A Beti headsman might send his son or a brother further inland to obtain an elephant tusk, leaving a woman or child as a guarantee until the transaction was completed. The Beti would then take the ivory to the original middleman, and receive partial payment in European goods, such as a rifle and powder. A date would be established to complete the transaction. Meanwhile, the Duala or Basa would deliver the ivory to the Germans and pay off the Beti, who in turn would send goods or money to the person from whom the ivory was obtained.[17]

The inland trade was flourishing by 1895 and the number of interior caravans grew each year. At that time Dominik said rifles, powder, iron implements, copper for body adornment, tobacco, rice, cloth, European clothes, umbrellas, petrol lamps, rum, gin, and salt were being imported to the interior. By 1908 in a single day more than a thousand carriers passed through Lolodorf, an important crossroads on the Kribi-Yaoundé road. Several improvised units of measure were employed in the coastal trade, such as the Kru, Beloko, Keg, Piggin and Bar. After 1984 the German government tried to introduce the metric system and payment in German marks, but here again, met opposition from the rigid German traders who preferred the open barter system.[18]

The inland trade spread through the Beti regions, but the Beti never became a trading people. This is because the role of the trader was simply outside what a Beti headman believed himself to be. Beti headmen were taught from birth to be brave and hospitable; presiding over a compound and keeping good relations with other headmen was a full time occupation. Their ancestors did not trade, neither did the Beti headmen. Thus, the Beti did not acquire the new skills needed to compete with the Duala and the Germans. When trade, like the commerce in ivory, was conducted by the Beti, it was not through the headmen, but through their brothers or sons who had not yet acquired the means to establish their own compounds, with the headmen receiving a portion of the profits. This was important because it meant that headmen received tribute but lesser compound-dwellers had a more active role in commerce.

As the German presence opened the interior to the coastal traders, it also did the opposite, allowing the Beti to move freely to the coast for the first time. In fact, the Beti had gradually been migrating southward toward the coast, 'in search of salt', at the same time as the Germans arrived inland. Some Beti became rubber plantation workers, others became porters; the latter could remain close to home and family, earn money, and remain near familiar food and climate. In 1894 Dominik wrote 'The Yaoundé people are scattered throughout the colony, engaged as soldiers or personal servants of the Europeans'.[19]

The growing German presence also brought the beginning of an inland railroad, but it had hardly moved from Douala and Edea on the coast before the start of World War I. By then, more than 5000 African day or contractual labourers were at work on the project, many of them Beti. This was much less attractive employment than being a carrier or plantation labourer. The work was hard, the rate of death and illness high, and the railroad work camps were often situated in unhealthy climates near the coast.

The Roman Catholic missionaries

The German missionary presence among the Beti was largely through the Pallotine Order in the twenty year period, 1896–1916. Initial Beti contact with the missionaries came in 1896 when Dominik sent several young people from his interior station to the mission school at Kribi; by 1899, seventy-four boys and one girl had attended the school.

The first German missionary to arrive in Yaoundé was Heinrich Vieter, apostolic prefect of Cameroon. He and two other Pallotine Fathers made the sixteen day trip from Kribi to Yaoundé, arriving on 13 February 1901, and renting two rooms from a Duala trader who was just leaving for the coast.[20]

The mission's record was one of constant expansion. There were a handful of converts at the German school in Kribi in 1896; by 1916 there were more than 20000 living Christians, many of them in population centres, along routes frequented by the Germans, or in enclaves near the mission station.

Some of the educational work among the Beti was done by the Pallotine Sisters, who arrived in 1903. They taught Beti women basic Christian doctrine, household skills, health care and sanitation. Catholic doctrine advocated monogamous marriage, which caused conflict with polygamous headmen who wanted numerous offspring as warriors, workers, and means of increasing their compound's size and their wealth through bride price.[21] The Pallotine curriculum mixed catechism and brickmaking, doctrine and sewing, the rudiments of reading, writing, and mathematics with masonry, carpentry, and manual work at the mission station to pay for tuition.[22]

An Ewondo catechism was published in 1910, and this Beti dialect became a required language for the German missionaries. When the missionaries spread elsewhere in Beti lands, Ewondo catechists and school teachers accompanied them, and Ewondo gained widespread use among other Beti groups, like the Eton, Bane and M'velle.

The Germans also created several Christian villages, such as Nkol Bisson and Mvog Ada, where presumably the nascent Christian communities could support one another and avoid pagan influence. However, as the number of Christians rapidly increased, the practice of isolating them in special villages was discontinued.[23]

The missionaries' success was aided by a supportive German administration, something that was often not the case with French Roman Catholic missionaries and administrators, who quarrelled frequently. Dominik sent the first Beti students to mission schools in Kribi in the late 1890s. He also sent women and children, seized on punitive raids, to the German nuns for education and upbringing. Dominik liked the 'straightforward, practical German Christianity' the mission taught, and said the sisters worked beside their students in the fields.

The Beti became Christians enthusiastically and in large numbers. The rapid expansion of the German times was multiplied in the 1920s and 1930s, which some described as a 'Cameroonian Pentecost'. Beti enthusiasm for Christianity is not difficult to explain. The Beti traditional world view was largely compatible with Christianity; for example, Beti veneration of ancestors differs little from the Christian idea of the communion of saints. In both instances, the living community draws strength from the wisdom and example of those who have preceded it.

The Beti found in Christianity a completion of themes left only partly explained in traditional religious thought. Moreover, the Beti found in the Christian world view an explanation of how the world was created, a code of personal conduct and a way of bearing suffering and difficulty. One searches in vain for resistance to Christianity, or for the lingering on of syncretic practices, or the mixing together of old and new beliefs, as might be true of other societies.

Notwithstanding, there were two stress points in the Beti missionary relationship: one concerned the abolition of the *Sso* rite, the second concerned polygamy. There are two versions of the ending of the Sso rite 'in the time of Major Dominik'.[24] A German missionary account recalled that in 1901 a young Christian convert was struck by a Sso candidate who was armed with a machete. The young person lost a finger in the dispute.

The Beti tell a different story.[25] They say the young man, uninitiated in the Sso rite, tried to enter the Sso candidates' compound, which all Beti knew was forbidden under pain of death. The interloper, the Beti say, was a student at the mission school, anxious to show his opposition to pagan practices, and lost a finger while being evicted by the candidates.

The incident resulted in a ban on the Sso rite, but effects of the ban took several years to realise. The Sso rite ceased in the Yaoundé region within a few years, and among the Bane, southwest of the station, there are isolated accounts of it continuing until 1910. In 1935, when a French administrator interested in ethnography wanted to film the ceremony, he had to visit Eton country, north of the capital where old men revived the ritual for him. By then, Beti Christians around Yaoundé believed that the Sso rite was a holdover from pagan days and opposed even a one-time revival for filming.[26]

What was the impact on Beti society of the abolition of the Sso rites? Sso symbols provided many Beti images of religion. The hunter's quest for the antelope that never died was an important image to Beti men. When the rite died, young men who had been trained as warriors were left in a society where military action was replaced by the tedium of guard duty. In the Sso rite, they were also trained as hunters, but large animals were disappearing, and they were left with less fulfilling work as farmers. And now there was no clear way to work the passage from youth to manhood. Learning Sso songs and dressing as a candidate gave way to learning German songs and wearing European dress.

Politically, the Sso rite gave headmen of traditional society valuable networks and alliances. Lavish extended hospitality was part of the Sso process. It gave a headman wide contacts, cemented friendships, and neutralised potential enemies in a fragile society. No new way was devised by the Beti to create such alliances, but by the end of the period, such bonds lost much of their importance with the general diminishing of the headman's role. Partial replacements came through church ceremonies, such as first communions, confirmations, and patron saints' days, occasions for men to extend hospitality and expand their networks.

The second important issue in Beti-German mission contact was over the issue of polygamy. Like the Sso rite, polygamous marriages were ways a headman could establish power, claim wealth, and consolidate relationships. Monogamy struck at the heart of such a social system. Wives were workers, child bearers, and instruments of alliance. Plurality of wives helped to compensate for high infant mortality and infertility. And if a headman became a Christian, and kept one wife, freeing the others to return to their original compounds, what should he do about the elaborately negotiated bride price he probably had spent by now?

The movement against polygamy was considerably less successful than that which abolished the Sso rite, for polygamy remained an issue for decades. The German administration did not officially oppose polygamy, but instituted a tax on plural wives. They tried to control bride price, and opposed the sale of young girls, with no visible effect.

The local courts heard many palavers over the status of women. In an attempt to regulate marriage practices, the government created a register for non-Christian marriages in 1914. The Christian marriages were recorded by the missionaries. The fee for dissolving a marriage was fifty marks.

The missionary impact was just making its mark when World War I came. The number of Christians was high, and the young people the missionaries educated were already moving into positions of importance, as clerks, translators, teachers and soldiers in the administration.

Beti-German relations in 1914–1915

What was the state of German-Beti relations in August 1914, on the eve of World War I? The German commercial presence was solidly established with profitable trade lines expanding far to the north. While Beti headmen did not become traders, headmen received tribute from German and African caravans crossing their lands and thousands of their kinsmen became porters and plantation workers. Military resistance had long since ceased, and several hundred Beti youths had passed through German schools. Thousands of Beti became devout Roman Catholics, abandoning traditional beliefs and practices as pagan. A class of 'mayors,' then chiefs, was superimposed on the headmen of this acephalous society, and government clerks, school teachers, catechists and militiamen became important, gradually contesting the power of traditional headmen. It would appear that Germany's fifteen year presence among the Beti was reaping the success of hard work and careful planning. Then came World War I.

Atangana's emerging leadership

Under the German administration, the most powerful office an African could aspire to was Paramount Chief. No such position existed in traditional Beti society, but for the Yaoundé region it was given to Karl Atangana in 1914. He was in his mid-30s at the time, and had, as we have seen, worked his way up from an insignificant position in his own lineage group to become first, houseboy to the Germans, then student at the mission school, assistant tax collector and aid-interpreter. In 1911 he was made head of the local Ewondo-Bane court, which resolved most African civil disputes, including land and marriage issues.

Atangana's writings suggest that this sensitive, intelligent young man tried to become the African equivalent of a model German administrator. His handwriting shows almost an engraver's script; he spoke excellent German, was a devout Roman Catholic, and developed a preference for German food. He wrote about himself when he said 'To dare to approach the Germans it is necessary to abandon the traits which displease them, to become their friend and then be valued by them'.[27]

Those who write their own histories favour themselves, and Atangana was no exception. He claimed descent from a royal lineage, when none existed among the Beti; he said his father, Atangana Essomba, was Paramount Chief of the Ewondo and Bane, when he was but a struggling headman among hundreds of peers, and translated the word for headman, Nkukuma, as 'chief' and later 'king'.[28]

Atangana was named *Oberhäuptling*, Paramount Chief, of the Ewondo and Bane on 25 March 1914. The appointment would be permanent after a year if ratified by both groups. A Beti associate of Atangana said the actual nomination made little difference to the Beti, as they knew by now that any contact with the Germans would have to be made through Atangana.

It is instructive to consider the means Atangana employed to broaden his influence. He used hospitality as a way of controlling people, as did the traditional Beti headmen. Visiting chiefs from elsewhere in Cameroon, or Beti headmen coming to Yaoundé were invited for a meal or, if important enough, to stay in Atangana's large European-style house and have a horse put at their disposal. Since most of the clerks at the Yaoundé station were Beti, placed there by Atangana, this meant that he was always well-informed about what was going on at the post as well.

Shortly after his return from Germany, Atangana created a twenty member band with German uniforms and instruments. They learned military and promenade music at Kribi on the coast, and Atangana sent them to play at weddings, religious ceremonies, and other gatherings.[29] Atangana did not charge for their services, but only he could tell them where to play. A favour was thus extended to others, who ended up in Atangana's debt.

Atangana did the best he could for his people. His own fortune improved constantly, but he was a skilled politician who frequently intervened on their behalf. An elderly informant, brother of an interpreter, said that the latter had accidentally fired his gun in an altercation with a German soldier. The interpreter faced a prison sentence, but through Atangana's intervention, was only required to carry a large load back to his village, a loss of face for someone in such a position, but at least not a jail term.[30]

It was not easy for Atangana to satisfy both Germans and the indigenous population, but he tried to do so. His skills were put to the test in 1914 when several important Cameroonian leaders asked him to join in a planned uprising against the Germans. The Duala, who had lost part of their valuable coastal land to the Germans, led the effort. They had sent a secret emissary to Berlin, petitioned the Reichstag, and hired German lawyers to present their case. It did not go well for the Cameroonians, four of whom were executed by the Germans.

What did Atangana do? Beti informants say he knew of the coastal peoples' plans, but did not reveal them to the Germans. Meanwhile, he tried to persuade them from taking on the Germans, for he believed their effort was futile. The incident was a serious one for Germany and Cameroon, but Atangana kept in the good graces of both sides.[31]

What is Atangana's place in Beti history? Consider his temperament, the times, and the options available to him. His personality was that of a negotiator, and balancer of contending forces, someone to whom persuasion was important. He worked hard to build a following among Beti headmen through his control of the tax collection process. And he did many favours for individual Beti. He was not a warrior, and he was convinced from his youth onwards that armed resistance was futile. So he joined the Germans, learnt their language, and modelled his behaviour on them. He believed that Roman Catholicism, schools, roads, European trading goods, and improved health and sanitation conditions were desirable, and worked without hesitation for them. He is the single most important Beti to gain a position of leadership in this period, emerging as neither a legendary hero nor a faceless collaborator, but as an agile pragmatist and skilled administrator, who did the best he could, considering who he was, and the historical situation in which he found himself.

'The White Man's War'

On 27 September 1914 the German forces in Duala blew up the telegraph station there, surrendered the coastal port without a fight, and withdrew to the interior. They made Yaoundé the provisional capital, where they would remain for the next fifteen months.

The Germans and Africans in the armed forces employed what would later be called guerilla tactics, retreating gradually through the rain forest, where they ambushed and harrassed the advancing allied units. Aided by loyal Beti troops, who knew the terrain, the defenders could control where the fighting might occur, an advantage in such warfare. But they never had a chance. The German-African force was only 4000 men in 1915 with no prospect of resupplying their numbers. The Allied forces opposing them were more than twice the Germans' strength.[32]

The Allies hoped to encircle Yaoundé as quickly as possible in a pincer movement. It was slow going, and the Allies took nearly nine months to move to within fifty miles of Yaoundé. In June 1915, they were pushed back by the German-Beti forces, sustaining a twenty-five per cent casualty count, plus the ravages of dysentery and fever.[33]

The rains came in July and warfare was suspended; in November, a final dry season offensive was launched on the capital. The British-led troops, advancing from the west, despite heavy resistance, came within sight of Yaoundé by late December 1915.

An elaborate system of trenches had been dug to defend Yaoundé, but there was no battle. The German-African soldiers once more withdrew into the rain forest. It would have been pointless for them to fight, for they would have sustained heavy casualties and the station, carefully built over a long period, would have been destroyed.

On 1 January 1916 the British entered Yaoundé unopposed; within the next ten days French and other Allied units entered as well. The last military encounter of any importance in Beti lands was near the Nyong River on 8 January 1916, a rear-guard action at which the retreating German-African force returned the Allies' African and European prisoners of war. 'All had received fair and humane treatment during their capture', the British commander noted.[34]

When Mora, the last northern stronghold still under German control, surrendered on 18 February 1916, World War I ended in Cameroon.

It was Karl Atangana, accompanied by seventy-two Beti chiefs, and several thousand Beti, who helped the Governor, General Ebermaier, southward through the rain forest, which they knew very well. Estimates of the number of African supporters who made the trip range from 14000 to 20000. The Beti did not believe the Germans would lose Cameroon and expected their return as part of a peace settlement. Before leaving, Atangana and the other chiefs appointed as replacements weaker kinsmen whom they thought would vacate their positions when the incumbents returned.[35]

In February 1916, the Germans and their African allies turned themselves over to the neutral Spanish in what was then Spanish Guinea. The Spanish received them well, and the Beti were given land at Bekoko near San Carlos, where many spent the remaining war years. On 16 April two Spanish ships carried 797 Germans from Fernando Po to Holland. Others were taken to Spain.

The war's effects

World War I was a traumatic time for the Beti. Their own feuds had been of short duration, involved small groups, simple arms, and less devastating results. Moreover, the Beti had believed that the Germans were invincible, but now they had been routed by another European power. Finally, the fabric of Beti society had been torn at a time when it was facing profound stress. A Beti who lived through the period wrote 'the First World War made a bad impression on the Beti. They spoke with horror of the white man's war. They had never seen anything like it. Their own wars involved only a few people over a short period of time and were consequently less destructive'.[36]

The breakdown of traditional and externally imposed order produced seismic shocks in Beti society. There was an increase in vandalism, and impostors wearing police costumes roamed the countryside extracting payments. Witchcraft accusations increased, and a new secret group, the 'Leopard Society' was formed. Its members resorted to witchcraft and robbery. They wore palm branch tails, painted themselves with leopard spots, wore calabashes on their heads, and carried wooden leopard's paws with nails for claws. They scratched the ground in front of someone's hut to tell them 'you are in trouble with the leopards'.[37]

The Germans invited Karl Atangana and six other Beti chiefs to Spain in 1918. The Germans lodged them in the Hotel Aurora and gave them a stipend. Germany never thought it would lose its colonies as part of the Versailles settlement, but had the question of the treatment of colonial peoples arisen, the Germans could have called on the Beti leaders to testify on their behalf. Also, the Beti wanted to recover a million to a million and a half marks which fifty Beti chiefs had banked through a Swiss Protestant group, the Basel mission.[38]

The Beti spent two years in Madrid and a month in Barcelona. Through the German embassy, their accounts were repaid in Spanish pesetas later changed to French francs. They met four times with the Spanish king, Alfonso XIII, and asked Nkukuma (chief) Alfonso to intercede on their behalf with the French.

The Beti learnt a great deal about Spain. They were twice dinner guests of the royal family, visited several high Spanish government officials, including the Foreign Minister, and discussed how what they saw of European government and industry might apply to their country. 'We talked and talked about what we saw', Max Abé Foudda, who made the trip, recalled half a century later, 'and asked among ourselves how we could bring these things back to our country'. The Beti had numerous photographs of themselves, taken in Madrid, which Atangana's family preserved.[39]

The Beti were allowed to return to Cameroon by the French on 8 June 1920, four years after they had left their country. Atangana brought with him several money orders from Germans who had fathered children in Cameroon, and who wanted to provide for their education. The Beti chiefs' ship docked for several hours at Las Palmas on their return voyage. Max Abé Foudda was struck by the design of a Spanish two-story hacienda, sketched a plan of it, and had a replica built when he returned to Nkolbewa, forty miles southwest of Yaoundé. Other Beti chiefs used the basic model for homes as well, some of which still stand in the rain forest. At the same time, the Beti who had been living in Spanish territory, began to filter back home, bringing with them new sorts of banana plants, pineapples, and macabos found on the coast.[40]

In 1922 Cameroon became a League of Nations mandate, and a new era in Cameroonian history began. France received a large section of Eastern Cameroon. Although the British had seized Douala, Yaoundé, and a sizeable section of the coast and rain forest, they abandoned most of this land simply to add a portion of Western Cameroon to their Nigerian territory. This land included the former German capital of Buea and the rich farming land around Mount Cameroon.

A final thought

Beti history begins with oral traditions. These include an explanation of their origins, the names and deeds of leading figures, and a recollection and interpretation of their encounter with the Germans. European colonial history helps add dates, events and differing interpretations to the encounter of two peoples. Both forms of history are incomplete when standing alone; taken together, they help complete the picture of two particular people and their relationship over a relatively brief (1887–1916) but event-filled period. The history of this era is not a meeting of impersonal force, but of living persons, like Dominik and Atangana, who greatly influenced the character of this encounter.

Within the span of two generations Beti society experienced the intrusion of new political leadership, new economic forces in the form of tax collections and long distance trade; a new religion, Roman Catholicism; a new language, German, and the transcription of an important Beti dialect, Ewondo, as a written language. Warfare ended, but a world war broke out, and everything was turned awry at the end of this period. No happy endings, just more change, as the French entered the scene, to stay as protectors for the next four decades.

Substantial recent contributions have been made to social, economic and religious history among the Beti. More biographies are needed; so are studies of groups about whom little has been written, such as catechists and missionaries, African clerks and school teachers, and German traders. The study of songs, proverbs, fables, and tales demand the sort of inquiry that will bring traditional Beti culture closer to historical interpretation by linking it to specific times, people, and events, to the extent that the material will allow.

Finally, two themes deserve greater explanation. The history of the Beti in the 1887–1916 period suggests them: shock and resilience – the shock is that produced by the tremendous changes a society experienced from its outer political structure to the depths of its collective psyche. And resilience? The Beti, and much of their culture, emerged intact from the colonial encounter, with powers of absorption and accommodation that served them well during a period of profound change, one which could have witnessed the fragmentation of a less adaptive people.

Notes

1   H.R. Rudin. *Germans in the Cameroons, 1884–1914*, New Haven, 1938, pp. 18 ff.; Curt Morgen, *Durch Kamerun von Sud nach Nord*, Leipzig, 1893, p. 49 ff.

2   'Expedition von Hauptmann Kund', in Freiherr von Dankelman, (ed.), *Mittheilungen von Forschungsreisenden und Gelehrten aus den Deutschen Schutzgebieten* (henceforth MFGDS), Berlin, 1899, pp. 61 ff.

3   H. Schnee, *Deutsches Kolonial-Lexikon*, vol. 1, Leipzig, 1920, pp. 128–129; 'Reise von Lieutenant Tappenbeck von der Jaunde-Station über den Sannaga nach Ngila's Residenz', MFGDS, vol. 2, 1890, pp. 109–113; G. Zenker, 'Jaunde', MFGDS, 1895, No. 8, pp. 38, 44–52. Two richly annotated works are P. Laburthe Tolra, 'Yaundé d'après Zenker (1895)', *Annales de la Faculté des Lettres et Sciences Humaines*, Université de Yaoundé, II, 1970, and *À travers le Cameroun du Sud au Nord, Traduction de l'ouvrage de Curt von Morgen*, Yaoundé, 1972.

4   F. Quinn, 'Beti Society in the Nineteenth Century', *Africa*, 1980, vol. 50, No. 3, pp. 293–304; Théodore Tsala, 'Le gouvernement des beti', MS in private possession, Mvolye, Cameroon, 1968. The late Abbé Tsala, one of the first Beti to be ordained a Roman Catholic priest, was a scholar and folklorist of note, with an extensive collection of material on Cameroon history in general and on the Beti in particular.

5   See entry on 'Dominik' in H. Schnee, *Deutsches Kolonial-Lexikon*, Vol. I, p. 471, also Hans Dominik, *Kamerun: Sechs Kriegs-und Friedensjahre in deutschen Tropen*, Berlin, 1901, and his *Vom Atlantik zum Tschadsee, Kriegs-und Forschungs-Fahrten in Kamerun*, Berlin, 1908.

6   Oral interviews: T. Tsala, Mvolye, 6 June 1968; Pierre Mebe, Yaoundé, 30 November 1967; François Atangana, Yaoundé, 2 May 1967.

7   Dominik, *Vom Atlantik zum Tschadsee*, p. 32: oral interview, Max Abé Foudda, Nkolbewa, 23 December 1967.

8   F. Quinn, 'Charles Atangana of Yaoundé', *Journal of African History*, vol. 21, 1980, pp. 485–495. Oral interview: T. Tsala, Mvolyé, 18 July 1968.

9   Oral interview: T. Tsala, Mvolyé, 4 May 1968.

10   Rudin, pp. 341–342.

11   Schutzbrief, Yaoundé 29 August 1905, reproduced in 'Charles Atangana and the Ewondo Chiefs, a Document', *Abbia*, 1969, XXIII, pp. 83–102. Many Beti headmen kept metal trunks under their beds with personal documents, awards and decorations, photos and souvenirs of the French and German colonial periods.

12   Document No. 1526, p. 8. Archives Nationales, Yaoundé (henceforth abbreviated to ANY).

13   Rudin, pp. 192–195; Dominik, *Kamerun*, p. 231; T. Tsala, personal communication, 8 April 1969.

14   Rudin, pp. 225–227.

15   *Ibid.*, p. 224

16   G. Zenker, 'Yaoundé', *MFGDS*, 8, 1895, pp. 64–5.

17 Oral interview: François Atangana, Yaoundé 2 May 1967.
18 Rudin, pp. 256–8.
19 Dominik, *Vom Atlantik zum Tschadsee*, pp. 35–36.
20 H. Skolaster, *Die Pallottiner in Kamerun, 25 Jahre Missionarbeit*, Limburg, 1924, pp. 121 ff.; H. Vieter, 'Erinnerungen aus Kamerun, 1890–1903', MS. ANY.
21 Oral interview: T. Tsala, Mvolyé, 3 March 1968.
22 Skolaster, p. 309.
23 Oral interview: T. Tsala, Mvolye, 3 March 1968.
24 Dominik, *Vom Atlantik zum Tschadsee*, Berlin, 1908, p. 37.
25 Martin Heepe, 'Jaunde-Texte von Karl Atangana und Paul Messi, nebst Experimentalphonetikschen Untersuchungen über die Sprache', *Abhandlungen des Hamburgischen Kolonial-Instituts*, XXIV, 1919.
26 M. Heepe, *Jaunde-Texte*, pp. 107–111.
27 F. Quinn, 'Charles' Atangana', p. 96.
28 Oral interview: Max Abé Foudda, Nkolbewa, 23 December 1967.
29 Oral interview: Pierre Elon, Mvolyé, 1 August 1968. A few members of the band were still alive and playing in the mid-1960s at restaurants and at airport farewells. I once asked them, outside a restaurant, in 1966 to play *Deutschland Uber Alles*. 'We know how to play it, but the French wouldn't like it', a musician told me, *sotto voce*.
30 Oral interview: Max Abé Foudda, Nkolbewa, 23 December 1967.
31 *Ibid*.
32 E.H. Gorges, *The Great War in West Africa*, London, n.d., pp. 145–152.
33 *Ibid*. pp. 237–239.
34 *Ibid*. pp. 237 ff.
35 Skolaster, 1924, p. 293.
36 T. Tsala, personal communication, 8 April 1969.
37 Oral interview: T. Tsala, Mvolyé, 2 February and 6 May 1968.
38 Oral interview: Max Abé Foudda, Nkolbewa, 23 December 1967.
39 Oral interview: Max Abé Foudda, Nkolbewa, 23 December 1967. Photographs in possession of Max Abé Foudda; family of Charles Atangana, Mvolyé.
40 Oral interviews: Pierre Mebe, Yaoundé, 24 May 1967; Martin Mballa Foe, Mbalmayo, 14 March 1968.

Chapter Five

Colonial élitism in Cameroon: the case of the Duala in the 1930s

Jonathan Derrick

The Duala, one of a group of related peoples called Sawa living in the coastal area of Cameroon, traded with Europeans for centuries until the coming of colonial rule in 1884, when their treaty with Germany began the colonial occupation of the area later called Cameroon – a term originally applied to the Duala home area by the estuary of the Wouri river. After long contact with Europeans through trade, the Duala under German rule were ahead of other Cameroonians in all forms of development along Western lines. They were soon in the lead in all élite activities.

The Duala had begun to accept Christianity before 1884 and in the German period were largely converted to Protestant Christianity, which was henceforth a major force in their lives. At the same time Western education was pursued keenly by the Duala, with some going to Germany for schooling. As the most educated of Cameroonians they held an élite position and had an influence far greater than their small numbers would suggest. They were particularly important as clerks and other junior staff, in both the government and business firms.

The Duala's élite position was enhanced by their success, from about 1900, in running plantations along the rivers in the area, such as the Wouri, Mungo, Dibamba and others, for growing cocoa and producing palm oil and kernels for export. They made good money as planters and also as traders, even though much of their earlier trading activity was curbed by the Germans. From the German period onwards many leading Duala built modern houses.

Amid all the rapid changes under colonialism, the chiefs retained prestige and authority, which they have continued to enjoy. Most important were the heads of the four 'maximal lineages' of the Duala: the 'Kings' or, as they were called after the colonial occupation, Paramount Chiefs, of Bell, Akwa, Deido and Bonaberi (or, to use the correct traditional names, the rulers of the Bonadoo, Bonaku, Bonebela and Bonaberi). Below them were many district chiefs. Famous 'Kings' in the German period were Tete Dika Mpondo of Akwa, called 'King Akwa'; 'King Bell', Ndoumb'a Lobe, who died in 1897; and Ndoumb'a Lobe's grandson, Rudolf Douala Manga Bell, who headed the Bonadoo from 1908 to 1914. All Cameroonian schoolchildren now know how Rudolf was put to death in 1914 after opposing the Germans' expropriation of his people's land on the Joss and Bali plateaus in the urban area. Opposition to that was the most celebrated of many acts of opposition to colonial rule, in which Dika Mpondo was also prominent.

Under the French Mandate the Duala remained the leading élite people in Cameroon, maintaining their lead in Western education and clerical employment, and continuing to run their plantations profitably until the slump.[1] They also remained highly critical of colonial rule. Many called for self-government at the time of World War I and the Treaty of Versailles, and the idea was often voiced later. In the early 1920s many joined the Native Baptist Church, which was revived then under the leadership of Pastor Adolf Lotin Same (1882–1946) in opposition to the Protestant Mission of the French *Société des Missions Evangéliques*. Then a number, especially among the Bonadoo, concentrated for years – especially from 1926 to 1931 – on efforts to secure the return of the land expropriated in 1914, which the French government refused to give up, saying it had legally inherited what had (so it said) legally become German government property.

Going beyond that land protest, some Duala called for self-government and appealed to the League of Nations. A petition on 19 December 1929, signed by the four Duala paramount chiefs, called for self-government, and some anti-colonial activists contacted the left-wing movements against imperialism which were formed in Europe at the time. On 22 July 1931 women in Douala protested, in a major demonstration against the extension of the head-tax to them. This activity, a little-known episode in early African nationalism,[2] had the support of many Duala.

All that activity failed, however. The French agreed in 1926 to allow the Bonadoo, who had been moved in 1914 to New-Bell, to have free plots of land at Bali and money for building modern houses there, while the government kept the Joss plateau for its own use. For years the Bonadoo refused to accept this, but in mid-1931 their resistance collapsed. They took the plots of land at Bali and built their houses there, while the position of New-Bell, as the home of the increasing population of African Strangers in Douala, was confirmed. Also, by 1932, radical anti-colonialism had virtually died away among the Duala, and at the same time the Slump affected Duala cocoa plantations, though many continued to run them until 1940.

The Duala in the 1930s

After the collapse of organised protests the Duala seem to have established a working compromise with the government, in which leading chiefs were given a role by the French and were no longer pushed into opposition activity by their people. As in other parts of Africa, the early 1930s were the heyday of colonialism, with resistance virtually absent for some years. Douala in those years affords a picture, typical in some ways but exceptional in others, of an African city in the Indian Summer of colonial rule.

A major Duala activity, following directly on the failure of the protests, was building. The surrender made by the Bonadoo in accepting the land offered at Bali led to a change in the urban geography of Douala. The building bonuses were used to good effect and Bali became a major upper-class Duala residential area. As such it extended to adjacent Koumassi and to the districts occupied by the former inhabitants of Bonapriso and Bonadouma and called after their old home districts. Today this large area, with Deido, is the main district of typical well-to-do Duala housing. The housing consists of bungalows of pale-coloured masonry, attractively designed with verandahs often going all round. They are laid out along straight grid-pattern roads which were, until the 1970s, untarred but well shaded with mango and other trees. The building of such houses began in the 1930s in Bali and, as the money for building was presented as a gift, added greatly to the number of modern houses built by the Duala.

Many of the occupants of new plots at Bali had their titles confirmed later under the provisions of two decrees on African property in French Cameroun, issued on 21 July 1932. One supplemented a decree of 20 August 1927 providing for *constatation* (recognition) of customary law rights to land. After 1932, as before, this was sought by some property owners, but many others did not bother, as it was not vitally necessary; Africans' land had always been treated as their own in the towns for all practical purposes, including leasing. The other 1932 decree, applied only from 1934, provided for full French-law registration, *immatriculation*, of landed property. Only a few Duala applied for this in the next few years.

Applications for *constatation* tell something about the Duala élite:

about its members, with well-known names such as Mudute Bell, Lobe Manga Priso, Toto Ngosso, Samuel Dimithe and others, and some less well known, appearing in the gazette in connection with applications; and about the size of its landed property. Confirmation of land titles did not indicate any precise sort of development of the land, but in the Bonadoo resettlement area this commonly took the form of house building, which continued in other areas too. Customary tenure had always been secure enough for individuals to invest, since the German period, in solid houses, whose continued spread was noted in 1929.[3] Such investment must usually have paid off, as besides living in the houses, people could let them out or mortgage them. The 1932 Circonscription Annual Report said, 'The Duala, feckless people, mortgage their possessions to obtain money which they waste. A number of buildings are mortgaged. The Duala owners will perhaps never recover them'.[4]

In 1933 two plots of land with houses were seized from Mudute Bell under a court order, presumably as foreclosure for his chronic debts (not for the first or last time). One covered 157 square metres; the other was much larger (129 hectares) with a two-storey masonry house leased to Mme Bellanger. The notice of the court order said bidding for auction of the seized properties would start at 30 000 francs for each.[5] It is not clear whether Mudute Bell actually lost those properties, of which the larger, at the crossroads of the then rue Cumberland and rue George in Bonanjo, may have been the one he was allowed to keep in 1914.

Someone like Franz Mudute Bell (1882–1942) − a leading elder of the Bonadoo, brother of the paramount chief, a former government official, a big property owner, and with a son studying in France − can unquestionably be put in the Duala élite. But more generally, who constituted that élite?

The French administrators themselves took an interest in it, but their views could be rather odd. A report in 1935 spoke of 5000 planters and separate groups of 'chiefs and their *familiers*', the 'clerks', and no less than 8000 fishermen.[6] Such classifications show little knowledge about the Duala, itself a suggestive fact about French rule over them. Some office workers and probably all chiefs had plantations and chiefs, clerks and planters were of the same families. The number of fishermen is unlikely to have approached 8000, but there were probably many more fishermen than the mere 300 estimated by the Chef de Circonscription in 1929.[7] Living for much of the time on their temporary camps in the creeks, and valuing their freedom, the fishermen could easily evade being counted. Some fishermen and other Duala were not élite people at all. But some fishermen, and some traditional craftsmen such as ivory workers, were definitely so, and rich. Whatever its exact number, the Duala élite, by any reasonable definition, was an unusually high proportion of the tribe's total numbers, because of its exceptional history and circumstances. They were, in a way, a whole élite tribe in relation to other tribes. More narrowly, one can assess the number of chiefs, elders, clerks, other office staff, important traders and businessmen, pastors and other church workers, and planters, with their families, at half at least of the total population of 15–20 000 Duala.

Such a number is indicated by a careful study made by the Douala Circonscription authorities in 1930.[8] There were 1490 skilled and specialised paid African staff; 224 government and business clerical and office staff; 91 African workers with the Missions; 181 traders; and 349 planters and major property owners, in Douala Circonscription. Not all were Duala but most of the government clerical staff probably were, as well as many of the government technical staff, almost all of the planters, and all of the urban landlords; only among the business staff and traders were other Africans (mainly non-Cameroonian) important. The government report called them 'European-trained and mainly literate people', which is fair enough if all sorts of modernisation and contact with new influences are considered. The following is a list of the main categories of the African élite in Douala, possibly excluding traditional chiefs and elders but perhaps including many of the planters and major property owners. In 1930 trade licences were given in Douala to:

64 retail traders
61 petty traders (*colporteurs*)
39 tailors
22 transport operators
18 shoemakers
17 jewellers
11 photographers
10 bakers
8 woodworkers
5 mechanics
5 ivory workers
2 mattress-makers
1 clockmaker
1 weaver[9]

There were many non-Duala among these. The Duala among them included élite people such as one of the mattress-makers, Martin Lobe Bebe Bell, cousin of Rudolf Bell whose business did well especially since he became a government contractor. (He is also remembered as the composer of *Tet' Ekombo*, a nationalist song written about 1929, in memory of Rudolf Bell.)

The important change in the Duala élite noted by the official who headed Douala Circonscription from 1926 to 1933, Louis-Julien Cortade, was the growing proportion of it which came under French rather than German influence.[8] This was certainly important, though it had not gone so far in 1930 as Cortade thought. Otherwise there was little change in the character of the élite after 1916, at least for three decades or so. No new professional categories were added; not until after 1943 would there be African doctors or lawyers in their home town of Douala, such as there had been in Lagos since the 1880s. The Duala were doing the same work in 1935 as in 1905. 'The dream of every Duala is to succeed, by way of examinations or competitions, in penetrating the administration', wrote Cortade in 1930,[10] and there had been much truth in this since the German period. But the same official had noted in 1929 that not all worked in office jobs: 'The young Duala seizes jobs in offices or shops, overseas his plantation, takes to commercial enterprise, and also practices crafts'.[11]

Cortade could have added that the Duala often combined more than one of those occupations. There were no clear divisions among the Duala élite. Chiefs, elders, planters, clerks were from the same families, and married each other's daughters. Within each of the four major traditional divisions (officially called 'Cantons') of the Duala the leading élite people were related by blood or marriage and knew each other. The élite was in fact small enough for people to know each other even more widely. The associations called *miemba* (see below) helped in this. Intermarriage among the four main divisions was not uncommon. As one example, one daughter of Pastor Manga Elokan of Deido was married to François Dika Bekombo, a government official from Akwa (who worked for the Sûreté for 30 years from 1939); the other daughter was married to another Deido man, Léopold Moume Etia, son of the civil servant Isaac Moume Etia.

Élite life

The results of a survey made in 1937–38 of nutrition and other aspects of life for the Africans in the Wouri Region (as Douala Circonscription had been renamed in 1935) give plenty of valuable information.[12] The sections on food and agriculture show the importance the Duala still attached to food farming and cash-crop plantations in the late 1930s.[13] The survey also produced some estimates of typical income and expenditure, notably by the élite of the Duala. Théodore Lobe Bell, Paramount Chief of the Bonadoo from 1927 to 1952, gave this estimate for a well-off family with plantations:

Income:	Sales of cocoa (2 fr per kg)	3000 francs
	Sales of bananas (500 fr in all), cocoyams (300), sweet potatoes (150) and maize	1050
	Sales of animals, and income from trading or craft	nil
		4050
Expenditure:	Fish and other food	960
	Men's clothing	890
	Women's clothing	600
	Children's clothing	300
	House building and repairs	300
	Lighting	100
	Receptions, hospitality	100
	Church contributions (men 24, women 12, children 6)	42
	Customary expenses (gifts, sacrifices, etc.)	50
	Expenses for children: education, initiation, puberty rites, marriage	15
	Taxes and other dues	120
	Miscellaneous, including pay of labour	500
		3977*

* There are puzzling aspects of these figures; that for 'expenses for children' was very low.

Paramount Chief Betote Akwa envisaged a budget twice as large for a family, again with plantations but with no salaried income, consisting of a man of 50, his wives aged 38 and 32, and two children of 20 and 12. He estimated that they would earn 12 950 francs per year from the sale of cocoa (5000), sweet potatoes, groundnuts and coffee; not many Africans grew coffee or bananas on plantations, but Mandessi Bell (see below) had had a coffee plantation and Betote himself had a banana plantation.

The typical ways of spending money of the élite were much the same in the 1930s as in the German period, but there was undoubtedly a steady rise in durable purchases, except in the First World War period. In 1929 the authorities in Douala issued 26 building permits to individuals, for buildings worth 2.3m francs, of which

290 000 came from 'native capital'.[14] Some Duala bought cars, motor-cycles, and bicycles, and many spent money on entertainments. Women bought expensive clothes; in 1926 Pastor Rusillon, head of the French Protestant Mission in Cameroon from 1922 to 1938, wrote that they ordered clothes from Samaritaine or Bon Marché in Paris for 400, 500 or 700 francs.[15] Betote Akwa estimated that an élite family would spend 6500 francs per year on clothes in 1938.

Very central in the lives of the Duala and their élite was Protestant Christianity, which most followed, whether they adhered to the mission church (as a majority did, including both Evangelicals and Baptists) or the Native Baptists. In 1931 there were 16 116 Evangelical and 4451 Baptist communicants under the Protestant Mission at Douala, possibly including the nearby rural areas where the famous Duala (Bell) pastor, Modi Din, was actively making converts then. Discipline was severe and there were many excommunications. But there were still many converts, as indicated by the figures for catechumens: 1610 being taught by the Evangelicals and 852 by the Baptists.[16]

The Mission was still concerned about traces of the traditional religion. There were many such traces, including the rites surrounding the canoe races (see below), and possibly the strong belief in witchcraft and traditional protection against it.[17] One of the Mission's school-mistresses, Idelette Allier, wrote in 1932 that her girl pupils were 'at heart very pagan'.[18] Pastor Rusillon was troubled by the semi-pagan mourning customs of the Duala:

> How many times have I not passed long hours of the night in some hut where a young Duala was at his last rest, a government interpreter, a civilised man. There, on a big bed covered with spotless sheets, lay the corpse of a young man dressed in new clothes, with his hands crossed, holding a bouquet of roses, a silk handkerchief in his jacket pocket, and delicately placed at his side a note-book, a book, often even his New Testament. On one side of his bed, old women, dressed in their black dresses covered with black neckerchiefs, danced gloomily, recounting to some unknown deity all the acts and deeds of the dead man, seeking to attract pity in advance from evil spirits, and above all insisting, one as much as another, on the fact that they had nothing to do with the death of him who lay there. But, beside these women who lamented, children played, men talked of a thousand other things, laughed and smoked; and when the dances had finished, and the night was advancing,

everyone slept in the dead man's room to await dawn, one on the damp earth, one on a native chair, one beside the corpse ....[19]

But the missionaries in some ways treated the Duala not as a Mission flock but as ordinary sinful Christians. 'The Duala', said Rusillon in 1935, 'is no longer a child, he leaves his father's house'.[20] The Duala showed a spontaneous vigour and initiative in the Church. This had led to the breakaway of the Native Baptist Church (NBC) which was becoming more active and vocal after 1930. But among Protestants still following the Mission, it was reported in 1933 that the churches had never been so full, with lay associations flourishing: men's choirs, a lay movement for young men, *Male me makom m'ebasi* (Union of friends of the Gospel), and a women's association, *Ndol'a penya* (new love).[21] In 1935 Rusillon spoke of the 'crowd of associations' but said they must be directed and closely watched;[22] and later the Annual Report for the Mission said that in Douala, 'the Churches are alive. But this liveliness itself becomes worrying, for it often reveals itself in initiatives which the missionary cannot sufficiently control. Societies of men and women multiply there, sometimes under the impulse of separatist and tribal preoccupations'.[23]

The phrase '... which the missionary cannot sufficiently control ...' indicates that normal missionary attitudes remained strong, with European churchmen not unhappy at being able to control people more than they could in a European parish. In Douala there were regular sessions where Christians reported on each other so that the Mission could take disciplinary action.[24] The question of discipline imposed by the missionaries had led to the growth of support for the Native Baptist Church in 1921–2, and the same apparently happened ten years later, when the Mission was worried by the support given to the expanding Native Baptist group.

But there were many keen Christians, and the Duala who worked full time for the Mission were said by one missionary to be 'for the most part admirable'.[25] The catechists and teachers gave up a part of their salaries, never very large, at the height of the Depression.[26] Squads of *Eclaireurs* went around Douala at night to keep people from sin.[27] The YMCA held weekly meetings attended by about 50 people in 1931. In that year Max Mpacko, a government school teacher, attended the YMCA International Conference in Toronto.[28] Mpacko was one of the laymen prominent in church affairs; there were many others, such as the businessmen Mandessi Bell and Njo Eteki. Among the pastors Manga Elokan had to be restrained by the missionaries; he was so zealous that he refused to accept the bride price for his daughter.[29] To the sorrow of the Mission he lived for only four years after his consecration, dying on 24 April 1930.[30]

The 'doyen of the Cameroun pastoral corps', the old Pastor Alfred Tobbo Eyoum (Tobbo Deido), died on 28 January 1932.[31] By then the Mission had more pastors; at Easter in 1931 Kouo Issedou laid hands on Martin Itondo and Martin Bapek in Douala.[32] Pastor Itondo of Bell (1892–1955) was one of the most famous Duala churchmen; he had worked for the Evangelical church for some time before becoming a pastor. He composed many well-known hymns and possibly the music for *Tet' Ekombo*. Gottlieb Munz Dibundu, younger son of Yoshua Dibundu, followed his father and his brother, Alfred Tongo Dibundu, into the Baptist ministry on 23 October 1932, when he, Otto Epale and Pierre Ebumbu Tanga were consecrated by five missionaries and ten African pastors.[33] In 1931 the Protestant Missions in Douala had, besides the pastors, nine evangelists, 126 catechists and 27 assistants for the Evangelicals; two evangelists, 35 catechists and one assistant for the Baptists. The Catholic Missions (of the Sacred Heart Father in Bonaberi, the Holy Ghost Fathers in the rest of Douala) had Duala followers, much fewer, but including, for example the catechists Andreas Mbangue (died 1932) and his son Benoît.

Besides the churches and the organisations they sponsored, the Duala also had voluntary associations, known as *miemba* (singular *muemba*), which were very important in élite life. By the Mandate period there were two sorts: Age-Sets, i.e. groups of people born in the same year or within two years of each other, and the Tribal or Clan Associations. Both were important social organisations, which helped people by giving them something to belong to and which particularly aimed at helping them to face modern life against a background of tradition.

The *Musango ma Bonadoo*, an association of the Bells, said its aim was to help the authorities in 'the accomplishing of the great work of civilisation', and to seek 'the social and moral progress of the country, as well as the material condition of the natives' among the whole Duala community, not only the Bonadoo.[34] Its announcement of all this in 1934 also said Africans were not sufficiently grateful to the white man for his efforts to civilise them. These were almost servile words of flattery, and in 1935 the new Chairman of the association, the Customs officer Michel Epee 'Papa' (1900–1975), declared on taking office, 'Long live the French administration! Long live Cameroun! Long live the Bonadoo!'[35] But behind such words lay a more subtle attitude.

Michel Epee also said, 'The chiefs will have in us a consultative chamber, the people will have us as an intermediary, and the high Administration asks for no more than to have in us a trusted interpreter'.[36] This expresses well what seems to have been the Duala's outlook then: after unsuccessful confrontation, compromise must be sought — but true compromise, with the people's leaders and spokesmen making their wishes known to the government, not only vice versa. Insofar as *miemba* had this aim and also the one of reviving interest in traditions, their ideas were similar to, but not the same as the government's. Studying the Bell Duala traditions was certainly one aim of the *Musango ma Bonadoo*.

The Bonadoo also had a special cultural association, the *Idubwan a Belle Belle*, which was different from ordinary *miemba*. Like the *Musango ma Bonadoo* it included the Bonaberi as well as their cousins the Bonadoo; the *Idubwan a Belle Belle* was in fact based at Bonaberi. It organised plays to illustrate Duala history and its great achievement was the writing of the history of the Duala people, in Duala, completed about 1930.[37] For many years the chairman was a tribal elder and fisherman, Ndoumbe Eboue.[38]

Akwa's counterpart to the *Musango ma Bonadoo* was the *Jemea la Bonambela* (Akwa loyalty), an association for entertainment, mutual aid and other purposes.[39] Mutual aid seems to have been a general aim of *miemba*. Deido (Bonebela) had two associations. *Ebele o Basu* (Deido Forward) was an association organising meetings and parties, which may have composed the Deido anthem (there were also Bell and Akwa anthems). Possibly begun under the Germans, in about 1927 it split into two, the breakaway branch being called *Ebele Mbale* (Deido Truth); the two were rivals until they both died out in or about the late 1930s.[40] Deido association members wore khaki uniforms, so that people used to refer to *Bonebela mabole kaki*, that is 'the Deido people who wear khaki'. The Bell and Akwa associations wore white uniforms.

The Age-Sets, a very old institution, had now been reformed to include among their purposes the inculcation of standards, to some extent based on European ones. An unsigned note written about them in 1934, apparently by a French official, said their aims were always practical and their members were usually, though not always, youths of from 15 to 20.[41] It added that their membership was irrespective of class, tribe or origin; certainly it cut across the division into 'Cantons', for Soppo Priso of Bell and Léopold Moume Etia of Deido (after his return from France in 1939) both belonged to one association, *Mon'a Muemba*, having been born in the same year, 1913.[42]

The note mentioned above said the Age-Sets included some European-style innovations such as written statutes, and officers (secretary, inspector, treasurer, etc.) and membership subscriptions. It went on to give details of organisations which seem to have been derived from the examples of both the Age-Sets and some other associations (of clerks, for example) not otherwise described in the document. Office-holders were elected by modern methods: ballot papers and boxes, and polling booths. The voting led to 'palavers and discussions'. The founder was Chairman, and he appointed his friends to other offices; meetings on the filling of posts 'are in general very agitated, and on these occasions is revealed the taste of the black man for grandiloquent, pointless discussions . . .' Generally an association held meetings in a member's house, but it could be in the open air. At meetings attended by about fifty people there was 'Disorder and confusion worthy of the French Lower Chamber'.[41]

Some associations kept minutes; the unknown author of the note enclosed an extract from the minutes of a meeting arranging the funeral of a member named Mouandjo, of the Moudy Association of Akwa (it is not in the file now). An important function of such bodies in many parts of the world is to arrange and pay for members' funerals. For this and other purposes the Duala *miemba* raised money by subscriptions and fines.

There were probably very many small associations formed, especially by younger educated Duala. In Akwa, in 1933, an organisation called *Elokon a Muemba ya Bonambela* was formed for boys born between 1915 and 1918 and girls born between 1918 and 1924, for them to know and help each other and put forward progressive ideas. In 1940 a *Kod'a Muemba ya Bana ba Bonambela* was formed, also in Akwa, for men of 23 to 25, helping them with, for example, allocations of 100 francs for a marriage and 250 for a burial.[43]

Clearly the *miemba* existed mainly as social organisations for younger Duala, for parties, organisation of plays (very popular among the Duala, and organised by the *Musango ma Bonadoo* for example), and other social events. But most of all they existed for helping members to adapt to conditions strongly influenced by European, and above all French, culture. There can be no doubt that it was a spontaneous sort of organisation. The official who wrote the report in 1934 clearly saw the *miemba* as a semi-secret institution which needed to be investigated. He even said they were comparable to the Freemasons and Carbonari − something of an exaggeration. He suggested that the statutes shown to Europeans may not have told all the stay, and the expenses also may have been partially concealed from white men. The government, however, showed favour to at least some associations.

The Duala in the 1930s were as keen on sport as at any time before or since. Modern versions were fast growing but old sports were far from dead. Traditional wrestling remained very popular among the Duala, and so did canoe racing. There are countless references to canoe races, *pembisan*, from the nineteenth century. That was their time of greatest development, when the boats raced from Suellaba roads to the Beseke mouth. In the German period the races were held once a year, on the Kaiser's birthday, 27 January. Under the French they were held twice yearly, on Bastille Day and Armistice Day.

The canoe races[44] were much influenced by the old Duala religion, with traditional rites including divination for the benefit of the crews on the night before the event. But after the conversion of most Duala to Christianity a pastor normally came to pray for the crews on the morning of the race. A family at nearby Jebale island, however, retained the exclusive control of rites to summon the *miengu* (mythical semi-human water beings of Duala tradition) to help the races. The canoes were between 20 and 28 metres long, made of *Pterocarpus* tree trunks, with no keels; each had a name. The figureheads, elaborately carved by skilled craftsmen, could be in the form of human beings or real or legendary animals and birds.

An article signed 'Un Duala Français' in 1937 said the races had been organised among the Bonadoo since 1919 by an Association formed, for mutual aid and promotion of business, before the return of the famous Prince Alexandre Douala Manga Bell, also called Ndoumb'a Douala. This *muemba* may have been one called *Alexanderbund* in 1919, or another one formed in honour of the Prince. The article said it had paid-up members and income from gifts and collections, and thus paid for training of canoe crews, who were usually fishermen. The canoeists had an elaborate hierarchy with captains, other ranking officers, and crewmen, the local chief being traditionally the honorary Commander. Each crew had a captain, a 'swimming chief', five team leaders, and four teams of ten men each, with one or two more teams sometimes added. Active canoeists were between 20 and 30 years old. In principle every district had its own canoe. The writer of this article said, 'The Federation of Canoeists, the Alexandre and Andre Association (*sic*), and the Bonadoo Tribe Peace Association have the same aim . . .'[45] He made it clear that the races among the Bonadoo were linked with the *miemba* and with the cult figure of Ndoumb'a Douala.

That article may well have been written by Douala's most famous son, Rudolf Bell's son Alexandre Ndoumb'a Douala, himself; he had by then applied for French citizenship (to be accorded in 1939) and could well call himself 'a French Duala'. Prince Alexandre certainly took a prominent part in the canoe races. At the 1934 Armistice Day races he took a paddle himself and trained the other crewmen of his boat, the *Ndumb'a Bolo* (Ndoumbe's Canoe); it won the main race,[46] and there is no reason to suspect 'fixing' as he was by all accounts a man of varied talents. In the special races for his birthday shortly afterwards the newspaper report did not mention him as joining the crew of the *Ndumb'a Bolo*, but it referred, without naming her, to a girl of 15 who was present to encourage the crew and was called the 'Siren of the Ndumb'a Bolo'.[47] Earlier the prince had ordered 'reparation' after a fight between Bonaberi and Bonendale people over the 1934 Bastille Day races; it is not clear whether the fight, in which fists, spears and canoe paddles were used, was between the crews, or fans, or both.[48]

Horse racing was popular in Douala, and Prince Alexandre competed. Football in the 1930s was fast becoming the passion it now is in Cameroon. Blaise Diagne, the famous Senegalese politician who became a Minister in Paris, is said to have urged the authorities in 1932 to encourage football among the Africans.[49] They did so, after years of official disapproval of the efforts of Goethe George, the Sierra Leonean photographer well known in Douala, and others to develop local football teams. The *Union Sportive Indigène de Douala* (USID), founded in 1926 by Goethe George, Ebole Bile and Mpondo Dika, was now 'taken over' officially;[50] it had a committee of four Europeans and four Africans.

Besides sport, dancing was a taste well provided for in Douala. The expatriate businessmen Fischer and Nassif (a Lebanese) ran bars plus dance halls for Africans. Doumbe-Moulongo recalls[51] that the Maringa was brought to Douala by Gold Coast immigrants in the nineteenth century and was apparently related to High-life. It was danced 'until 1935 at the latest', as was the Ambas-Be, a sort of quadrille introduced from the Ambas Bay area (Victoria) about 1910 and danced to guitar accompaniment. The Ashiko (from Pidgin 'I'm shake'), a fast dance introduced in the 1920s from Lagos, remained for long popular in Douala.

Élite figures

The élite was obviously increasing, with the annual graduation of its sons from the various available schools continuing regularly. By the same process the élite was becoming more and more French in culture. Although the German-era generation was to remain powerful until the Second World War, inevitably many of its leading members were removed from the scene in the preceding decade by death or retirement.

An outstanding personality of the Duala élite, David Mandessi Bell, died on 14 November 1936. An adoptive son of King Ndoumb'a Lobe, a very successful import-export businessman, a processor and exporter of timber, owner of many plantations, owner since 1897 of a fine modern house at Bonanoo, an early financial backer of the land agitation movement and a pillar of the Protestant Mission, he was certainly one of Douala's leading citizens in the German and French periods. He was buried at the Bonadoo community's Njo Njo cemetery, with Rusillon and Modi Din conducting the service.[52]

Mandessi Bell sent his daughter Maria to Germany for her education, and later sent his sons Sam and Jean to France. Maria's marriage to Mamadou Diop from Senegal was among the most distinguished of many marriages between the Duala élite and Africans from other territories (another was between Goethe George and Christine Etonde Duala, a niece of Betote Akwa). Diop, the most prominent of the Senegalese in Douala, was earning 56 525 francs per year, including allowances, in 1931. He often visited France with his wife, and their son, the poet David Mandessi Diop, was born there in 1927. On 17 August 1935 Mamadou Diop died on leave in France.

Sam Mandessi Bell returned from France in 1931, and on his father's death inherited the Bonanjo house and other property. David Mandessi Bell made provision in his will for spending income from rents from houses and land, on the education of children, of whom 20 were named in the will. Rent from one house, let to the French businessman Grenouilleau, half the income from a coffee farm, and income from plantations had to be used to pay a debt to the Credit Français.[53]

Erdmann Njo Eteki was another aristocratic businessman. In 1934 his daughters, Irma Makongue and Laurance Malady, returned[54] from schooling in France, where their sisters went later. Makongue, who became a teacher, later married Sam Mandessi Bell. Malady married first a West Indian, then a Senegalese; she worked as a midwife.[55]

Two other Duala businessmen, both from Deido like Eteki, were prominent in the early 1930s. Samuel Moundo Esoukan was by then a leading import-export businessman and a member of the Chamber of Commerce, with a house by the historic Silk-Cotton Tree of Deido (said to have been planted by the Basa before they sold the land to the Duala). He was called Sam Black Deido but was not

related to Sam Deido, a famous businessman of earlier years.[56] He
was to go on flourishing until recent times, and to acquire properties
in Akwa, including one by the Paramount Chief's residence there.[55]
Then there was Eitel Kondo Ebele, formerly a clerk under the
Germans, then a timber contractor and import-export entrepreneur
under the French.[56] In 1935 he was appointed to the Chamber of
Commerce (an almost wholly European body, founded in 1921)
with Paul Sonne, a Mungo (born 1905), who was to be another
leading African businessman in Douala until recent times.

Nseke Diboti, another Deido import-export businessman, was
appointed a member of the Conseil des Notables (an official consultative body for Africans at Circonscription/Region level) in 1930
and a Court Assessor, for the 2nd-degree Court, in 1933: typical
indications of the status of these Duala businessmen. Bema
Mouangue, of Bonakwamwang, was an active Duala member of the
Chamber of Commerce in the 1930s. Other prominent Duala
businessmen at that time included Isaac Doumbe Edimo (a member
of the Chamber) and the Eboumbou brothers, Moukoko, Din and
Koma.[57]

Later there was the famous Paul Soppo Priso, a Bell man, born in
1913. As a junior official in the Public Works and Mines Depart-
ments he began − at the age of 18, so he recalls[58] − to build houses
to let out. He was to go far, much further than his elder brother
Nfon Priso who was also a businessman; today he is the leading
property tycoon in Cameroon. He married Lisette Eteki, another
daughter of Njo Eteki who had studied in France.

Of the other children of the Duala élite sent to school in France,
Gaston Kingue Jong returned from there in 1931 and so, about the
same time, did François Kouo, son of Pastor Kouo Issedou. That
pastor was a true élite figure, with a large income, particularly from
plantations, which upset the missionaries. François Kouo entered
the African civil service like many young Duala emerging from
French schools, particularly the Ecole Supérieure in Yaoundé.

In the African civil service Isaac Moume Etia was for long the
outstanding figure. Besides his main work he also wrote many books,
particularly on the Duala language and traditions. In 1926 he wrote
La Langue de Douala par Vous-Même, forwarded to the Commissioner (governor) with praise by Cortade; in 1928 a *Lexique
Français-Douala* and *Quelques Renseignements sur la Coutume locale
chez les Doualas (Cameroun)*; in 1930 *Fables de Douala (Cameroun)
en deux langues: Français-Douala* and *Grammaire abrégé de la langue
Douala (Cameroun)*. For his linguistic studies and his aid to 'France's
work of civilisation in Africa' the clerk-interpreter from Deido was

created, on 21 October 1929, a *Chevalier de l'Ordre Universel du Mérite Humain* (an order based in Geneva). Of his sons, Léopold was in France for studies from 1927 to 1939, and Abel followed his father into the African civil service.[59]

Moume Etia came under suspicion in 1930–1, but later he received important new postings outside Douala from 1931 to 1935. He served in the Bamileke country, at Dschang, Bafoussam, then Dschang again, and finally, from 13 May 1933, at Bafang. On 21 October 1935 he retired, though he was only 45 years old; he died four years later. His was a major loss to the ranks of the German-trained older generation of the élite in government service. Others were still serving, though two who were very prominent in the 1930s – Albert Mpondo Dika, posted to Bafia in 1934, and Guillaume Jemba, who after serving in the Commissioner's office joined in 1936 the Secretariat of the Chef de Région in Douala, having reached the rank of Commis d'Ordre et de Comptabilité, First Class – had worked under the Germans only very briefly before the First World War.

The French, the Duala and the Chiefs

Moume Etia's writings were one indication that the spread of French culture did not mean any serious loss of interest in the Duala language and traditions. On the contrary, the continued interest in these prevented a breach between the generations and limited and eased the adaptation to French culture. Not that the French seriously tried to uproot the Dualas' attachment to their traditions, although they insisted on teaching in French alone. They encouraged Moume Etia's work, while other African officials were encouraged to write about their people's traditions in *La Gazette du Cameroun* (a government-sponsored periodical) and many did so. Many also contributed, in 1934–5, to a private newspaper in Douala which was for Africans and was published partly in Duala.

This was *L'Eveil des Camerouniens*, or *L'Eveil des Camerounais*, started in 1934 by Eugène Schneider, editor of *L'Eveil du Cameroun*. A rather irregular fortnightly, it was not a journal of record; it had some articles on recent events, and some often well written reports of canoe races and other sporting events, but it did not report news at all regularly. There were limits to what such a newspaper could or would publish, but it did provide another outlet for writing by Duala and others of the élite, usually if not always of the government junior staff. The venture lost money and Schneider, who was its editor (a Duala, Alfred A. Musinga, was assistant editor), warned in the issue of 25 February 1935 that that would be the last issue but one for lack of money. But he also said the government had been asked for permission to publish a four-page newspaper in African languages – Duala, Bassa and Ewondo or Boulou – and French. Permission was evidently given, and on 23 March 1935 there appeared *Jumwele la Bana Ba Kamerun/L'Eveil des Camerounais*. There were parts in Bassa, Ewondo and Bulu, but much longer ones in Duala.

After the first multi-lingual issue, however, the amount of the newspaper in African languages steadily declined, until it was very small in the issue of 25 May 1935, one of the last before the newspaper collapsed. The Africans had not shown much apparent interest in it as a vehicle for writing in their own languages, as the editor complained in the final issue of 1 June 1935. But the Duala of the younger generation were literate in Duala, and the French were fully reconciled to such attachment to custom, as they showed by many measures in the early 1930s.

Besides deciding in 1933 to record the major tribes' unwritten customary law of the major ethnic groups the French administration, soon after the appointment in 1933 of Commissioner Bonnecarrère, started official studies of Cameroon African languages, and an *Arrêté* (ordinance) of 21 April 1933 fixed bonuses for officials learning them.[60] It noted, without any indication of concern or dissatisfaction, the spread of Duala outside the Douala region: 'Richer than the neighbouring languages, Bakoko and the various dialects of Basa origin, Duala is tending bit by bit to superimpose itself on these and to be the commercial and official language of the Circonscriptions of Nkongsamba and Yabassi and the Subdivisions of Edea and N'Dikinimeki ... grouping 200 000 individuals'.[61] This was due very much to the Protestant Mission's extensive use of Duala. The continual use of their language in church helped the Dualas combine traditional and modern culture as they did.

Duala were already a minority in their city by the early 1930s. African immigrants outnumbered them by 1929, when a sleeping-sickness vaccination campaign showed that there were already about 20 000 immigrants, twice as many as the government counted in its censuses, and already more numerous than the Duala.[62] Immigrants from the interior apparently found it easy to reach Douala in spite of the many influx-control regulations, and to remain there in defiance of the government, whose censuses they naturally evaded. Many were regularly rounded up and sent home, but the number may never have stopped growing.

New-Bell was the home of most of the Cameroonian immigrants by the late 1920s. In 1935–6 the government moved some there from Akwa and Deido.[63] This was no doubt another move to apply the general French policy in Douala of removing non-Duala Africans from the influence of the Duala and their chiefs. Those Strangers who still lived in Duala residential areas, as some did, were in some sort of social subordination to Duala. Their increasing numbers in fact eventually made the Strangers more effectively independent of Duala influence. French policy of removing any sort of Duala influence over other Africans in the city had started in 1920, when new artificial chieftaincies were created for the Strangers, both those from other parts of Cameroon and those from other African territories.[64]

Those immigrants from other parts of Africa were prominent in the city. Unlike the Cameroonian immigrants, at first commonly labourers, small traders or unemployed, the Nigerian, Dahomean, Gold Coast (Ghanaian) and other West African immigrants tended to be high-ranking clerks, important traders, or leading craftsmen. While socially important − and on a social level with the Duala élite − they were not numerous. Among the far more numerous Cameroonian immigrants the Bamileke, today the largest single group, were already coming to the fore in the 1930s. The other immigrants were commonly Beti ('Yaoundé people') and Basa.

On 24 December 1933 an *Arrêté* grouped the Strangers' chieftaincies into two new Paramount Chieftaincies, for '*New-Bell: Etrangers à Douala*' and '*New-Bell: Etrangers au Cameroun*'. The first holders of these posts were respectively Marcous Eteme and Joseph Paraiso. They were officially equal to the traditional Duala 'Kings' in ranks, while Paraiso, a Dahomean, was in his own right a prominent citizen of Douala for decades.

The position of the more traditional Cameroonian chiefs, including the Duala chiefs, was the object of concentrated attention from Bonnecarrère, Commissioner for French Cameroon from 1932 to 1934, and his successor Répiquet (1934−36). Soon after assuming duty Bonnecarrère sent a Circular saying, 'As you know, our administrative action in this country rests on native authority; our policy has been aiming with perseverance, for several years, in the Southern regions at least, to reorganise and strengthen that authority.[65] He called for each Chef de Circonscription and Chef de Subdivision (the Subdivision was the administrative unit below the Circonscription level; but in Douala there was only one Subdivision) to keep a list of chiefs, and the said chiefs must be educated and their prestige upheld; no judicial proceedings could be started against a chief without the Commissioner's permission. Apart from saying that small chieftaincies must be replaced by larger and more powerful ones, which would go against tradition, the Circular was an indication of a policy more favourable to chiefs.

There may have been momentary doubts about applying such a policy to the Duala. Cortade, repeating views expressed before, spoke in his Annual Report for 1932 for Douala Circonscription of the 'feeble influence' of the chiefs,[66] and the Annual Report to the League of Nations for French Cameroon, apparently reflecting Cortade's ideas in this case, said Douala was 'in fact subject to a regime of direct administration'.[67] As stated, this was an exaggeration, no doubt based on the authorities' inclination to bypass the chiefs to get things done. Cortade's views were at one point shared by the new Commissioner, who in December 1932 wrote to him to confirm 'my way of thinking on the timeliness of studying without delay for the urban centre of Douala the substitution, for a native authority system whose impotence does not need further proof, of a system of direct administration, based on the use of native staff suitably salaried and officered'.[68]

This idea may have been influenced by the case of the Paramount Chief of Deido, Eyoum Ekwalla, who was charged with embezzlement of tax money. On 29 November 1932 Bonnecarrère told Cortade he needed more information before allowing the prosecution of Eyoum Ekwalla. He asked particularly for information on the tax collection system.[69] Approval was given for the prosecution and on 29 December 1932 the Paramount Chief was convicted. The Commissioner's unfavourable view of Duala chiefs at this time may also have been influenced by Lobe Bell's role in the land protests. In his letter of 20 December he asked Cortade for details of Lobe Bell's appointment, saying he had found nothing about it in the files. Bonnecarrère was clearly doing his homework on the chieftaincy question. The outcome was to be in line with his 28 October circular; his ideas about Douala after that were soon dropped.

On 9 February 1933 a *décision* proclaimed that 'Théodore Lobe Bell, chief of the village of Bonanjo, is appointed Paramount Chief of Bell, to replace Richard Manga Bell, whose resignation has been accepted'.[70] As Richard Bell's resignation had been accepted in 1927, this proclamation must have puzzled people who did not know that the new governor was evidently trying to bring some new order into the situation of chiefs. His government waited two months before dismissing Eyoum Ekwalla. This was eventually done by a *décision* of 1 March 1933 which also dismissed Ntepe Priso, chief of Bonapriso, who was also convicted of tax embezzlement.

Two other Duala chiefs were also dismissed, for the same reason, by *décisions* of 12 April 1933: Maniania Nyungu, chief of Bonendale II in Bonaberi, and Essaka Ntone, chief of Bonamoudourou in

Deido. This was quite a little purge; the convictions may have been correct, though Eyoum Ekwalla's offence may not have been the real reason for his removal as he had been briefly gaoled for nationalistic activity in 1931 and his successor, his uncle Eboa Epee, who had already ruled Deido from 1919 to 1927, had also had a criminal conviction, for illicit alcohol dealing. But although removals of chiefs for tax embezzlement were to continue now and then (with some others quite possibly allowed to get away with the same thing), and while the new Chief of Bonapriso, appointed in 1933, was removed the following year for political reasons, the sackings in 1933 were not the prelude to an anti-chief policy.

On 4 February 1933 a new *Arrêté* laid down the status of chiefs, dividing them into three groups: Paramount or 'Regional' chiefs, Chefs de Groupement and village chiefs.[71] Chefs de Groupement were apparently appointed in other parts of the territory, and among the Duala the main change in title was that the title Chef de Région, applied for some years hitherto to certain Paramount Chiefs (those of Akwa and Bonaberi), was apparently an alternative title for the Chefs Supérieurs. The real innovation of the new *Arrêté* was a specific provision for the choice of chiefs from the traditional families if possible, with consultation. Chiefs' uniforms were also prescribed.

In a Circular at the end of 1933 Bonnecarrère spoke of the need to educate chiefs and their sons, and added, 'I would even say that so long as a feeling of social hierarchy based principally on birth remains among the peoples of Cameroon, the necessarily limited numbers attending our school establishments must be recruited, for preference, among the families of chiefs and elders'.[72] This circular referred principally to the chiefs in Northern Cameroon in particular; in Douala many chiefs had for long been educated men anyway. But the Circular was a further indication of the new emphasis in policy. This policy continued under Répiquet, and in 1936 the government told the League of Nations that its 'native authority' policy was based on four principles:

1) Respect for customs, and the need to have a middle-ranking authority so that chiefs should be 'an essential cog in the administration of the territory'.

2) A dual obligation of chiefs, to inform the government of the people's needs and wishes, and to inform the people of the government's advice and orders.

3) A consistent aim of increasing chiefs' authority and helping them act as 'guides, advisers and leaders', but also controlling them and if necessary restraining abuses by them.

4) An open-minded approach to hierarchy except for attention to

tradition; on this principle no new chiefly authorities would be created.[73]

In Douala an exception was made to the new policy in the non-traditional chieftaincies and, from 1933, in the Paramount Chieftaincies of the Strangers. But the chieftaincy *Arrêté* of 4 February 1933 ended, among the Dualas, the untraditional higher status given for many years (but perhaps with little effect) to the Akwa ruler.

For seven years after the dismissal of Eyoum Ekwalla of Deido no Duala Paramount Chief was sacked. Lobe Bell and Betote Akwa were to retain their posts for 20 years (Betote Akwa for 44 years) after 1932, and to be outstanding figures among the Dualas. The French encouraged chiefs and others to act as interpreters between them and the people; among the others were the *miemba* described above and one businessman, Doumbe Edimo, who in 1935 was decorated for his 'ardour' in defending African interests in the Chamber of Commerce of which he was a member.[74] Signs of favour to the chiefs included the award in 1934 of the *Mérite Indigène* (a government decoration for Cameroonians in the Mandate era) to Lobe Bell for 'giving satisfaction' and to the Bonaberi Paramount Chief, Mbappe Bwanga, for his plantations, as well as the appointment of Lobe Bell to the Chamber of Commerce, as a planter, in 1935. From 1934 regular meetings between chiefs and other Africans and French officials were organised to explain policy, with the aid of film shows.[75]

Respect for tradition and chieftaincy among the Dualas was taken by the French as far as encouragement and sponsorship of popular shows of feeling towards the elder son of Rudolf Douala Manga Bell. Prince Alexandre Douala Manga Bell (1897–1966), after his return to a hero's welcome from Germany (where he had spent nearly all his childhood) in 1919, remained popular even though he took no part in the protest movements and was utterly loyal to France. He was a well-known 'character' of wide accomplishments, and became the most prominent Duala of his time, serving after the Second World War as a *député* in the French parliament. But despite his pro-French feelings the French for long denied him the succession to his father's Paramount Chieftaincy. However, in the 1930s, while still recognising Lobe Bell as the Bell Paramount Chief, the government approved of popular respect for Prince Alexandre as the true heir to the throne. Jean Michel, Chef de Circonscription from 1933 to 1935, not only served as patron of the *Musango ma Bonadoo*, but lent his patronage to a spectacular celebration on 9 December 1934 of the 37th birthday of Prince Alexandre Douala Manga Bell, organised at Bonaberi by two associations, the *Male ma N'Doumb'a Douala* and *Muemba ma Nyango Andre* (the latter named after his wife). On 8 December, the Associations organised a march down the main street of Bonasama, 'to the sound of the Bonadoo anthem'.

Subsequent press reports said there was a torchlight procession and all-night singing 'to the accompaniment of two bands and guitars'. One franc was charged for admission to a preliminary party, where sandwiches and other refreshments were served. Then, at 8 a.m. on 9 December, the beach at Bonaberi was crowded for the landing of Prince Alexandre and M Michel with other guests of honour, filling two steam launches. A canoe race was held, and a religious service where Pastor Rusillon preached. A ceremony was held under the historic *Bongongi ba Belle Belle*, the baobab tree under which rulers of the Bonadoo had been crowned and Ndoumb'a Douala himself had, at the age of 4, been the object of another ceremony in 1902. Later people went to the Prince's house at Bali, where the anthems of Bell, Akwa, Deido and France were played.[76]

The report of this event written by Michel Epee in *L'Eveil des Camerouniens* is full of interest. More remarkable than the popular veneration of Prince Alexandre, something of a symbol of tradition for all his modern-style accomplishments, was the ceremony — whatever it actually was — under the baobab tree, and the presence there of the senior French government representative. The Bonadoo were out to show their acceptance of Ndoumb'a Duala as the real 'King', and the French to show that they did not mind him being considered so. This indicated their cultivation of the prince at this time, which can be linked with other signs of positive official interest in traditions, chieftaincy included.

In 1934 Ndoumb'a Douala (his traditional name) was appointed to the Administrative Council of French Cameroon. But in that same year the Prince clashed with the government over his land. As the government, for all its favouring of him, opposed him on his land claim, this case must have raised still further the Prince's standing among the Bonadoo. The report on the case given later, and now in the French Colonial Ministry archives, does not fully explain the details. Certainly Ndoumb'a Douala started in 1934 by claiming *constatation* of customary-law rights over seven plots of land, all with buildings on them, which had been occupied by the administration for twenty years. The government opposed his claim on the ground of 'effective occupation', and on 28 February 1935 the Douala Court of First Instance upheld its case and rejected Alexandre's.

However, a French presidential decree of 30 June 1935, applied by *Arrêté* of 2 February 1936 in Cameroon, placed that territory under the jurisdiction of the Court of Appeal of French Equatorial Africa, abolishing the separate Appeal Court of French Cameroon, Prince Alexandre then appealed to the Court in Brazzaville, and won.[77] This was on 5 March 1937.

More needs to be studied about this triumph of Ndoumb'a Douala over the French in the courts, for it is a puzzling case. The seven plots of land had all been inherited from his father by the prince in 1914. Presumably the French occupation of them had been a part of the general occupation of land seized by the Germans in 1914, the plots having been covered by the Bonanjo expropriation. But how, in that case, could the French occupation of the land claimed by Prince Alexandre be ruled illegal, as it clearly was, without the entire French occupation of the land seized by the Germans in 1914 also being overruled? Research is necessary to determine how the court in 1937 conceded the prince's claim without accepting the whole case fruitlessly argued for years by the Bonadoo. It is possible that the French occupation of that land had been separate from the other, wider occupation of the land expropriated in 1914; though it is hard to see on what other grounds they could have occupied it.

Anyway, his triumph in his land case was another step on Prince Alexandre Douala Manga Bell's way to becoming the outstanding figure of the Duala élite and an unofficial leader of the whole Duala community. He had become something like that by the later 1930s, partly, no doubt, because the anti-colonial movement from which he had stood aloof had proved useless, leaving his alternative course, of greater collaboration, the only one apparently likely to lead anywhere. (It must not be forgotten, though, that some other leading Duala élite figures had always upheld French rule stoutly, such as Robert Ebolo Bile and Kunz Kwa Moutome.)

On 8 March 1935 the remains of Rudolf Douala Manga Bell were re-interred behind his old house at Bonanjo, *La Pagode*. Michel attended the ceremony,[78] and this was not an empty gesture at all. Duala Manga was a symbol of resistance, remembered above all as a martyr in the cause of the Bell land; for the government's main representative in Douala to attend what must have been a very emotional occasion as his reburial showed a really positive attitude to tradition, especially as it was just a few days after the rejection of the claim by Rudolf's heir to land he had bequeathed in 1914. A year later, on 8 August 1936 (the 22nd anniversary of the execution), an Obelisk to the memory of Douala Manga was inaugurated by the tomb. His widow Emma Engome, died not long afterwards, in November 1936.

In March 1935 a monument to Tete Dika Mpondo, 'King Akwa', was inaugurated in Akwa with a speech by his son Betote Akwa.[79] The aim of these ceremonies, of course, was to enlist traditional sentiments on the side of the French. Two years later Betote led his people in submission to large-scale evictions (but without loss of property rights) in Akwa.

Continued dissent in Church and State

Not everyone followed Prince Alexandre's policy. The acquiescence of Duala under French rule after the failure of the major protest activity was not complete or unconditional. It seems, in fact, that the revived Baptist Church agitation reached a peak between 1932 and 1934. However, a close study of this, using the Cameroon Archives, is needed to determine exactly what happened then, as the published material gives a confusing picture.

It is clear that the Native Baptist Church sought some sort of legal status or recognition, being unsatisfied with mere *de facto* freedom to operate, and that its efforts to achieve this were backed by a strong state of feeling among the Duala, noted with alarm by the Protestant Mission.[80] Then an effort at a reconciliation between the NBC and the Mission was made in 1932, but unsuccessfully.[81] The breach continued to widen, partly because a new Decree on religion, dated 28 March 1933, made religious buildings subject to authorisation, and the Mission obtained this for the use of all the Protestant churches in Douala. The NBC, whose efforts to secure a fuller legal status may all along have been made partly with the control of existing churches in mind, challenged the allocation of churches to the Mission in the courts, but its action was dismissed on 15 May 1934.[82] The government was hostile to the NBC as always, and Bonnecarrère and Michel are said to have been particularly so.[83] But the Church remained free to operate in practice and in 1935 Lotin Same consecrated some pastors, including Johannes Njembele Ekwe, the Bonadoo Elder and former Customs officer.

Further research is necessary to fill out the story thus outlined of the revived NBC agitation in the early 1930s and its outcome. It is also necessary to supplement the information on political activity in those years.

The continued lack of really submissive feelings among the Duala was indicated by their reluctance to show deference to Europeans they passed in the street, which led to a minor flurry when in 1933 Michel issued a circular quoting with approval a European newspaper's views on the subject.[84] It was also shown by the continued

French apprehension over left-wing and German activity. The former was apparently less important after 1932. In 1933 the Nazi seizure of power in Germany, besides depriving many anti-colonial left-wingers of a base (including Joseph Ekwe Bile, a Duala, who had been a left-wing activist in Europe, but who now had to leave Germany and in 1935 returned to Douala),[85] made many of them tone down their opposition to Britain and France because of the common Nazi-Fascist danger. The same event, however, led to increasing French fears of support in Douala for the movement for restoration of the German 'lost colonies'.

In 1933—4 the French uncovered a secret organisation including Duala, some Batanga and a Malimba, all German-educated, which was called the *Kamerun Eingeboren Deutsch Gesinnten Verein*, meaning, in ungrammatical or 'Pidgin' German, the 'Cameroon Natives' German-Thinking Union'. A prominent member was Edinguele Meetom, who had escaped arrest as a leading anti-colonial activist in 1931. In 1934 he escaped from his Douala hiding place to British Cameroons.[86] Others, whose role was discovered in the same year, included Peter Mukuri Dikongue and Paul Muduru Dibongo, Akwa men like Meetom. They escaped arrest, apparently fleeing to British Cameroons; Meetom may have fled there following those police discoveries. Felix Etame Joss, chief of Bonapriso and previously a clerk under the Germans and the French, was dismissed as an accomplice, and interned along with nine other people.[87]

The KEDGV, whose members swore oaths to the Kaiser, was probably a sort of 'old boys' association' of veterans of German government service, rather than a movement for restoration of German rule. Edinguele Meetom was probably always a true nationalist. Planters, traders and urban landlords who were veterans of the German era had been at the heart of the nationalist movement (though many of that class, as noted, had been pillars of French rule); the KEDGV may simply have been a continuation of the same movement by a few of them. They may have contacted the Germans, who were suspected of having agents in Douala, but the Duala must have known about the character of Nazism from people like Ekwe Bile.

Even so, the French were to be very worried about 'pro-Germans' among the Duala for years. They were said to have encouraged some opposition to the Akwa evictions of 1937. It was to counter the German call for a return of the former colonies, and suspected sympathy for this among some Duala, that the *Jeunesse Camerounaise Française* (Jeucafra) was started, mainly by young Duala, in 1938. This was the first legal African political body in Cameroon.

Conclusion

Soon after this came the Second World War and the dramatic changes it brought to French Cameroon. In Douala a major event was the witch-hunt of alleged 'pro-Germans' by the Free French regime which took over in August 1940; one was executed (Theodore Dikongue Meetom) and fifteen or more imprisoned in 1941.[88] This persecution, born of runaway security men's paranoia, culminated years of French hostility to the older Duala élite − the planters, urban landlords and other independent élite men, veterans of the German era when many had had office jobs which they were suspected of wanting to restore.[89] In fact many of them were true nationalists, like Ferdinand Edinguele Meetom who was among those gaoled in 1941.

The mass punishment of these people hastened the end of an era in Douala. True, some of the German-trained generation were still important after the Second World War, while some, before and after then, were never involved in anti-French activity. But things were no longer the same. And the war years, because of the disruption of overseas trade and special Anglo-Free French arrangements which favoured white planters, brought the final blow to the Duala élite's plantations.

In addition, the rapid changes which began in 1944−5 in French Cameroon reduced the role of the Duala in the country. They had already begun losing their predominance in clerical employment, with the steady spread of education in other parts of Cameroon; this process continued and accelerated after the war. As for politics, the rapid growth of political parties and trade unions after 1944 was different beyond recognition from the protest movements in which Duala had taken the lead. Individual Duala were prominent in politics and trade unionism in the Trusteeship era and after independence, most notably Soppo Priso. But now their role in politics was nearer to what their numbers would suggest.

So as in much of Africa, an era ended in the Second World War for the coastal élite communities which had grown up since the nineteenth century. Those peoples, such as the Creoles of Freetown and the indigenous Lagosians, are far from totally eclipsed even today; but their great era ended after the 1930s. Until then they flourished as the most educated Africans, taking the majority of clerical jobs under the government and business firms. As a people they adopted Western culture, built Western-style houses, and bought Western consumer goods. Often, as pioneer converts to Christianity, their churches were a central feature of élite life (Islam, though important in Lagos and Freetown, was absent in Douala, except for immigrants). The Duala had much in common with coastal élites in other parts of Africa. They differed from the élites of British West Africa in three major ways. First, the narrower possibilities for higher education under French rule meant that in the Mandate era there were no Duala lawyers and doctors in their home town (one, Stephan Dualla Missipo, who went to Germany before 1914 became a doctor there but did not return); the leading role of the liberal professions among other African élites was therefore absent. Secondly, French rule did not allow the development of African newspapers such as those which flourished in Nigeria, Gold Coast and Sierra Leone for decades. Thirdly, Duala had an activity — cash crop plantations — which the other élite peoples largely did not have: an important source of income and of a certain amount of independence.

On the other hand, the Duala's position was very different from that of other Cameroonians. The Duala never felt the full weight of French Mandate rule. The Indigénat was in force in Douala, and so was the official forced labour (the Prestations), although the Duala normally commuted this for cash. But the much wider use of forced labour common in the interior, remembered with horror by many Cameroonians, was not experienced by Duala at first hand. Even their protest activity was seldom punished and not, by French colonial standards, very severely until the persecution of 1941.

Politics was only one part of élite life, and a minor one for many. In almost every other respect the Duala élite continued to develop with considerable freedom under colonial rule. After the settlement of the Bell land question the main French attack on the Duala's rights was massive eviction of Africans in Akwa in 1937. But a vital difference from the 1914 expropriation was that Duala retained ownership of the land where they were forbidden to live. They submitted to the measure and those lands, with others, have continued to provide ever multiplying revenue for the indigenous inhabitants of the largest city and commercial metropolis of Cameroon.

The Duala are still important today, notably as owners of land in a city of over a million people; their language, understood by many Cameroonians, is also still important. But their heyday was fifty years ago, in the period described in this chapter.

Notes

1   See J. Derrick, 'Douala under the French Mandate, 1916–36', Ph. D thesis (unpublished) School of Oriental and African Studies, University of London, 1979. Most of this chapter is extracted from the thesis.

2   *Ibid.* pp. 286 ff.
3   Douala Circonscription Annual Report 1929, p. 28ff., file Affaires Politiques et Administratives (hereafter APA) 10005/A, Archives Nationales, Yaoundé [ANY].
4   Douala Annual Report 1932, file APA 11757
5   *L'Eveil du Cameroun*, 15 February 1933. This was a Europeans' newspaper founded in Douala in 1928.
6   Douala Circonscription Annual Report 1935, quoted in Gouellain, *Douala: Ville et Histoire*, Paris 1975, p. 239–40. French Cameroon was then divided into fifteen Circonscriptions, Douala Circonscription consisting mainly of the Douala urban area.
7   Douala Annual Report 1929, p. 46–7, file APA 10005/A.
8   Douala Circonscription Annual Report 1930, p. 2, file APA 10005/A.
9   *Ibid.*, p. 40 ff.
10 Douala Annual Report 1930, p. 23 (see note 8).
11 Douala Annual Report 1929, file APA 10005/A.
12 The full results of the survey are preserved in an isolated file in the ORSTOM library at Yaoundé.
13 See summary of findings in Derrick, p. 436–447.
14 Douala Annual Report 1929, file APA 10005/A, pp. 2ff., 27 ff.
15 *Journal des Missions Evangéliques* (hereafter abbreviated to *JME*), Paris, 1927, p. 154.
16 *JME*, 1932, p. 648 ff.
17 E. de Rosny, *Ndimsi*, Yaoundé, 1974, describes the survival of these beliefs today.
18 Mlle. Allier (later Mme Dugast, the anthropologist) letter published in *JME*, second half of 1930, p. 274–6.
19 Rusillon in Mission Report for 1931–32, *JME*, 1932, p. 645,
20 Quoted in J. van Slageren, *Les Originer de L'Eglise Evangélique du Cameroun*, p. 231.
21 *JME*, second half of 1933, p. 566.
22 *JME*, 1935, p. 551.
23 Annual Report for 1937–9, *JME*, 1938, p. 694.
24 Interview, Pastor Rusillon, Geneva 1973. In retrospect Rusillon disliked the practice.
25 M. Scheurer in *JME*, 1932, p. 30.
26 *JME*, 1932, p. 30.
27 *JME*, 1929, p. 238.
28 *JME*, 1931, pp. 564, 625 ff.
29 *JME*, first half of 1930, p. 392–3; second half of 1930, p. 275.
30 *JME*, 1932, p. 213; Léopold Moume Etia papers, Douala.
31 *JME*, 1931, p. 468 ff.
32 *JME*, 1932, p. 640.
33 *JME*, 1932, p. 648 ff.
34 *L'Eveil des Camerouniens*, Douala, 10 September 1934. (See below on that newspaper.)
35 *L'Eveil des Camerouniens*, 1 June 1935.
36 Interview, Michel Epee, Douala.
37 M. Doumbe-Moulongo, 'Les Dualas du Cameroun' (unpublished), p. 2; Gouellain, *Douala*, p. 56.
38 Interview, Louis Mbappe, Douala.

39   Interview, Jacques Kuoh Moukouri, Douala.
40   Doumbe-Moulongo, *op. cit.*, p. 110.
41   'Report No. 111 131' (no other specification) in ORSTOM files, Yaoundé: an isolated document apparently from the archives.
42   Interview, Léopold Moume Etia, Douala.
43   J. Guilbot, 'Les Conditions de Vie des Indigènes de Douala', *Etudes Camerounaises* 27–8, September-December 1949, p. 207–8.
44   See full account in P. Harter, 'Les Courses de Pirogues Coutumiers chez les Dualas', *Recherches et Etudes Camerounaises*, 1960, no. 1, p. 71 ff
45   'La Fédération Ancestrale des Piroguiers de Douala', *L'Eveil du Cameroun*, 23 November 1937.
46   *L'Eveil des Camerouniens*, 10 November 1934.
47   *L'Eveil des Camerouniens*, 10 January 1935.
48   *L'Eveil des Camerouniens*, 10 January 1935.
49   Interview, Jacques Kuoh Moukouri.
50   Interviews, Goethe George, Albert Mpondo Dika, Douala.
51   M. Doumbe-Moulongo, 'Musique et danse chez les Dualas', *Abbia*, no. 22, Yaoundé, May-August 1969.
52   Notes (unpublished) on pastors and leading Christians of Douala by Pastor J.-R. Brutsch, Geneva.
53   Will of David Mandessi Bell. I am grateful to Dr. R. Austen for showing me a photocopy of this will.
54   *L'Eveil des Camerouniens*, 10 September 1934.
55   Interview, Léopold Moume Etia.
56   Interview, Johannes Sam Deido, Douala.
57   Interview, Léopold Moume Etia.
58   Interview, Paul Soppo Priso, Douala.
59   L. and A. Moume Etia, *Notice Biographique sur la Vie de Monsieur Isaac Moume Etia*, Douala, 1940.
60   Annual Report to League of Nations, 1933, p. 89.
61   *Ibid.*, p. 91.
62   Derrick, p. 400.
63   Gouellain, p. 232.
64   Derrick, p. 401–4.
65   Circular, Bonnecarrère to all Chefs de Circonscription 28 October 1932, reproduced in Annual Report to League of Nations for French Cameroon, 1932.
66   Douala Circonscription Annual Report, 1932, file APA 11757.
67   Annual Report to League of Nations, 1932, p. 73.
68   Bonnecarrère to Cortade, 20 December 1932, file APA 12395.
69   Bonnecarrère to Cortade, 29 November 1932, same file.
70   *La Gazette du Cameroun*, 15 March 1933.
71   *Journal Officiel du Cameroun, JOC*, 15 February 1933.
72   Circular letter of 31 December 1933, *JOC* 1 January 1934.
73   *Annual Report to League of Nations*, 1936, p. 42.
74   *JOC*, 15 January 1935.
75   Permanent Mandates Commission, Report of 38th session (2–12 September 1939), Geneva. A report (by Paraiso) of one of the first meetings appeared in *L'Eveil des Camerouniens*, 10 November 1934.
76   *L'Eveil des Camerouniens*, 10 January 1935.
77   Commissioner Brunot to Minister of Colonies, 16 December 1938, and related handwritten note on case; Box Cameroun Affaires Politiques (hereafter abbrevi-

ated AP) II 29 & 30, Archives Section Outremer (hereafter abbreviated SOM), Paris.

78 *L'Eveil des Camerouniens*, 25 February 1935.

79 *Jumwele la Bana ba Kamerun*, 25 March 1935.

80 *JME*, 2nd half of 1932, Annual Report for French Cameroon Mission; *JME*, 1933, p. 168.

81 J.-R. Brutsch, 'Origine et Dévelopment d'une Eglise Indépendante Africaine', *Le Monde Non-Chrétien* no. 12, October-December 1949, Paris; L. Moume Etia, 'Lotin Same et L'Eglise Baptist Camerounaise', *La Presse du Cameroun*, 12 November and 9 December 1971, Douala; A. Mpondo Dika, 'A la mémoire d'Adolf Lotin Same', unpublished MS, Douala.

82 Brutsch, *op. cit.*; J. van Slageren, *Les Origines de L'Eglise Evangélique du Cameroun*, p. 195.

83 Mpondo Dika, *op. cit.* and interview.

84 Senator Lémery to Bonnecarrère, Paris 28 November 1933; Minister to Bonnecarrère, 28 December 1933; Commissioner to Minister, 23 February 1934; Box Cameroun AP II 29 & 30, Archives SOM, Paris.

85 Minister to Commissioner, 27 March 1935, file on J.E. Bile in Box Cameroun AP II 28, Archives SOM, Paris; *Jumwele la Bana ba Kamerun*, 10 April 1935.

86 Interview, Edinguele Meetom, Douala.

87 Report by head of Secretariat-General, Yaoundé, quoted in Répiquet (Commissioner) to Minister, 2 November 1934; translation of German document by Mukuri Dikongue; report by head of Sûreté, Douala, Oct. 1934; Box Cameroun AP II 30, Archives SOM, Paris. Also isolated undated note in Box Cameroun AP II, Archives SOM, Paris; *JOC*, 1 September 1933, 1 October 1933.

88 J. Derrick, 'Free French and Africans in Douala, 1940–1941', *Journal of the Historical Society of Nigeria*, Vol. X, No. 2, June 1980, p. 53–70.

89 J. Derrick, 'The Germanophone Élite of Douala under the French Mandate', *Journal of African History*, Vol. XXI, No. 3, July 1980.

Chapter Six
The French administrative system in the lamidate of Ngaoundéré, 1915–1945

Daniel Abwa

The French imperialist administrative system in the lamidate of Ngaoundéré, from 1915 to 1945, was full of ambiguities and contradictions. Firstly, there was ambiguity in its relations with the Lamibbe and with the people of the lamidate. Secondly, there was ambiguity because the system did not correspond either to the direct rule idea, preferred by the French, or to the British system of indirect rule.

The system enforced in the lamidate of Ngaoundéré cannot be identified with the direct rule system, one feature of which was to break the power of pre-colonial kingdoms, examples being the kingdom of Abomey, the empire of the Morho Naba in present-day Burkina Faso, and several former states in the Chad region.[1] It cannot be identified, either, with the indirect rule system which made the local chief an important element in the administrative machinery by giving him wide responsibilities such as the running of a Native Treasury into which variable amounts of the taxes and duties collected in the name of the African traditional authority were paid.[2]

The contradiction in the French administrative system in the lamidate of Ngaoundéré lay in the political methods used in dealing with the Lamibbe and the people of the lamidate. Our aim in this chapter is to illustrate the ambiguities and contradictions in this administrative system, in its relations with both the Lamibbe and the people.

Relations between the Lamido and the French administration

After its rapid victory over the Germans and occupation of Ngaoundéré on 29 June 1915, the French administration very quickly realised that success for its colonial rule must involve the help of the local chiefs. It understood that its authority, if it were founded on that of the traditional chiefs, would be more easily accepted by the people. Its choice fell on the Fulani chief, the Lamido. This can be attributed to the German colonial background, the political structure of the lamidate, and sympathy for Islam among the French.

To administer the lamidate of Ngaoundéré, the Germans relied on the Lamido, leaving him full authority over the peoples of the area; they were content to maintain now and then a reminder of their presence. The French, direct successors of the Germans, had to do as they had done, to avoid discontent by a radical change.

The well structured organisation of Fulani government may have swayed the French too. As a political and religious leader, with authority over the majority of the peoples of the lamidate, and endowed with definite prestige, the Lamido seemed a valid spokesman, and the obvious auxiliary for the French. In addition, the shortage of staff among those who had defeated the Germans could only encourage them to choose the chief who had no lack of staff. One may recall that the Lamido, who went ahead of the French on the Garoua road, showed himself from the outset an admirer of the victorious side.

Finally, the choice of the Lamido as an auxiliary of the government can also be attributed to a definite sympathy that Europeans felt for Islam, based on their previous experience in Muslim North Africa. Froelich says on this point:

> Islam was something convenient and reassuring; Muslims knew how to receive and honour the white man, while the Animist peoples showed evidence of duplicity and treason.[3]

However, all the factors advanced in favour of the choice of the Lamido as auxiliary were factors which could act against the French. By his position in his territory, the Lamido of Ngaoundéré could at any moment arouse against the foreigners a people which had learned to obey him. Aware of this, the French adopted an ambiguous and contradictory policy in their dealings with the Lamido, a policy of accommodation, of supervision, and of division.

The policy of accommodation

The Lamido of Ngaoundéré, traditionally the sole master of his subjects in the lamidate of Ngaoundéré, had, after the French conquest, to submit to an authority other than his own. To enjoy the advantages of his voluntary co-operation and make him give the maximum expected of him, the colonial power, instead of breaking this chief, showed him consideration in many ways. Its benevolent approach, which sought to win the Lamido over, involved a policy of generosity and a policy of upholding the ruler's authority.

By the policy of generosity the French sought to win the goodwill of the Lamido and derive advantage from his co-operation. It also involved conferring many political gifts on him. The strategy was adopted from the beginning of the French occupation, for in 1916 the Commandant of the Ngaoundéré Circonscription laid down that it was good policy to show publicly, at every opportunity, marks of the confidence of the French in the Lamido and the leading chiefs of his entourage. This would win the gratitude of the Fulani people and the Lamido towards the colonial power. 'This way of dealing with the chiefs', he said, 'is therefore one of the major conditions for the people remaining peaceful as they have been since our recent occupation'.[4]

The political gifts which were offered to the Lamibbe of Ngaoundéré were of two sorts and had complementary aims. The first sort was intended to win the goodwill of the Lamido alone, while the second aimed not only at that but also at the goodwill of the people of the lamidate as a whole.

Gifts in the first category were offered discreetly to the Lamido as an individual. Generally they involved satisfying requests from him or showing the government's generosity towards him. Thus, during the visit of the Commissioner Lucien Fourneau (1916–19) to the North Cameroon region in 1917, he received an application from the Commandant of that region, Compérat, to obtain for Lamido Issa Maigari a special permission to buy champagne for his personal consumption.[5] To back up the application Compérat told the Commissioner that

> this permission will both give the Sultan of Ngaoundéré pleasure, through satisfaction of his request, and also provide some sign of your trust and goodwill, to which the Sultan would attach great importance.[6]

The permission, which was granted the same day, was aimed at showing the French colonial rulers in a favourable light. In another step, by letter no. 976 of 1 February 1919 the Commissioner confirmed in writing the verbal instructions given during his tour in which he allowed 'various Sultans to communicate directly with him without prior reference to any of the local administrative authorities'.[7]

These instructions show how much the authorities desired to secure the co-operation of the Lamibbe in their work of colonial government, contrary to the habit of the French administration, normally so devoted to extreme centralisation, to give so many prerogatives and so much autonomy to traditional authorities. In 1925, for example, when a fire accidentally broke out in the *tata*[8] of Lamido Yaya Dandi, the French authorities in Ngaoundéré took the opportunity to make a political gesture in favour of the Lamido. They took no account of the damage caused by the fire, but instead asked that the Lamido be allowed the maximum tax refund even if he had not brought in all the taxes of the lamidate at the date fixed.[9] This action reflected once more the policy of accommodation because it had definite political repercussions; any contrary action would have brought an obstinate response from Yaya Dandi, and this would have been harmful to the aim of co-operation pursued by the French administration from the beginning of its rule. Even so, the human aspect of this gesture is not to be entirely disregarded.

The policy of gifts for different Lamibbe by the French administrators was carried out in proportion to each one's desire for co-operation. That desire was stronger under Issa Maigari because it was necessary to give France an attractive image, different from that of Germany which, during the war, had made itself hated by its requisitions.

Political gifts in the second category were those which, given at carefully chosen psychological moments, could win the sympathy of both the Lamido and his subjects. They were made publicly, before all the people of Ngaoundéré and its surrounding area. The moments chosen for making those gifts were the French national day, 14 July, and the installation ceremonies for the Lamibbe of Ngaoundéré.

The French national day was celebrated in the lamidate of Ngaoundéré as well as over French Cameroon. The peoples of the lamidate, who were French subjects and not French citizens, were invited to join in the celebration as if it was their own. The people considered it as one more occasion for festivities. That may have been why that day was chosen for the making of political gifts to the Lamido. In highlighting the dignity of the Lamido's office, the French government enjoyed the sympathy of the ruler himself and his subjects. On 14 July 1919, Lamido Issa was given the award of Officer of the Black Star of Benin before a great crowd. Although the award for the Lamido had been requested on 5 August 1918 at the same time as a bugle,[10] by an official telegram[11], Issa could not receive it before then. Here is how the Chef de Circonscription described the ceremony:

On 14 July, the Cross of the Officer of the Black Star of Benin was solemnly conferred on Lamido Issa Maigari. This honour, which greatly flattered him, produced an excellent impression among the population not only of Ngaoundéré, but of the whole area, and in the festivities which followed the award, many people came to congratulate him who, until then, would not have bothered. It is certain that his prestige and authority have been greatly enhanced.[12].

Lamido Mohammadou Abbo (1929–1939) was also given that award, in more or less the same circumstances.[13] Offering political gifts on the French national day had a definite impact. Not only were the prestige and authority of the Lamido enhanced, but the French national day was celebrated with general gaiety and the French government gained in popularity.

The other psychological moments chosen by the colonial rulers of the lamidate of Ngaoundéré were the investiture ceremonies for Lamibbe. On the occasion of every new appointment of a Lamido, the investiture ceremony was carried out in two phases – the letter of appointment and the handing over of gifts.

The letter of appointment was to confirm officially and publicly the appointment of a new Lamido. All the Lamibbe, after the death of Issa, received one: the Lamibbe Yagarou or Iya Garou (1922–1924), Yaya Dandi (1924–1929), Mohammadou Abbo (1929–1939) and Ardo Aliou (1939–1948). The letter was handed over in public, as is shown in the case of Yaya Dandi's letter:

> The letter of appointment of Yaya Dandi was handed over to him in front of the principal family heads at Ngaoundéré. Yaya Dandi and his elders showed a lively gratitude towards you and great pleasure.[14]

But, although it was handed over in public, the letter of appointment was not a political gift; on the contrary, it carried the implication of submission to French authority.

After the letter of appointment, the French administration then offered the Lamido of Ngaoundéré a political gift in the form of a turban. In this way the French government showed its knowledge of the history of the region. The Lamibbe of Ngaoundéré still retain fresh memories of the sumptuous gifts, including turbans, which their predecessors received from the Emir of Yola as a sign of their vassalage.[15] The ceremony of the conferring of turbans was carried out in public in the presence of the elders and was always followed by popular festivities. Its aim was to accommodate a new Lamido to the colonial order and to flatter his vanity, that of his elders and that of the people as a whole.[16] By this policy of favours, the French sought to win over the Lamibbe so as to enjoy their co-operation, which was indispensible; without it, success for French colonial rule would have been difficult. This reality was deeply impressed on the consciousness of the French authorities; thus the Commandant of the North Cameroon region made the following reflection:

> It is contrary to our own interests to treat a Sultan, however humble his real situation may be in comparison with the high-sounding title, as a black houseboy.[17]

Does this mean that the Lamibbe were ready to surrender their authority for a few presents? It seems not, because the French administration did not rely on friendly gestures alone. It also took measures, of considerable political importance, to uphold the authority of the Lamibbe of Ngaoundéré.

The policy of upholding the Lamido's authority was the second facet of the accommodation policy. The Lamido of Ngaoundéré appeared to the French as an indispensable intermediary, through whom every administrative act relating to the peoples of the lamidate had to pass. The chief was the screen preventing the French from having direct relations with the mass of the people of the lamidate. To allow him to give the best performance, the French government had to avoid anything which might affect his authority. Thus not only had his authority to be upheld, it also had to be protected against all internal or external dangers. In this policy France, in the lamidate of Ngaoundéré, gave up its favourite system of direct rule. If it had applied that system, it would instead have taken advantage of any elements liable to reduce the Lamido's authority and exploited them to impose its authority. In fact, it showed itself on the contrary very vigilant in thrusting off any possible threat to the Lamido's authority. Several events in Ngaoundéré between 1915 and 1945 show the continued application of this policy; we have chosen a few examples.

The Dalil affair

In September 1916 Dalil,[18] who had reigned as Lamido of Ngaoundéré from 1903 to 1904, but had been deposed by the Germans in favour of Lamido Issa Maigari and banished in 1904, took advantage of the French occupation to try to regain his throne. Warned of the presence of the former rival of Lamido Issa Maigari, the French rulers took the latter's side and banished Dalil once again. The Chef de Circonscription gave as the reason for this his wish to avoid the return of the old quarrels which had divided the two rivals for ten years. With that aim, he said:

I had him sent for on the pretext of protecting him from the hostility of the people, and on 1 October I sent him to Yaoundé under escort ...[19]

By coming down in this way on the side of the incumbent Lamido the Ngaoundéré Chef de Circonscription, Captain Popp, increased the Lamido's prestige and upheld his authority. He increased the Lamido's prestige by showing that Issa was the sole rightful Lamido of Ngaoundéré and that his authority must not be contested in any way. He upheld his authority because Dalil's presence would have caused a split among the people of the lamidate; Dalil's supporters could have rallied round their former chief and thus created a situation of rebellion which Issa could not have opposed because he no longer had the right to make war on his own account. Three former supporters of Dalil, at Tibati, had already gone to join him at Galim, where he had withdrawn; the movement could have spread.[20] So Captain Popp reinforced the Lamido's authority, because inaction on his part in this case could have been seen as weakness by Issa's supporters. We need no further proof of this than the demonstrations of joy and loyalty by the chiefs, the elders and the people which took place all over the country after Dalil's deportation.[21]

This decision against Dalil was also taken against Modibo Bouhari, a former dignitary of Lamido Yaya Dandi. In 1933 Bouhari, who had been banished eight years earlier and had been the inspiration of certain intrigues against Mohammadou Abbo, asked to return to Ngaoundéré. To preserve Abbo's power, the Chef de Circonscription, Roland, refused permission to return and wrote:

Later, and on a request from the Lamido, we can envisage this old madman's return to Ngaoundéré.[22]

The Ouham-Pende affair

In February 1917, Lamido Issa was accused by Lieutenant Pinassaud, Chef de Circonscription of Ouham-Pende, of organising a raid in his administrative area and kidnapping a considerable number of men, women and children. He had reached this conclusion from information given by prisoners, saying that a gang of raiders had been organised under the auspices of the Lamido of Ngaoundéré and its principal leader had been chief Alim of the village of Lobo.[23] He was so fully convinced that he announced his wish to have a heavy compensation demanded from the Lamido.[24] The accusations against Issa were plausible because the Ouham-Pende region had been, in pre-colonial times, the scene of raids organised by the Lamibbe of Ngaoundéré.

However, faced with such a serious charge made with such assurance by a French officer, Captain Popp refused to institute an inquiry. An inquiry on that subject would have meant large-scale harassment of the Lamido; this would doubtless have been noticed by the elders and dignitaries of the Lamido and could have reduced his authority over them. This incident could have been an ideal opportunity to break Lamido Issa. But in fact, to avoid any risk of harm to the Lamido's authority, the Chef de Circonscription not only refused to institute an inquiry, but came to the Lamido's defence. In reply to Lt Pinassaud, he wrote:

> In any case, I think it is advisable not to place faith in the words of your prisoners who have an obvious interest in putting the blame for their misdeeds on others, in this case the Lamido.[25]

Captain Popp went even further: he gave Issa the task of having the principal people charged put under arrest, including chief Alim.[26] Can one then be surprised to learn that Alim could not be found? And can one be surprised when a year later, the new Chef de Circonscription, Captain Ripert, reported that Alim, wanted by Captain Popp and Issa, went to his village the previous year and he (Ripert) had only known after he left?[27] This attitude on Captain Popp's part shows how important the Fulani chief's place was in the French administrative set-up. His authority must not be reduced under any circumstances, and must be safeguarded if necessary, because it was a vital stick to lean on. By taking Issa's side Captain Popp showed that he was an indispensible auxiliary who had to be accommodated. By such action the French administration took another step yet further away from the direct rule system.

Abolition of the post of policeman in the lamidate of Ngaoundéré

After their conquest of the lamidate in June 1915, the French installed there most of the elements universally recognised as necessary for normal administration. So they appointed to Ngaoundéré a Senegalese to serve as a policeman. The presence of this policeman did not please the Fulani chief, who considered him as a spy sent by the government to watch over his every act. In fact there was duplication of work because the lamidate of Ngaoundéré had its own police force responsible for maintaining order. The Lamido's hostility corresponded with growing concern in the French administration, which realised more and more the embarassment the Senegalese policeman was causing for them. The Commandant of the North Cameroon Region, Audouin, spoke of the danger in these terms:

> As the police post and the village are about 8 km apart, the policeman, who does not feel the effect of any immediate supervision over him, has a tendency, natural to a Senegalese above all, to consider himself superior to the Sultan himself.[28]

The African policeman stationed near the Lamido's side could, by some excesses causing displeasure, compromise the government's task. So, to avoid the risk of seeing its policy compromised by faults on the part of an African, the French administration preferred to sacrifice an important pawn and leave the Lamido's own police to cope alone. The police post was therefore abolished as from 1 January 1918.[29] Thus, as a precaution, the French removed an element which could harm the Lamido's authority. However, the police post was to be established again in 1939 at the expense of the Lamido's traditional police force, which was abolished.[30] This was certainly decided because the French felt sufficiently well established in the region.

The case of Adjia Halamadou and Lamido Yaya Dandi

European rule in the lamidate of Ngaoundéré gave rise to new functions such as that of Adjia. The holder of that title was charged with errands between the Lamido and the administration. This agent for carrying out the Lamido's orders was generally chosen from among his close entourage, and more particularly the non-Fulanis. So he was a man who owed his rise to the Lamido's will alone and not to birth, and thus had to be devoted to the ruler.

But in August 1924 Adjia Halamadou, of Laka origin, rose in open rebellion against Lamido Yaya Dandi. Halamadou had held the title of Adjia since the French conquest and had since then done many services for the government. In 1922, when Administrator Bru put forward to the Commissioner for French Cameroon names of natives who were particularly deserving and had given real services, he was one of them. He was recommended in these terms:

> This dignitary of Lamido Issa served during military operations against the Germans as a guide and as a leader of guerrillas and scouts for the Brisset Column. He showed himself a devoted and brave auxiliary. Since our occupation he has acted as

liaison between the Circonscription authorities and the native chief. He has always shown himself as devoted to his chief as to ourselves; all the successive Chefs de Circonscription here have appreciated his real services.[31]

In 1921 and 1922, he was for me a constantly devoted and active auxiliary. During my tours in the Baya country, he, by his knowledge of the country and his constant zeal, smoothed over many difficulties and forestalled resistance which I, without him, would have had to overcome and break by force. He is a remarkable and alert intelligence agent, truly intelligent and sincere.[32]

From 1915 to 1924, Halamadou appeared as a devoted, active, brave, intelligent and sincere auxiliary for the French. All that praise suggests that this Adjia could look forward to a well earned retirement, peaceful and without worries. To achieve this, he had to be doubly careful, to avoid displeasing either the Lamido or the colonial power. Nonetheless Halamadou rebelled against the Lamido, Yaya Dandi, the man who had retained him as one of the most important dignitaries of the lamidate. How can one explain such a blunder by this man who was so 'intelligent' and 'devoted'?

The first explanation can be found in the fact that Halamadou did not owe his appointment to Lamido Yaya Dandi. He was part of the heritage of Issa and his son Yagarou; so he did not have cause to feel much obligation to Lamido Yaya Dandi.

Secondly, the rebellion can be explained by actual hostility towards Yaya Dandi on the Adjia's part. Portalès tells us that Halamadou was opposed with all his might to the appointment of Yaya Dandi, whom the colonial authorities had before banished to Banyo. This second reason, following from the first, shows that the Adjia was in Yaya's service only because Yaya hesitated to remove him. That can be explained by the new Lamido's awareness of how the Chefs de Circonscription appreciated the Adjia's zeal. In fact the Lamido had admitted to the Chef de Circonscription for a long time his wish to dismiss the Adjia.[33]

A third reason for the Adjia's rebellion would seem to be resistance to being deprived of his title. Having heard of his master's desire to remove him from his post, Halamadou decided not to let himself be sacked without reacting. So he started, with his men, a campaign of intimidation in the lamidate. These men told whoever would listen that their leader would not leave his post except by force, and that if it was necessary as a last resort, they would fire on the Lamido.[34] This intimidation campaign succeeded because Yaya

Dandi, filled with fear, with the help of his *doghari* (traditional guards) and the complicity of the Imam, had the Adjia arrested, disarmed him on 21 August and confined him in his *tata* until 23 August, when the Chef de Circonscription returned from a tour of Galim.

The French official, who was given a report on the events, confirmed the facts and indicated that an army Browning of 27 calibre, loaded with seven bullets, had been found on the Adjia.[35] This attempt at a revolt by Halamadou was a bad example for the Lamido's other dignitaries and a danger to the maintenance of the chief's authority. So the French government took a firm stance, on the side of the Lamido. Without any more formalities, Portalès, the Chef de Circonscription, on his return imprisoned the Adjia as a trouble-maker on 23 August 1924, and set about arresting his servants who had fled to the Dourou country.[36] The services that the Adjia had rendered no longer counted for much from the moment that the Lamido was weighed in the scales against him. Attacking the Lamido automatically meant heavy punishment. Halamadou was banished away from Ngaoundéré to prevent him from intriguing and plotting against the Lamido, by *Arrêté* no. 104 of 23 September 1924.[37] That showed how much the French cared about the Lamido's prestige. Halamadou had given many services, he could have given more, but he was no longer worth much from the moment he attacked the government's protégé.

All the facts set out above go to show that France did not practise the direct rule system in relations with the Lamibbe of Ngaoundéré. Instead of ruining the Lamido's authority, it aimed rather to reinforce and safeguard it, as if to declare that he was an essential pawn in the administrative system. However, the facts noted above are not the whole story. The French authorities missed no opportunity to help the Lamibbe to maintain their authority. Thus, at every appointment of a new Lamido, French presence at his side was a guarantee of his prestige and authority. During the tours by the administrative officials in areas far from the headquarters of the lamidate, they called on the people, through their advice and in the course of discussions, not to break away from the authority of the Lamido.

The policy of accommodation in the lamidate of Ngaoundéré was a very subtle one. Instead of seeking to obtain the Lamido's cooperation by strict measures, the French government preferred to make allowances; it used kindness to win the sympathy and hence the co-operation of the Lamido. In addition, it opted for the upholding of his authority. Thus it placed the Lamido in its debt.

Every time that the Lamido received attention in this way, the government expected concessions in return. Thus, after the Adjia Halamadou incident, the Commissioner, Marchand, asked the Chef de Circonscription to derive advantage from it.

He wrote:

> You will also take advantage of the incident which has occurred to encourage the Lamido to show himself more forceful towards his entourage, and to push him insistently, showing him that it is in his own interests, to reduce substantially the number of those dignitaries who show so little dignity.[38]

The policy of accommodation had a precise aim: to safeguard and increase the Lamido's authority so as to favour his voluntary co-operation, to obtain the best results from him in the administration of his lamidate. This policy was applied to all the Lamibbe of Ngaoundéré, but particularly to the first who came into contact with the French, Lamido Issa Maigari. The special concern over him can be explained by the very recent occupation of the lamidate by France and the need to make the Lamido always to regard the French as better colonisers than the Germans.

However, to carry on the administration of the lamidate of Ngaoundéré successfully, the French authorities were not content only with this certainly subtle policy which recalls the British system of indirect rule, whose success was not always guaranteed. A change in the French official in charge of the area made the Lamido feel no longer under obligation to the new official in charge. The French also applied other policies towards the Lamido, which we have called policies of supervision and of fragmentation of the Lamido's authority.

The policy of supervision

The Lamido, as the centrepiece of the French administrative machinery in the lamidate of Ngaoundéré, was subject to firm and constant supervision by the administrative authorities. The watchword of this policy was supervision and guidance. Carde, Commissioner for French Cameroon from 1919 to 1923, in letter no. 95 CF of 1 October 1920, gave the following instructions to the Chef de Circonscription of Ngaoundéré:

> It is therefore the task of the head of the Circonscription to place the Lamido under permanent supervision and to orient

him towards our administrative ideas. These rule out all display of any authority other than our own, except by specific delegation ... That the use of the traditional chief as an intermediary is a convenient expedient for our government, that it is in our interests to make use to our own advantage of the existing framework of a native organisation which is certainly imperfect but which is accepted by the people, is an obvious fact. But in no case should the Lamido think that he has a special role above or alongside us.[39]

These instructions from Carde left no room for misunderstanding. Although obliged to take account of the Lamido for the government of Ngaoundéré, the French refused to recognise him as holding any power of his own. The policy of supervision therefore involved permanent intervention by the French government in all the Lamido's acts, and a permanent watch kept to avoid and head off any inclination towards autonomy on his part. The government, by this policy, wanted to submit the Lamido to its authority and make him understand that he was only there to carry out orders and, if he had by custom full authority over his people, the government on its part had full authority over him.[40] The contradiction which might have existed between the accommodation policy and the supervision policy was thus avoided. The government agreed to recognise that the Lamido was the chief of his people and therefore accommodated him while also upholding his authority; but it denied him any right to believe that the power he had over his people allowed him to make demands.

The permanent supervision over the Lamido was shown in practice by some measures taken by the French authorities: a weekly visit by the Lamido, effective presence near him (the administrative post being moved from Tison to the village); surveillance of and hostility towards the Fulani chief's entourage, appointment and dismissal of the Lamido.

Until Administrator Bru assumed duty on 3 December 1920, the Lamido of Ngaoundéré only went to the administrative post when summoned. Anyway, he had appointed the Adjia to receive all instructions and complaints. However, when Bru took over in the Circonscription, he passed on an order to Lamido Issa to come to his office at least once a week, or more often if he thought it necessary.[41] This practice was made regular and applied by all Bru's successors in regard to all the Lamibbe.[42] During these visits, the Lamido received instructions, which he had to follow to the letter, for the good running of his lamidate, relating to the supply of porters and labourers, repair of roads and bridges, improvements to the town, extension of food cultivation fields, or greetings to be made to the Lamido.[43] This new strategy on the part of the Ngaoundéré administrative authorities had a definite psychological effect. The Lamido of Ngaoundéré behaved from then on like a good subordinate who, after doing a job, went to his superior to make his report and receive new instructions. The subordination of traditional authority to administrative authority was from then on clear; the Lamido could not evade this obligation easily, for to do so would by itself reveal hostility to French rule on his part.

After the German conquest of the lamidate in 1901, the administrative post was built at the place called Tison,[44] on the Meiganga road 8 km from Ngaoundéré, the seat of the Lamido. This separation of the German post by a distance from the native chief was typical of the political system employed by the Germans. That system, known as the 'Protectorate' system, consisted, for the German authorities, in leaving to the Fulani chief the task of ruling over his territory, while they on their side were content to maintain a notion of their presence. The French did not have the same political ideas as their predecessors. They thought that effective supervision over something was not possible if one was far removed from it. They therefore decided to move the administrative post from Tison to the village of Ngaoundéré.

However, they gave humanitarian reasons for this move, instead of the political motive of watching over the Lamido more closely. One of these reasons was a concern to see an end to abuses and arbitrary acts by the Lamibbe which, for a very long time, had weighed on the peoples of the lamidate without the administration's knowledge.[45] So, it was suggested, it was for the people's benefit that it was decided to move the post. On the other hand, Dr Moureau, in a health report sent to the Commissioner, complained of the bad conditions in which Europeans had to live in the camp at Tison:

> The huts of the European camp (besides being German-built) are nearly all humid and badly ventilated and...the post was generally set up in bad conditions.[46]

This report adds a new aspect to the decision to move the post. The move was necessary not only because abuses by the Lamibbe needed to be limited or even eliminated, but also because the Europeans in the lamidate had to live in healthier conditions. However, if we cannot deny that the humanitarian considerations just mentioned played an important part in the moving of the post, we think even so that the move was decided upon above all for political and administrative reasons. We need no further proof of this than a statement by Bru, in the course of a complaint to his superiors accusing the military authorities at Ngaoundéré of opposing his authority, that the Ngaoundéré post has been placed where it was for exclusively political and administrative reasons.[47] So the moving of the post from Tison nearer to the village was a political measure whose aim was to keep a better check on the Lamido's entourage. Issa Maigari understood it in this light and opposed it in 1918.[48]

The Lamido of Ngaoundéré's entourage was the object both of close surveillance and of a strong hostility. Surveillance was directed above all at Stranger elements who succeeded in living close to the Lamido. Information was secretly collected to prevent adventurers from joining the people who approached the ruler. The French believed that an administrative set-up like that of Ngaoundéré, which centralised all powers in the hands of the Fulani chief, ensured that in his territory there could not be any uprising unless it was ordered by him. To ensure against this, it was necessary to know who was living near him and what influence he might have over the Fulani chief. In 1921 the presence among the people surrounding Lamido Issa was an Arab, who said he was a *Sharif* and a member of the family of Mahamad Mouktar al Kouti, caused dismay among the administrative authorities in the area. The Chef de Circonscription wrote to the Commissioner to inform him of the presence of this man, answering to the name of Sharif Mohamed Ali ben Mohamad Mouktar al Kouti, although he recognised that the man's behaviour seemed to be not at all objectionable.[49]

In that letter Administrator Bru relieved himself of any responsibility in the event of the man leading the Lamido into unfriendly acts towards France. The Commissioner wrote to the Governor-General of French West Africa,[50] who in turn wrote to the Lieutenant-Governor of French Sudan. All this letter-writing was aimed at finding who this Sharif was and what attitude should be adopted towards him.[51] That was the attitude of the administrative authorities towards those who surrounded the Lamibbe of Ngaoundéré. The moving of the post near to the headquarters of the lamidate certainly definitely contributed to the reinforcing of this surveillance. But the surveillance was carried out very discreetly, as the Fulani chiefs were very sensitive about their freedom.

In contrast, the Lamido's dignitaries who lived near him were the object of almost permanent open hostility in the application of the policy of supervision. The Lamido of Ngaoundéré, to be better able to reign over his people, surrounded himself with an impressive court consisting of chiefs of subject tribes, dignitaries, and house slaves, who were both his contact men and his advisers.

The chiefs of subject tribes, such as the Dourou, Baya, Mboum, Maka, Laka and other tribes, lived at the Lamido's court. They only returned to their subjects for solemn occasions such as tax collection, the religious festivals of their tribes, conscription of labourers, etc. That is what the Chef de Circonscription tells us in his general political and administrative report for 1916:

> Lesser chiefs do not exist, one may say, and village chiefs only bear that name because we give it to them. The real chiefs, the ones who are obeyed, do not live in their home areas, but with the Sultans. The latter, following custom, surround themselves with a numerous following consisting of all the major chiefs of the regions subject to their authority.[52]

Also among the people surrounding the Lamido were the chiefs of the major Fulani towns, the *djaoro'en*. They, like the chiefs of subject tribes, did not live with their subjects, and only went among them for important duties imposed by the European administration. Very soon the French authorities at Ngaoundéré were unable to accept this residence of chiefs around the Lamido, which, in their view, brought more problems than advantages. As early as 1917 Compérat, then Commandant of the North Cameroon region, said on this subject:

> I do not share the ideas of the Commandant de Circonscription on the subject of the residence [at the Lamido's court] of lesser and greater chiefs. It gives good results, I admit, but it remains to be seen whether they would be better if each chief stayed in the area he governed, among the people he ruled. Thus he would be less under the orders of the Sultan, because he would not wait on him straight after rising each morning. To my knowledge, the system of chiefs living far from the place of their chieftaincy has always had to be abandoned, the problems being real, the advantages illusory.[53] (translator's brackets)

So all the Lamibbe were recommended to send the chiefs back to their respective areas of authority. But the Lamibbe were aware of the power that the presence of these chiefs gave them. As they were given food, housing and clothing by their master, and also received gifts from him from time to time, they were submissive and loyal to him. The Lamido could, if only to show his power, forbid them to give service to the government. A letter of Sergeant Gerriez, complaining of non-cooperation by Lamido Issa, clearly illustrates this idea.[54] The Lamibbe of Ngaoundéré wanted to keep this means of pressure on the administration. However, after the Baya revolt of 1928–29, the French authorities succeeded, by themselves appointing other chiefs, in obliging chiefs to live near their subjects.[55]

The government's hostility was directed also against the Lamido's dignitaries, who were both his advisers and his administrative agents. Generally, in the lamidate of Ngaoundéré there were two groups of dignitaries, Fulani and non-Fulani Matchoube. The Fulani dignitaries, though not very numerous (twelve according to Froelich[56]), were all members of the *Faada*, the council of elders which chose the Lamido. They were not objects of the French government's hostility. In contrast the government, with a few exceptions, rarely showed any tender feelings for the Matchoube dignitaries, who were however more numerous, and who, in the Lamido's entourage, retained high posts at the expense of Fulani dignitaries. The essential peculiarity of the Lamido's court was indeed the existence of many Matchoube dignitaries occupying high posts, possessing much wealth and power. They were the closest associates of the Fulani chief and they provided the strength to protect him from his rivals.[57]

These dignitaries were both the Lamido's advisors and his agents for administration. Among them were the Adjias, the heads of the traditional police, the head of the palace, the chiefs of the slaves and of agriculture, a large number of archers and riders, musicians and servants of all sorts. All these people were chosen by the Lamido and gravitated around him. They received no official or regular pay; the Fulani chief recognised their services by favours — providing them with clothes and food, lending them one or more horses from time to time, and sometimes giving them lavish presents. Why was there such hostility to people who had nothing in the world but the confidence and goodwill of the Lamido? Why the desire at all times to see the Lamido reduce their number? The French authorities gave various reasons to explain it. The first was that the confidence placed by the Lamido in those people would be an obstacle to harmonious development of Fulani society.

The Lamibbe of Ngaoundéré placed more trust in non-Fulani dignitaries than in those of their own tribe. The non-Fulani could never claim the throne and therefore could not plot against the person who had chosen them. They knew that the Lamido's fortunes were linked to theirs, and that they could never be sure that a new Lamido who might be appointed would keep them around him.

That explains their loyalty to him, who had made them dignitaries, and why he trusted them. The French government did not see things in the same light. In its view the Matchoube dignitaries were only irresponsible people who claimed the right to guide the Lamido's decisions and policies in the direction indicated by their own interests; they were the main obstacle to the development of Fulani society.[58] So they were people who formed a barrier between the administration and the Lamido. Every instruction from the government was discussed in a circle where no Frenchman could penetrate.

According to the French, the Matchoube dignitaries prevented the Lamido from realising that they brought him 'civilisation'. But in reality, the insistence of the French authorities on getting rid of the Matchoube elders or reducing their number concealed another consideration: the filling of the vacancies which would be left if this were done. In reality the French authorities coveted the position and role held by those dignitaries around the Lamido. By ridding himself of many of those dignitaries the Lamido would free a number of positions which the colonial government would quickly fill so as better to guide the Fulani ruler who, without his dignitaries, would no longer be able to struggle against French influence. However, as the French government could not oblige the Lamibbe by force to act in the way they wanted, and as the Lamibbe refused to consider all demands in that sense, the government took certain measures to bring them to reduce the number of their Matchoube dignitaries.

On the occasion of any political event when the French government played a role favourable to the Lamido, it took advantage of this either to remove by banishment some particularly influential dignitaries close to the Lamido, or to invite the Lamido to get rid of a number of them. Thus during the disturbances at the time of the moving of the post from Tison to Ngaoundéré in 1918, the military administrator, Captain Ripert, seized the opportunity to get rid of Lamido Issa Maigari's most intimate and influential dignitary by banishing him to Campo.[59] Similarly, after coming down decisively on the side of Lamido Yaya Dandi in the case of Adjia Halamadou, the government asked him to reduce the number of these dignitaries substantially. In addition, on the occasion of every removal or appointment of a Lamido, France took the opportunity to deflate considerably this group of dignitaries and ask the new Lamido to reduce their number. Thus Mohammadou Abbo was called 'intelligent' by Froelich because he reduced their number.[60]

Finally, to reduce the influence of these dignitaries, the French authorities set up a parallel organisation, the Consultative Commission of Elders of Ngaoundéré,[61] whose members were carefully chosen by the same authorities. In that council Fulanis had a large majority relative to non-Fulani. In his letter of 5 January 1924, Administrator Bru proposed 22 elders in all, including 14 Fulanis, two Mboums, two Hausas and two from Borno – no Bayas.[62] So while the Lamido preferred to surround himself with Matchoube dignitaries, the French authorities preferred Fulanis. In reality that Commission was a means of putting pressure on the Lamido, because he could not easily argue with decisions taken in that council consisting of elders of his lamidate. So, to have a decision accepted, it now sufficed to have it taken in that Council, instead of putting it to the Lamido who, with his advisers, might or might not agree to carry it out.

The Ngaoundéré Consultative Commission was, if René Costedoat is to be believed, the origin of the Council of Elders (*Conseil des Notables*) set up by *Arrêté* of 9 October 1925.[63] He says that:

The creation of the Councils of Elders (9 April 1925) ... originated in a measure taken on the occasion of the dismissal of the Sultan of Ngaoundéré during the year 1923.[64]

Everything seems to confirm Costedoat's claim that the creation of the Councils of Elders was only the application to the whole territory of an institution which had already proved itself at Ngaoundéré. The dismissal of Lamido Issa's successor, Yagarou, took place during 1923 and could have given the French rulers the opportunity to set up that Consultative Commission on 15 December 1923. The omission of the Lamido from the list of elders put forward for membership of this body argues in favour of this thesis.[65] In addition, it seems that the creation of the Council of Elders followed the spirit of the Consultative Commission, for in its first version, its membership was not open to any Paramount Chief or regional or Canton chief in other parts of Cameroon. Only after another *Arrêté* on 12 November 1925 were those chiefs accepted as members of the Councils, without the title of Lamido, however, being mentioned in the *Arrêté*.[66]

So the first reason for the administrative authorities' hostility to the Matchoube dignitaries in the lamidate was therefore that they prevented the French from manipulating the Lamido at will. The French exercised their wits to have them removed, but the Lamido, feeling very exposed without that cohort of people praising him and acknowledging his power, refused to get rid of them.

The second reason given by the French authorities was the generous gifts which the Lamido gave to those dignitaries and the abuses which resulted from this, or were committed by the dignitaries. The very large number of the dignitaries meant that their master had to have considerable resources for their upkeep. This often forced the Lamido to make requisitions from the people of the lamidate. Captain Ripert, in 1918, reported that the Lamido was obliged to make requisitions from various people, concentrating on the non-Fulani who were timid and fearful and could not go to the administrative post.[67]

So it was to avoid these abuses by the Lamibbe that they were very soon urged to limit the number of their dignitaries of slave origin. The Europeans also explained their hostility by their desire to see an end to oppression of the people by those dignitaries. They suggested that these, taking advantage of the influence they had over the Lamido, went themselves to make requisitions from the people in the name of their master and, when it went very far, asked for things in the name of the white man.[68] Thus the more numerous they were, the more the people were subjected to ill-treatment to a worrying extent. The chiefs therefore had to be made to get rid of them. Looked at in this way, the Matchoube dignitaries appeared as 'parasites' who made others feel the burden of their upkeep.

However, the reasons given, though well founded, did not completely convince the Lamibbe of Ngaoundéré. They only agreed to get rid of their dignitaries when the government had a specific reason to force them to do so; but they systematically refused to live in isolation from those men whom they trusted and could count on. In truth the ill-treatment by the dignitaries or by the Lamibbe, given as a reason for the administration's hostility to the large number of Matchoube dignitaries around the Lamido, was above all a pretext. It was cited to justify the dismissal of Lamido Abbo in 1939 and to justify numerous banishments of some dignitaries of the Lamibbe. The administration's aim was to eliminate those prominent members of the native community which surrounded the Lamido and acted as an obstacle, and then itself to play the leading role in the councils of the Fulani chief. We need no further proof of this than the following statement from Lozet, Assistant Administrator, who after the banishment in 1922 of the dignitary closest to Issa, Djaro Yaoua from Borno, wrote:

> I must however point out that servants like the Hadjia, the Bareya and the Kaigama, if they often abuse their position to commit acts of oppression, are nonetheless excellent auxiliaries on whom we can count.[69]

This meant that certain abuses by the dignitaries could be accepted, from the moment when they were or could be used by the government. Others, those who were banished, were dangerous to the maintenance of French influence.

Finally, the policy of supervision made it necessary to separate the Lamido from whatever helped him maintain his own power. Only people contributing to the maintenance of pomp and circumstance, necessary to preserve his authority over his subjects, could be left with him. That was what the Commissioner, Marchand, demanded when he gave these instructions to the Chef de Circonscription of Ngaoundéré in 1924:

> To sum up, the Lamido of Ngaoundéré must be brought by you, with the necessary tact, to an exact idea of his true and unique role, that of the administration's intermediary and auxiliary. It is permissible for him, under your supervision, to keep up the appearances of a power whose reality is in your hands; if he has an escort of riders, if a parasol serves as a mark of his dignity in the eyes of the natives, that suits us perfectly. But he must — and you must lead him to this by the hand — steadily cast off the oppressive cohort of dignitaries who add nothing to his display (which is necessarily limited) but help to maintain a parasitical way of life which is very burdensome for the masses who have to feed them.[70]

However, the Lamibbe of Ngaoundéré kept their dignitaries and continued to reject completely the calls from the French government to cast them off. From 1939 to 1948 the last Lamido of our period of study depended exclusively on those dignitaries to govern his lamidate.[71]

The supervision policy followed by the French towards the Lamibbe of Ngaoundéré was also applied to two important political events in the lamidate: the appointment and dismissal of Lamibbe. These provided two ways of keeping a check on the Lamibbe's activities. They were closely linked and hung like Swords of Damocles over the various Fulani traditional chiefs. In this way the French administration tried to stamp out any impulse to independence among the traditional rulers; it used the appointments and dismissals of Lamibbe as a means of pressure and warning against them. The dismissal of a Lamido also served as a warning and a means of pressure on the new Lamido.

Traditionally, the Lamido of Ngaoundéré was chosen by a council of elders, the *Faada*, composed of both Fulani and Matchoube dignitaries, This assembly was sovereign and its choice was final as regards the selection of a Lamido.

role. It chose the new Lamido to be appointed, from among the family of the preceding chief — usually his brother or his son. However, from now on the choice was submitted to the French government for approval. The Imam submitted the name of the candidate proposed to the Chef de Circonscription; a choice only became definitive after approval by the Commissioner for French Cameroon.[72]

Some authors, such as Froelich, claim that France had no part in the choice of a Lamido, but left it to the elders to look for possible candidates and to present their choice to the French authorities:

> When the candidate who would be put forward to the French authorities for appointment as Lamido was to be chosen, the four or five most important dignitaries, after prior unofficial consultations, came to agreement and then summoned the rest of the Faada. When all members of the Faada were agreed, which was quickly achieved because of the prior unofficial discussions, the leading Matchoube dignitaries were informed of the Faada's decision.[73]

Froelich thus rules out any intervention. In 1939, after the dismissal of Lamido Mohammadou Abbo (1929–39), the Chef de Région stated on the same lines that members of the electoral council proceeded rapidly to the appointment of Lamido Aliou, without any administrative pressure being applied.[74]

According to these authors, from 1915 to 1945 the *Faada* retained its traditional powers in full. Convinced of this, Froelich, in dealing with the poor performance of Lamido Aliou, said the *Faada* was responsible for the poor choice; they chose him, he wrote, voluntarily but secretly, among the less deserving candidates.[75]

However, other authors suggest that the French administration had effective influence over the *Faada* in its choice. After the death of Lamido Issa Maigari a successor had to be found, and this, according to Costedoat, was how he was chosen:

> The death of Sultan Issa of Ngaoundéré left the succession to the Sultanate open. For centuries, such an event had always been marked by bloodstained clashes between the claimants to the throne. When the Sultan's death became known, some rivalries were aroused straight away; but it was enough for the Chef de Circonscription to announce that the deceased Sultan's choice of his son as successor had the approval of the French administration, for order to be fully restored and the life of the Sultanate to continue without problems or disturbances.[76]

Costedoat thus supports the idea that the administration influenced the choice of the Lamido. It exercised some supervision to see that the members of the *Faada* did not present it with a bad candidate. In view of this, Froelich's criticism of the *Faada* is not valid, and indeed seems unfair. He suggests that the *Faada* was responsible for Lamido Aliou not fulfilling the hopes placed in him, as it still considered his deposed predecessor as the sole true Lamido.[77] Certainly the restoration of Mohammadou Abbo as Lamido in 1948 seems to support this argument. However, his restoration can also be explained by the fact that France had then achieved the plan which he had opposed. However it may be, Costedoat's theory is much more credible, because it is unlikely that the colonial government, with all its concern to watch over the activities of the Lamibbe of Ngaoundéré, should leave their selection to the judgment of the *Faada* alone.

A question which could reasonably be asked is, why did the French authorities not put themselves in the place of the *Faada* and suppress it? They in fact kept the *Faada* and its traditional functions because it was very useful to them. The appointment of the Lamido in ways consecrated by custom guaranteed[78] first, that the candidate would be chosen in the region concerned and the people would be governed by someone of their tribe, an indispensible basis for sound administration; secondly, that the chief would have the authority, according to tradition, to speak and act in the name of his countrymen. The French administration took care not to lose those advantages, and preferred to influence the dignitaries' choice than to put itself in the place of the *Faada*.

By intervening in this way in the appointment of the Lamido, the French government exerted control over the political life of the lamidate. The Fulani chief knew from then on that he held that post thanks to the French government's approval. The supervision policy was thus made relatively easier because the administration's authority was recognised right from the appointment of the new Lamido. Thus the appointment was, from the outset, a means of pressure on the Fulani ruler.

Between 1915 and 1945, the French administration installed four Lamibbe of Ngaoundéré: Yagarou (1922), Yaya Dandi (1924), Mohammadou Abbo (1929) and Aliou (1939). Lamido Issa owed his appointment to the Germans and it was merely confirmed by the French after their victory. The French government was not fortunate in its choices of later Lamibbe; of the four enthroned, only one died in office, the other three were dismissed. In its first intervention in the appointment of Lamibbe, France picked on Yagarou, who showed hostility to French rule; he only stayed for two years on the throne.

The other two were dismissed after about ten years' reign: Mohammadou from 1929 to 1939, Aliou from 1939 to 1948. They may have remained for that long because they were good auxiliaries, or maybe the French had finally understood that it was:

> preferable to retain a chief, even if he turns out to be mediocre, whose faults are known, than to replace him by another who will have to satisfy his ambitions and those of his dignitaries, and maybe work off scores.[79]

The French authorities exercised their supervision in the choice of Lamibbe by the *Faada*; by that supervision they sought to place men who were favourable to them on the throne of the lamidate. Supervision was also exercised over the Lamibbe of Ngaoundéré by the weapon of dismissal.

The *Faada*, acting as the electoral council for the Lamibbe, traditionally had the exclusive right to pronounce the dismissal of a Lamido if he did not give satisfaction. However, it never made use of that right in living memory, and the Lamibbe's reigns generally ended with their death. Dismissal, which was something new, was introduced to the region by the Europeans. Its aim was to end the reign of a Lamido who was not a good auxiliary or intermediary for the government. It was also used as a threat to force the Lamibbe to work in the direction indicated by French interests. That threat comes out clearly in the letter which Commissioner Marchand sent to the Chef de Circonscription of Ngaoundéré about Lamido Yaya Dandi in 1924:

> Yaya Dandi is there because we installed him there; he is quite aware, his letters prove it, that his dismissal would be pronounced if he let himself fall into acts contrary to the dignity of our presence.[80]

Between 1915 and 1945, two Fulani rulers were dismissed at Ngaoundéré, one for incapacity, the other for acts of oppression.[81] Lamido Aliou, who came to the throne in 1939, was dismissed in 1948; he does not belong to our study, at any rate as far as his dismissal is concerned.

The first Lamido of Ngaoundéré to be dismissed by the French was Yagarou, son of Lamido Issa Maigari; he was sacked in 1923 for incapacity. Administrator Bru, speaking of this dismissal, said that Yagarou was not able to exercise the power conferred on him because his behaviour was unsatisfactory. He had been known, for example, to destroy all his family's archives and written traditions, and to burn banknotes.[82]

Bru shows therefore that Yagarou was dismissed for incapacity, because he behaved either like a child or like someone unbalanced; either way, the lamidate of Ngaoundéré could not continue to be ruled by an unfit person, a serious person was needed. René Costedoat gives another version of the events giving reason for Yagarou's dismissal:

> In 1923 the government realised that the Sultan of Ngaoundéré had a tendency to let himself be led astray by native traders and wasted the fortune of the lamidate, the Beitel mal (*sic*) or treasury, and the income from the Diakka (*sic*) on ridiculous purchases. The government found, therefore, that it had to intervene more closely in the Sultan's affairs; a petition was sent to the Commissioner by the elders and dignitaries of the lamidate calling for the dismissal of the Lamido.[83]

According to this author, the reason for the sacking of Yagarou was his maladministration of the treasury, which, it would seem, was so blatant that the elders felt obliged to call for his dismissal.

These explanations of the dismissal of Yagarou raise some questions. Was it really out of infantile or mentally unbalanced behaviour that Yagarou set about destroying the archives, the Korans and the written traditions of his family, and burned banknotes for fun? Maybe there was another reason for his dismissal? Yagarou was certainly very young at the time of his father's death in 1922.[84] One may wonder why the French were so insistent on making him the Lamido of Ngaoundéré. Was his choice not perhaps a manoeuvre by the government aimed at taking advantage of his youth to impose itself more fully on the lamidate through him? Information given by Bellaka Mbang Mboum can help us try to answer these questions. He tells us that:

> The real reason for Yagarou's dismissal was that he had shown very openly that he was hostile to the white people's rule. He had not done like his father, who knew what to accept and what to refuse.[85]

If we consider this statement, it appears that the acts of which Issa's successor was accused were above all reactions against French rule. Were they not perhaps due to his youth?

On the other hand, was the maladministration of the lamidate treasury, cited by Costedoat as the reason for the dismissal, a sufficient reason for the government to be obliged to intervene more closely in the Lamido's affairs? Was it not rather the young Lamido's refusal to let the white man intervene in his affairs that obliged the government to dismiss him? One can believe this, because it was after his dismissal that the Consultative Commission of Elders of Ngaoundéré was set up, in which the Lamido of Ngaoundéré had no place and the members were not proposed by the Lamido. Was it not perhaps his hostility to the creation of that body which led to his dismissal? It is very possible, because every time that a Lamido of Ngaoundéré came out strongly against a plan of the French, he was threatened with dismissal or simply sacked. That happened with Lamido Issa when in 1918 he opposed the moving of the administrative post from Tison to near the seat of the lamidate. Captain Ripert asked for his removal then and accused him of addiction to drink, weakness of character and not commanding the obedience of his subjects. It also happened with Lamido Mohammadou Abbo in 1939, when he opposed a plan to modify the method of levying the Koranic taxes, a subject until then reserved exclusively to the Lamido's jurisdiction. He was dismissed and accused of having carried out, with his dignitaries, many acts of oppression on the peoples of the lamidate; the plan was then put into effect.[86]

Dismissal was used by the French government as a safety valve. It had to have the power to end at any moment the reign of a ruler who could, by his actions, pose a danger to the success of French policy generally. This was one of the developments to which the supervision policy led; it was, as we have said above, a Sword of Damocles hanging over the heads of the Lamibbe of Ngaoundéré. It was brandished each time that the Lamido had to be scared and brought back to the 'straight and narrow'. To make sure the Lamibbe did not become too important, the French authorities were not content with just keeping a watch over them. It also practised a policy of fragmenting their authority.

The policy of division: fragmenting the Lamido's authority

From 1915 to 1945 the French government applied in the lamidate of Ngaoundéré, with a view to limiting the Fulani monarch's power, a policy of breaking up the Lamido's authority. It realised that the combined effect of the policies of accommodation and of supervision still left the Lamido wide scope for command which could be harmful if used in a sense contrary to French interests. To avoid risks the Lamido's authority had to be curbed. To that end the French attacked both the extent of his power and the resources which enabled him to live in style and maintain his court.

Regarding the extent of his traditional government's jurisdiction, the French administration wanted to limit it to the Fulani people of the lamidate only. The lamidate population, of course, included not only the Fulani but also non-Muslim peoples more or less subject to the Lamido's authority. To limit the Fulani ruler's power to the Fulani only, or at least to the Muslim peoples, was equivalent to removing the Mboum, Dourou, and Baya peoples from his authority. This was the *leit-motiv* of the administration in dealing with the subject peoples. Bru said on this subject:

All that I have been doing here for the past three years revolves around the plan for complete liberation of the enslaved families and the most rapid possible improvement of their situation.[87]

This French aim remained a mere plan for a long time because of the hostility of the Lamibbe of Ngaoundéré to it. A first step towards putting it into effect was taken in 1929, with the creation of a Subdivision for the Baya.[88] As for the other peoples, the government's efforts remained unsuccessful because of its desire not to alienate the Lamibbe completely. In 1933 the Chef de Subdivision of Ngaoundéré, Peyron, inspired by the example of Meiganga, wanted to create new chieftancies in that subdivision, i.e. in the Ngaoundéré lamidate. He suggested creation of chieftaincies for the Dourou first, and for the Kaka and even the Mboum in the more or less distant future.[89] Without awaiting the reply from his superior in the service, Peyron proceeded to carry out his ideas. This brought a reaction from Lamido Abbo which paralysed the French administration in the lamidate.[90] This unfortunate initiative by the Ngaoundéré Chef de Subdivision provoked this annoyed comment by Commissioner Bonnecarrère: 'I cannot fathom the attitude of M. Peyron ...'[91] The conclusion was drawn that the peoples of the Ngaoundéré were not yet ready for a system of government in which the Lamido would not have hegemony over the subject peoples.[92] However, that desire to free the non-Fulani peoples from the Lamido's authority, despite its failures, remained a constant theme in the French policy of fragmenting or limiting that authority.

In this the French administration was following the positive example of the separation of the Kirdi from Fulani sovereignty[93] which was being carried out in the North Cameroon region, more precisely at Garoua and Maroua. But its success in the lamidate of Ngaoundéré was very limited.[94]

To limit the Lamido of Ngaoundéré's power, the French also attacked the sources of his revenue from 1915 to 1945, and here they were successful. Many taxes were traditionally levied by the Lamibbe, and this allowed them to keep their hold over their subjects, and to keep up a lavish lifestyle and maintain a numerous court. They were the *oumoussou* or tax on taking of prisoners (a warrior who took three prisoners had to give one to the Lamido); the *diomorgal* or the conquered tribes' tax (a native who killed an elephant never had the right to keep the tusks, one went to his immediate master or chief, the other to the Lamido); the *tioffal* or emergency tax to add to the coffers of the *bait al-mal*; and the *zakkat* or religious tax levied on cattle and crops — the tithe.[95]

The French administration very soon ended the levying of some of these taxes, which had become anachronisms; the *oumoussou* was outlawed by the very fact of the subordination of traditional to colonial authority; the *diomorgal* and *tioffal* were abolished in 1921–22.[96] The French could not abolish the *zakkat*, which was levied by the Lamido until 1939. In that year the French authorities in the lamidate decided, instead of abolishing it, to modify the method of levying it and supervise its administration. The *zakkat* on cattle was thus transformed into a tax fixed at two francs per head of cattle; it was collected at the same time as the head-tax, and the government kept account of income and expenditure for the tax receipts, to prevent wasting of funds.[97] As for the *zakkat* in millet, which was formerly 10 per cent or one basket out of every ten harvested, it was fixed at one basket of millet per household, collected under the government's supervision. The proceeds of this tax in kind were placed in silos in the Adamawa region; a portion was paid to the Lamido, and the rest was used by the government to feed prisoners, labourers on worksites and native government officials and employees, at the rate of 1 franc per kilogram.[98]

By this measure the French authorities reduced enormously the Lamibbe of Ngaoundéré's sources of revenue. It was a very severe blow because the rulers of that lamidate could no longer dispose of the proceeds of the religious tax at will and keep up the same lifestyle as before. That alone caused them considerable loss of prestige.

Conclusion

The French administrative system just described here, in the relationship it established between the government and the Lamibbe of Ngaoundéré, was full of ambiguities and contradictions. In its policy of accommodation, the system was akin to British indirect rule. It was in fact very necessary to keep the Fulani rulers of Ngaoundéré as intermediaries between the peoples of the lamidate and the French government, because, to use the words of Governor van Vollenhoven:

The time has passed, in Africa as in other continents of the world, where authority can impose itself and maintain itself against the will of the people. Everywhere governments must have the formal or tacit consent of the masses whom they govern.[99]

To have that consent in the lamidate of Ngaoundéré, the French needed the Lamido; hence its strategies of generosity and upholding of his authority, under the accommodation policy. In the policies of supervision and fragmentation of the Fulani ruler's authority, we see on the other hand the influence of direct rule. By those other strategies the French authorities sought to limit the Lamibbe's possibilities of competing with their own power; the Lamibbe could have all powers over their subjects, but they should not retain such extensive power that they could think themselves able to rival or challenge the government. It was the oscillation of this system between indirect and direct rule which makes us speak of its ambiguous nature. However, it was nearer to indirect than to direct rule, for the French could never cross the threshold and abolish the Muslim chiefs who were necessary to them. The prudent attitude towards the Lamibbe of Ngaoundéré was due to the failure of earlier experiments by the French administration in using direct rule methods in dealing with chiefs of a political stature similar to that of the Lamibbe of Ngaoundéré. Georges Masson confirms this, saying that the abolition of the leading Muslim chiefs in Chad made the work of government very hard in that country, and the administrators had a difficult job keeping order among the multitude of turbulent rival chiefs which they had set up.[100] Indirect rule in the lamidate of Ngaoundéré was thus a necessity recognised by the French authorities; however, they could never shake off their devotion to the principles of direct rule, hence the attempts at complete subjection of the Lamido.

The contradiction between the policies used to achieve success for the French administrative system is one inherent in all government. France's merit was to succeed in doing violence to its own ideas and agreeing not to abolish the Fulani sovereigns of Ngaoundéré. The Lamibbe of Ngaoundéré, however, were not indifferent to this ambiguity in the French administrative system.

Notes

1   R. Cornevin, *L'Afrique Noire de 1919 à nos jours*, Paris, 1973, p. 69.
2   *Ibid.*, p. 65.
3   J.C. Froelich, *Les Musulmans d'Afrique Noire*, Paris, 1962, p. 85.
4   APA 11901/B (ANY), *Rapport général politique et administratif de la circonscription de Ngaoundéré pendant la période de juin à décembre 1914.*

5   APA 11901/B, letter no. 5, 29 January 1917. In 1918, Captain Ripert, then Commandant of the Circonscription, arguing in favour of the dismissal of Issa, accused him of addiction to drink, forgetting that this vice had been encouraged by the Europeans.

6   *Ibid.*

7   APA 11901/B, letter no. 976 of 1 February 1919.

8   *Tata* is a Manding word applied to clay-built fortifications built by peoples of the Western Sudan. In this context it refers to the wall-round the *saré* (household) of the Lamido of Ngaoundéré.

9   APA 11901/B, letter no. 31 of 23 February 1925; see also letter no. 3280 of 20 March 1925 from the Commissioner, who answered, in effect, that 'it would have been bad policy to want Yaya Dandi to pay for an act he did not commit'.

10 *Ibid.* T.O. No. 60 of 5 August 1918.

11 APA 11901/B, T.O. No. 101 of 5 August 1918.

12 APA 10956/B, Annual Report 1919. The conferring of medals was a favourite practice of the French colonial rulers. Its aim was to flatter every man who had consecrated most of his energies in the service of France (cf. Ferdinand Oyono, *The Old Man and the Medal*). In the case under discussion here, the French government sought less to reward the Lamido for services rendered than to draw the attention of the people of the lamidate to its cordial relations with the Fulani ruler.

13 APA 11625/M, staff correspondence 1926–1928.

14 APA 11901/B, letter no. 5 of 5 January 1924.

15 M.Z.Njeuma, *Fulani Hegemony at Yola (Old Adamawa)*, Yaoundé, 1978, pp, 150–160.

16 APA 11901/B, letter no. 282 of 15 December 1924 about the conferring of a turban on Lamido Yaya Dandi.

17 APA 11764/B, Tour Reports 1917–1918, Report of the Commandant of the North Cameroon Region on a tour in the Circonscription of Ngaoundéré, letter no. 24, CR of 29 October 1917.

18 Regarding the dismissal of Dalil, our informants recall that Issa, when staying at Maiduri, took the opportunity of a journey by Dalil to Garoua to go and set up residence in his *saré* with the complicity of the people. After occupying the *saré*, he reported his victory to the Germans at Garoua, Dalil was then arrested and dismissed. Issa thus succeeded in making the second palace revolution of the lamidate of Ngaoundéré, the first being that of Bello.

19 APA 11898/2, Monthly reports and annexed documents 1916–1918: Monthly report for September 1916.

20 *Ibid.* Those three supporters, named Yoga, Amadou and Bakary, were punished on 23 October 1916 with two weeks' imprisonment.

21 APA 11898/B.

22 APA 11635/B, Tour Reports 1933, Letter no. 240 of 11 February 1933.

23 APA 11808/I, Monthly report, February 1917.

24 *Ibid.*

25 *Ibid.* Captain Popp says further on that 'the request for a "heavy compensation" shows simply that he has acted too hastily, is very credulous and accepts uncritically information which in the circumstances is obviously false'.

26 *Ibid.*

27 APA 11899/6, Political and Administrative reports for 1916 and 1917, letter no. 5 of 23 April 1918.

28 APA 11766/D, letter no. 24 CR of 29 October 1917.

29 *Ibid.*, and *Décision* no. 783 of 14 December 1917 (APA 11901/B, letter of 13 December 1918).
30 APA 10800/14, Adamaoua, Half-yearly report 1939, first half.
31 APA 11901/B, letter of 24 June 1924. The assessments made by various Chefs de Circonscription took concrete form in the certificates which they awarded for good and loyal service. Until August 1924 there were eight of them, with those of Governors Fourneau and Carde and Colonial Inspector-General Meray.
32 APA 11901/B, letter no. 101 of 29 April 1922.
33 APA 11901/B, letter no. 213 of 30 August 1924.
34 *Ibid.*, letter no. 213. After the death of Issa and the dismissal of Yagarou, Adjia Halamadou created for himself a real court of armed retainers (20 men) and a considerable harem (32 concubines). It was with his retainers that the Adjia started his campaign of intimidation against the Lamido. This campaign by Halamadou occurred in the absence of the Chef de Circonscription, on tour to Galim, and Chef de Subdivision, who had left for Yaoundé.
35 *Ibid.*
36 APA 11901/B, letter no. 11250 of 21 October 1924. They were arrested in the Dourou country, tried, and sentenced on 2 October — Belandia to 30 months' imprisonment, Maisano to two years, Djabo to two years, and Dabron to one year.
37 APA 11901/B, *Arrêté* no. 104 of 23 September 1924. He was banished to Doume for two years.
38 APA 11901/B, letter no. 1125 C.
39 APA 11901/B, letter no. 95 CF of 1 October 1920.
40 R. Costedoat, *L'effort français au Cameroun: le mandat français et la réorganisation des territoires du Cameroun*, Besançon, 1930, p. 85.
41 APA 11901/B, letter no. 55 of 5 January 1921 and letter no. 1 of 30 August 1924.
42 Today, the Lamibbe of Ngaoundéré are still obliged to go once a week, on Saturday, to the sub-prefecture at Ngaoundéré. We were able to meet the present Lamido there on our research journey in August 1978.
43 APA 11901/B, letter no. 55.
44 Our informant tells us that the word Tison is a Mboum word meaning 'come out of our tribe' or 'another tribe has come to settle'.
45 APA 11901/B, letter no. 107CF of 21 May 1924
46 *Ibid.* Report by Dr Moureau, dated 22 May 1918.
47 APA 11901/B, confidential letter no. 6 of 6 April 1921.
48 D. Abwa, 'Le Lamidat de Ngaoundéré, 1915–1945', Master's Degree Thesis, University of Yaoundé, 1980.
49 APA 11901/B, letter no. 370 of 18 June 1921.
50 *Ibid.*, letter no. 133 of 5 December 1921.
51 Inquiries made by the Lieutenant-Governor of French Sudan about the self-styled Chérif found that the title had been falsely assumed. By a letter of 20 October 1921 he reported to the Governor-General of French West Africa that Mohamed Ali Ben Mouktar al Kounti was unknown at Timbuktu.
52 APA 11899/6, Political and Administrative reports for 1916 and 1917.
53 APA 11898/6, Observation on the general report, no. 84 CR of 1 April 1917.
54 APA 11766/B, Tour Reports 1919/1921, letter of 3 December 1919.
55 Before the Baya revolt, the chiefs of the subject tribes and those of the Fulani towns were appointed by the Lamido; usually he appointed men faithful to him.
56 Froelich, 1954, p. 34.

57 *Ibid.*

58 Froelich, 1954, p. 34.

59 APA 11901/B, letter of 30 November 1918.

60 Froelich, 1954, p. 22.

61 Arrêté no. 13180 of 15 December 1923, *Journal Officiel du Cameroun* (*JOC*) no. 89 of 1 January 1924, pp. 26−27.

62 APA 11901/B, letter of 5 January 1924.

63 *JOC* No. 132 of 1 December 1925, p. 460.

64 Costedoat, 1930, p. 91. The date of 9 April 1925 cited here is not that of the creation of the Council of Elders. This was set up by Arrêté of 9 October 1925.

65 APA 11901/B, letter no. 5.

66 *JOC* no. 134 of 1 December 1925, p. 521.

67 APA 11899/6, Political Reports.

68 *Ibid.*

69 APA 11901/B, letter no. 253.

70 *Ibid.*, letter no. 107 of 21 May 1924.

71 Abwa, 1980, pp. 133−178; and APA 11733, Annual reports 1942−1951: Annual Report 1942.

72 APA 11384/C, Returns and Reports: Regions of Ngaoundéré, Dschang, Ebolowa, As we have seen, this procedure was introduced into the lamidate by the Germans in 1901. The French thus continued a system already familiar to the Fulani.

73 Froelich, 1954, p. 34.

74 APA 10800/14, Adamaoua, Half-yearly report, first half of 1939.

75 Froelich, 1954, p. 39.

76 R. Costedoat, 1930, p. 86. The author speaks of this Fench intervention to show France's salutary influence over the political life of the lamidate of Ngaoundéré. However, the process used to impose the choice of Yagarou, son of Issa, was contrary to tradition. Our informants tell us: 'The Lamido cannot choose his successor. He can at the very most choose among the *Yerima* the one he considers the best and choose him as the chief of the Princes. That does not at all mean that that man will become Lamido'.

77 Froelich, 1954, p. 39.

78 APA 11384/C.

79 APA 11384/C.

80 APA 11901/B, letter of 21 May 1924.

81 APA 11733, Annual Report 1944.

82 APA 11901/B, letter no. 47 of 29 February 1924.

83 Costedoat, p. 85. This quotation was taken from the annual report for 1923. We have not been able to find this report in the Yaoundé National Archives.

84 Our informants (see Abwa 1980, p. X) say that Yagarou came to the throne of the lamidate at the age of fourteen.

85 Informant Bellaka Mbang Mboum, 1979.

86 Abwa, 1980, pp. 133−178

87 APA 11901/B, letter no. 47 of 29 February 1924; see also *Réactions des Lamibbe: Issa Maigari 1904−1922*; *Réactions des Lamibbe: Mohammadou Abbo 1929−1939*.

88 *JOC* 1929, p. 227.

89 IAA 11635/F, Inspector of Administrative Affairs: Mission Nord (November 1932−April 1933).

90 *Ibid.*

91   IAA 11635/F.
92   *Ibid.*
93   IAA 11886/1, Mission Nord (1930/1932).
94   Abwa, 1980, p. 129.
95   APA 10956/B, Annual Report, 1922.
96   APA 11901/B, letter no. 159 of 19 June 1924.
97   APA 10525/D, Lamidate of Ngaoundéré: Zakkat 1945.
98   *Ibid.*
99   Quoted by H. Crimal, *La décolonisation 1919–1963*, Collection U, 1965, p. 63. Van Vollenhoven was a well known Governor-General of French West Africa.
100 G. Masson, *La mise en valeur des territoires du Cameroun placés sous le mandat français*, Paris, 1928, p. 126.

Chapter Seven
British administration and nationalism in the Southern Cameroons, 1914–1954*

Emmanuel Chiabi

This chapter describes the administrative and political structures within which Britain administered Cameroon. It examines firstly, the beginnings of British administration in Cameroon because the circumstances which contributed to the British presence influenced the nature of the British administrative and political structures as well as British rule in Cameroon; secondly, the various administrative and political structures or stages through which Cameroon was administered from 1914 to 1954, in order to demonstrate how all these factors combined to enhance or inhibit the growth of nationalism. In addition the chapter focuses on native administration, giving an overview of that system of administration as well as examining the impact of the system on the growth of nationalism.[1]

British acquisition of Cameroon was not in response to calls by British adventurers, explorers, traders, or missionaries to establish a sanatorium and a 'breadbasket' in Cameroon. Nor was it in response to the British soldiers who fought so gallantly in Cameroon and continued to see it, or at least the coastal region, as an enchanted land and the Singapore of West Africa. The acquisition of Cameroon in 1914 resulted from a British-French military victory over the Germans and the expulsion of the latter from Cameroon. Because of this type of acquisition, we find that British administration and political structure reflected the circumstantial possession of Cameroon.

Administrative structure

Although the British, in 1914, brought with them personnel ready to take up administrative duties in Cameroon, they yielded a larger

---

* In this chapter, Southern Cameroons is used to refer to contemporary Northwest and Southwest Provinces of Cameroon, the area of British control during colonial rule.

proportion of Cameroon to the less-prepared French, and accepted a joint administration of Cameroon with France.[2] British administration in Cameroon, therefore, began as a condominium. The condominium required the two allies, Britain and France, to provide a provisional administration of Cameroon until the Germans had been completely expelled. This arrangement undoubtedly reflected the problems of the war and the uncertainties of a war-shaken and war-acquired Cameroon. Both the British and the French needed time to set up an administrative structure in a territory that had been disorganised by the war; a territory in which many of its inhabitants had abandoned their occupations and homes and some of its citizens had been taken to the nearby island of Fernando Po. Shortly after the German stronghold at Mora fell, the British and the French abandoned the idea of the condominium and decided to establish respective administrative structures. Consequently, by the agreement of 4 March 1916, the condominium which had existed since September 1914 (when the Germans departed from Douala) ended. The British set up their administration in Buea and the French established theirs in Douala.

From 1916 to 1919, when the status of Cameroon was discussed at Versailles, until the summer of 1922, when the Supreme Allied Council confirmed Southern Cameroon's status as a British Mandate, British administration remained provisional.[3] The period of provisional administration also reflected both the problems of World War I and British lack of interest in Cameroon. A military officer, General Charles Dobell, with no specific political title, ushered in the new administration in British Cameroon. Even when civil administration began on 1 April 1916, and the post of Resident (the highest British administrative post in Cameroon then) was created, many of the Residents were military men and their concerns remained related to the war and to arousing a British interest for Cameroon. No wonder, then, that Resident P. V. Young, in 1917, hoped as had Richard Burton in the nineteenth century, to convince Britain that:

In the British Cameroons we have a country which when developed could supply the West Coast of Africa with wheat, oats, barley, potatoes, and all the vegetables of a temperate climate while at the same time it abounds in palm oil forests, cocoa and the products of tropical countries; in few countries can there be such enormous possibilities for the development of wealth ....[4]

While it is true that Cameroon could have become the breadbasket of West Africa (Cameroon has great potential for agriculture), Mr Young's observation revealed that many of these early administrators were more concerned with arousing an official British interest for Cameroon than with administration of the territory.

During the period of provisional administration, the colonial administrators attempted to make their presence felt in Cameroon by the imposition of taxes. Prior to British involvement in Cameroon, Cameroonians had become accustomed to paying German taxes. But following British acquisition of the territory, Resident Duff, in 1916, increased taxes and a general resentment grew, especially among the emerging urban areas of Buea and Victoria. Cameroonians could understand neither higher taxes nor some of the British policies which followed. In another unpopular move, the British, in 1916, issued a proclamation which forbade the importation of liquor. Another proclamation in 1917 enjoined Cameroonians from tapping and selling palm wine. Needless to say that this particular measure was resented, especially among those people who not only consumed the wine but depended upon it as a source of income.

While the British administrators busied themselves with these immediate measures to make their presence felt in Cameroon, they engaged themselves in creating western institutions of a more permanent nature. During the period of provisional administration, the British opened many native courts throughout the region.[5] By the end of 1916 the British had established 30 native courts in Victoria Division although in 1917 they reduced them to 14.[6] It was important that native courts received early attention. The courts, as the report on the establishment of the Bamenda Native Court noted, were 'instructional courts for chiefs'. The chiefs' instruction in the native courts involved not only an understanding of criminal or judicial matters but, more importantly, a knowledge of the details of revenue and expenditure. Thus realising the economic importance of courts, the colonial administration continued to emphasise the creation and the usage of courts. But there was no official policy in the early period of colonial rule governing the establishment and functioning of these native courts.

The institution of a native court system and many of the policies aimed at cementing British administration in Cameroon from 1916 to 1922 reflected efforts of individual administrative officers rather than any planned or guided official policy. Commenting on the failure of a systematic policy, N. C. Duncan, a Divisional Officer (DO) in Cameroon in 1921, observed that policy was 'individual and uncontrolled' and pointed out that the 'political memoranda and the accumulated experience of senior officers was not available to guide the officers on the spot'.[7] Resident F. H. Ruxton confirmed in 1921 that policy consisted of the 'idiosyncrasies of individual

Residents and DOs with "Southern" or "Northern" Nigerian pro-clivities'.[8] The failure to design a definite administrative policy for Cameroon prior to and including the period of provisional adminis-tration may be explained, at least in part, by British lack of interest in Cameroon, and may also be assessed in reference to Lord Lugard's observation that Cameroon without Douala was an 'insignificant little strip... hardly worth reserving'. Lugard's comment and British lack of interest reflect both the events and outcome of World War I in Cameroon and as such a brief examination of World War I, here, is in order. Such an examination will help to show what guided British administration in Cameroon after 1916.

World War I

World War I broke out in Europe in August 1914. By the end of August and early September allied forces from the British territory of Nigeria and from the adjacent French territories had invaded Cameroon. By the end of September Douala had capitulated. In mid November, 1914, Buea, under the German District Commissioner, submitted and the Germans were ousted. In February 1916, Mora, in the Extreme North Province succumbed. Thus World War I ended early in Cameroon but the experiences and activities of some eighteen months influenced the nature of colonial administration and the direction and manner in which Cameroonian nationalism progressed.

The most obvious effect of World War I on Cameroon was the passage of Cameroon from Germany to Britain and France. To the Cameroonians this passage signalled the split of German Kamerun into British and French Cameroons, a split which meant the develop-ment of two Cameroonian political entities, one under French and the other under British tutelage. While the split could have been a catalyst to nationalism it did not turn out to be so.[9] The concerns of many Cameroonians at the time reflected the events of global war. Indigenous attitudes and reactions, as indicated in assessment reports and ascertained from interviews conducted in the summer of 1979, show that after the war many Cameroonians were filled with uncer-tainties. People wondered whether the war had indeed ended the German era which had been to some a period characterised by punitive and reprisal expeditions and gruelling work. Some remem-bered with awe the executions by hanging of their chiefs. In Mamfe Division, for example, where the chiefs of Foto, Foandong and Foangang had been hanged at the outbreak of the war, the general post-war attitude was one of uncertainty and fear. Such doubts probably caused the one-time courageous Chief Asonganyi of Fontem to go to the British and pledge that there 'shall be no more war between Europeans and his people'.[10] Chief Asonganyi's response epitomised the general attitude, an attitude which had left, in Mamfe, 'a people of docile taxpayers, a certain amount of orderliness ... and a (people with a) readiness to obey the direct orders of the administration'.[11]

The war not only left docile and more receptive individuals but contributed to general retrogression. As people retreated to their hideouts or homes of origins so they reverted to many of their traditional ways. Dr E.M.L. Endeley, a child of the war period, son of a chief, and an enlightened nationalist, remarked on this retrogression:

> After 30 years of vigorous German rule where the Cameroonians had imbibed German education and culture, brought up under a strict German economic system they now had to learn new ways ....[12]

In confirming this retrogressive impact of the war and explaining the reasons for the shortage of adequate Cameroon staff, the Resident of Buea wrote in 1920:

> It must be borne in mind that his (Cameroonian) original education was in German and that English is to him, a foreign tongue twice removed and his knowledge had to be acquired all over again ...[13]

Many Cameroonians in the post-war era were, therefore, wary of the future and how the change in colonial administration would affect their political relationships. In many respects Cameroonians, in the words of Dr Endeley, became 'orphans of the war, torn apart from their kith and kin ...'. They had, as the colonial administrators noted, become 'apprehensive of Europeans'.[14] The British, or at least the officers on the spot, were certain that they had replaced the Germans and, therefore, needed to make their rule authoritative and permanent. That is why assessment reports and the establishment of native courts became essential features of early colonial rule. Both were avenues of control.

Another adverse impact of World War I on Cameroon was the escalation of the problems for on-the-spot colonial administrators, particularly those of the provisional administration. One problem that arose from war-time acquisition was the absence of significant records on indigenous peoples. Some of the records had been destroyed during wartime, while the fleeing Germans escaped with many others. Consequently, the British administration had to begin almost afresh, compiling intelligence and assessment reports and studying the geography of Cameroon.

Also the home government, lacking interest in Cameroon, did not post sufficient political administrators to this region. Reports of the early period of British colonial administration in Cameroon are filled with complaints of an overwhelming shortage of staff. This shortage, which was very evident at the beginning of British rule, continued throughout the period of British administration there. In 1920 the problem was so intense that the resident in Buea suggested Britain maintain a larger staff in Cameroon even to the detriment of some of the provinces and divisions of Nigeria. This move was necessary for the British to make a marked contrast between the German administration and their own. The home government gave little heed to the residents' request. Consequently, some divisions such as Kumba often went without divisional officers for months, and the few officers who were in Cameroon could not adequately carry out assessment, intelligence, administrative and other duties. Nevertheless, many of these officers, like the missionaries, had to become jacks-of-all-trades. Colonial records abound with examples of administrative officers who functioned as magistrate, treasurer, or agricultural officer, in addition to their own administrative duties. In 1929, for example, the Assistant Divisional Officer (ADO), Buea, was in charge of the Provincial Prison, the Buea Treasury, and the Native Administration. The Resident was required to supervise the divisional administration, serve as magistrate and ensure the proper functioning of plantations.[15] While individual officers may have claimed credit for variegated careers, such jacks-of-all-trades did not provide for an effective administration of a territory.

Two other problems compounded that of inadequate staff. First, officers posted to Cameroon, especially during the provisional administration, were frequently changed or moved from one division to another. Between 1916 and 1921, Residents were moved with such frequency that few had time to gain a thorough knowledge of Cameroon. Between the beginning of civil administration in Cameroon in 1916 and the end of 1921, nine persons held the position of Resident. In 1921 alone, three Residents presided in Buea.[16] There was supposed to be, in theory, a specified number of colonial administrators in residence in Cameroon but in practice, this number was never maintained. In 1924, for example, the expected number of colonial administrators on duty in Cameroon was nineteen but, in fact, the actual number present at any one time on average was ten.[17]

As if to deplete further the colonial staff, officers were required to take a three months' study leave to Kano, in northern Nigeria. There they would study Hausa, a language required of colonial administrators, but one which was not essential to their duty in the Cameroon. The slow steamer transportation between Nigeria and Cameroon and annual leaves in England increased the length and frequency of official absences. Only later were colonial administrators encouraged to spend their leave periods in Cameroon. Also later, in 1926, it became necessary to settle the language question for administrators in Cameroon. At that time, Bali Mungaka and Duala were the possible alternative languages for colonial administrators in Cameroon. The British chose Duala because more printed matter existed in it than in Mungaka, and to the Europeans, it resembled Swahili, which was easier to learn.[18] In 1927, two administrators, B.G. Stone and E.A. Gaskin, took their language examination in Duala. In spite of such efforts, administrative problems remained and Cameroon continued to suffer from want of colonial administrators.

Another major staffing problem was the inexperience of many of the officers posted to Cameroon. The requirements stipulated that a Resident, for example, had to have been an officer with some 20 to 25 years of experience; one who had been in charge of various districts; and one who had periods of trial in an acting capacity. Also, DOs were to have had 9 to 20 years of experience. Yet, in Cameroon these stipulations were often ignored or violated. It was common to find a number of probationers − officers who were, so-to-speak, doing internships. In 1921, for example, Mr F.B. Carr, ADO of Kumba was a Probationer. So was A.G.T. Grier, ADO of Victoria.[19] These cadets were, of course, still attempting to master what they were expected to have acquired in training − language, law, colonial procedures, financial matters, and so forth.

The problem of the cadet or the probationer was so acute that, in 1920, when the Resident wrote to recommend administrators for Cameroon, he stressed that a:

> proportion of assistant divisional officers to be sent to Cameroon should have had previous experience since some sub-stations such as Wum and Menka could not be safely left in charge of new and inexperienced officers without risk.[20]

These risks were many and continued for a long time since experienced officers were sent to such places as India and Sudan. Qualified officers often remained stationed in those countries which presented the greatest economic potential and/or threat to the administration. Officers were often reluctant to go to Cameroon because working conditions were not enticing. Cameroon was also considered a dumping ground for Colonial Officers who were unfit elsewhere.[21] While these characteristics of Cameroon kept experienced officers away, the 'uneventfulness' of Cameroon and British disinterestedness in the territory undoubtedly enhanced Cameroon's suitability as a training ground for many cadets.

This state of affairs not only affected administration, but also the quality of records kept. In 1916, G.S. Podevin complained that the report for Bamenda was based on 'slight acquaintance with the people ...'[22] Meagre or sometimes inaccurate records resulted in incorrect appointments and improper management of newly created political institutions. This was particularly true in Kumba, the 'Cinderella Division', where insufficient assessment information led to the appointment of district heads who were not traditionally entitled to such appointments.[23] Also, in Bamenda, inaccurate information contributed to the appointment of Ndefru as the chief of Mankon in preference to Ndesso, whom many Mankon people knew to be the rightful heir.[24] Insufficient or incomplete documentation also detracted from the accumulation of information on which native administration could be based. In fact, the shortage of political officers in Cameroon in the early 1920s, led to the scrapping of those numerous native courts which the Native Courts Ordinance of 1916 had established in Victoria Division. Even as late as 1947, C.J. Mayne, the DO of Victoria, still complained that there were insufficient officers to visit the native authorities.

Ultimately, colonial administrators in Cameroon failed to develop a planned or definite policy, but continued to issue experimental and contradictory instructions and, for the most part, deployed policies which were being applied in Nigeria.

The Versailles Treaty, the League of Nations and Cameroon

Another major event that guided British administration of Cameroon was the creation of the League of Nations in 1919. Within the group of lobbyists addressing this League of Nations were individuals who not only supported the 'liberation' of former German colonies of which Cameroon was one, but who became quite vocal in their demands for self-determination of African territories. Amongst such advocates were W.E.B. DuBois of the United States of America and Blaise Diagne of Senegal. Also present in Paris at the time, although less involved than the others, was a Cameroonian – Alexander Ndoumb'a Douala Manga Bell. By 1920, Manga Bell had returned to Cameroon.[25] Although Manga Bell was not from British Cameroon it seems that upon his arrival he made contacts with some chiefs in Kumba Division to gain, in the words of the Resident, their support 'in the case of an eventual rebellion against the French'.[26] The fear of war with France probably did not concern British administrators as much as the fear that Bell had contacted some participants of the Versailles Conference; that he was aware of the Soviet Union's anti-imperialism; and that he had listened to the 'poisoning' views of the members of the Pan-African Congress which met in Paris in 1919.

Although Manga Bell was not connected with the progressive Cameroonian attempt to spark anti-British sentiment, the British always regarded him as a potential danger.

In his 1920 annual report, the Resident of Buea, complained that Bell had:

> returned obsessed with ideas of 'the self-determination of the smaller nations' and the 'Black man's country for the black man' and is now preaching his ideas of independence.[27]

And although no one comparable to Manga Bell emerged in British Cameroon, his visit to Kumba was sufficient to intimidate the Resident, who called for 'vigilance in Kumba', and cautioned fellow colonial administrators that Manga Bell's ideas were 'likely to lead to trouble in the future if not watched'.[28]

In connection with the British administration of Cameroon one significant outcome of the Versailles Treaty was the classification of Cameroon as a League of Nations Mandate. On 20 July 1922, Cameroon was officially declared a class 'B' Mandate. According to Article 2 of the Mandate Agreement, Britain became:

> responsible for the peace, order and good government of the territory, and for the promotion to the utmost of the material and moral wellbeing and the social progress of its inhabitants.[29]

Britain insisted on administering Cameroon as though it were an integral part of Nigeria, and made an annual report to the League of Nations' Mandate Commission concerning measures to satisfy the provisions of the Commission as stipulated in Article 2 of the Mandate Agreement. With this understanding, Cameroon remained a League of Nations Mandate but administered for all practical purposes as a region of Nigeria. It held officially the ambiguous designation of an 'integral part of Nigeria'.[30]

Consequently, by the Order in Council of 26 June 1923, the Cameroons Province fell under the charge of a lieutenant-governor stationed in Enugu, Nigeria. The British Chief Executive in Cameroon received the title of Resident and was stationed in Buea. He was responsible for the direct administration of Cameroon but was accountable to the lieutenant-governor, who, for his part, answered to the governor stationed in Lagos, Nigeria.

For ease of administration, the British separated Cameroons Province, a relatively large area with very poor roads, into four administrative divisions — Victoria, Kumba, Mamfe and Bamenda.[31] In each division, whenever economically feasible, the British appointed a divisional officer or an assistant responsible to the Resident. The organisation of Cameroon into these divisions was not a British innovation. With minor adjustments, Britain had maintained the political or administrative divisions as they had been when the Germans were ousted in 1916. What was new or, at least different, was that the administration of Cameroon took on a new twist or entanglement as an integrated part of Nigeria. Whereas the German Governor in Buea had direct contact with Berlin, the British Resident had to go through a host of officers stationed in Nigeria before reaching London.

Another effect of the Order in Council of 1923 was that the Nigerian system of governance became applicable to Cameroon. Of course, early British administrators in Cameroon, having no planned policies, applied those laws of Nigeria with which they were familiar or adopted some Nigerian ordinances such as the Native Courts Ordinance of 1914, the Native Authority Ordinance of 1916, and the policy of Indirect Administration in 1921. But after the League of Nations recognized the Cameroonian-Nigerian relationship, more laws followed which were intended to 'improve' the administrative structure in Cameroon.

In 1924, therefore, the British Cameroons Administrative Ordinance (No. 3 of 1924) was issued.[32] By the terms of this Ordinance, the Nigerian laws became applicable in Cameroon and superceded German legislation which hitherto was still in practice in some areas in Cameroon. This administrative step was technically illegal and, therefore, problematic because Nigeria was a British colony and Cameroon a League of Nations' mandate. 'Integration' of Cameroon with Nigeria meant that Britain would continue to administer Cameroon as 'British Cameroon' though their annual reports were to be examined by a Permanent Mandates Commission (PMC) of the League of Nations. This arrangement, by implication, if not explicitly, voided the mandate.

Nonetheless, so long as Cameroon theoretically remained a mandate, Britain was obliged to report to the League's Permanent Mandates Commission and, more importantly, was subjected to inquiries from Commission members on the status and administration of Cameroon. Inquiries by the PMC members centred mainly on the problems of British administrative integration of Cameroon with Nigeria. Many of the inquiries took the form of ineffectual attacks or charges, but they constituted a warning system to the British administrators that the administrative integration of Cameroon with Nigeria was fraught with problems. The British, however, often defended their administrative arrangement on the basis that it was neither wise, politically practical, nor economical to administer Cameroon separately. To this effect, during the mandate period, they had to collect data and prepare reports on Cameroon in order to defend themselves at the annual sessional meetings.[33]

One of the reasons which contributed to the ineffectiveness of the League system was that the structure and composition of the League was not that which could compel Britain or any other power to liberalise their policies. In the first place, the League of Nations, as Dr Nnamdi Azikiwe of Nigeria pointed out, was not endowed with the attributes of sovereignty and therefore, could not have a mandate.[34] In addition, the mandate had no functional mechanism to pressure British implementation of resolutions adopted at the PMC sessional meetings. Finally, and perhaps more importantly, the League of Nations' Western membership was still too conservative to pressure any of its members to introduce liberal policies in Third World countries. Consequently, British administration in the mandate period, 1922–1945, remained basically what it was prior to 1922. It was based sometimes on individual administrator's intuition and frequently proved to be contradictory and generally unplanned. Because of these defects of the League of Nations, neither liberal nor planned policies emerged during the mandate period. Liberal and planned policies began with the coming, but, especially, with the aftermath of World War II.

World War II
World War II broke out in Europe in September 1939 and, as had been the case during World War I, Cameroon became a centre of British concern. This time the British were not concerned with an offensive attack against the Germans in Cameroon, but were worried that the Germans who had remained in Cameroon – plantation owners, who had repurchased their former plantations in 1925, and some missionaries and traders – might rise against the British, or incite Cameroonians to do so, or both. By June 1940, the British had interned all enemy aliens. The internment of plantation owners and other Germans meant that most of the activities in which the

Germans were engaged, especially trade, virtually came to a standstill. But rather than take over the German functions, the British administrators became involved in war-related activities. Thus the period between 1939 and 1945 saw a paucity and, in some cases, a total absence of the once-annual reports. As the senior Resident, A.E.F. Murray, noted about those years, 'the energies of the administration . . . were devoted in the main to production for the war effort . . .'.[35]

In addition to expending energy on the collection of products, and despite the internment of enemy elements, the colonial administration established vigilance groups that made further demands on the administrators' time, for example, the establishment of the Pioneer Corps in the early 1940s.[36] The DO in charge of Victoria spent most of the year maintaining and supervising this group. Even the Resident was happy to report in 1943 that the recruiting for the Pioneer Corps had ceased, and that the local volunteer and the Air Raid Precaution Bodies (which had been taxing on the administration) had disbanded.

Although recruiting ended in Victoria it was continued in other places. In 1944, the DO for Bamenda was still actively recruiting for the fighting and vigilance services. He, like many officers, was still involved with fund raising, which had become a major occupation in the mid-1940s. In fact, as the demand for Cameroonian raw products diminished the need to raise funds to relieve the war-afflicted Europeans increased. Fund raising for relief, as Samuel Torimiro, a Nigerian police officer in Cameroon during World War II testified, was not easy. In Bamenda, for example, the people refused to respond, as was expected, to colonial inducements – subsidised prices, gifts of gunpowder, special facilities and bonuses for chiefs and village heads. It took, in 1943, the passage of the Wild Rubber Order which required that 'all able bodied males bring in 3 lb of rubber per head per month' to change the attitude of many people.[37]

The strains and changes brought by World War II were numerous and sometimes profound. The end of World War II, with respect to British administration of Cameroon, may be appropriately termed the beginning of the end, an end to the slumber and lack of interest that marked the period from 1914 through World War II. To the British administrators in Cameroon World War II had raised different questions and issues than had World War I. The administrators were now (unlike during post-World War I when they were primarily concerned with the question of the disposal of Cameroon) faced with substantive policy issues. They were concerned with the administration of plantations. The war had revealed the isolated and neglected state of Cameroon.

Yet some colonial administrators noticed the 'remarkable expansion in the desire of Cameroonians for educational facilities'. Resident Murray pointed out that this desire was due to the fact that Cameroonians had travelled 'more extensively than before'. Murray feared that the remarkable educational development which took place in the Owerri and Calabar provinces of Nigeria in the early 1920s would also occur in Cameroon. The educational development was not duplicated, but, undoubtedly, the outcome of World War II, especially the advent of the United Nations, led to a change in British policies and administrative structure in Cameroon subsequently.[38]

Native administration and nationalism

In their administration of Cameroon, the colonial administrators adroitly employed the system which became known as 'native administration'. Sir Frederick Lugard, a former Governor-General of Nigeria, developed the principle of native administration in Africa and the basic tenet of the concept is clearly stated in his *Dual Mandate in British Tropical Africa*.[39] The constitutional framework of the system hinged upon three ordinances – the Native Authority Ordinance, the Native Courts Ordinance, and the Native Revenue Ordinance. In every dependency, therefore, in which the system was introduced, Native Authorities, Native Courts, and Native Treasuries became vital instruments of native administration, local administration, local government, or indirect rule, as the system was variously called.[40] The system played an important role in the background to nationalism in Cameroon. In essence, the proponents of native administration hoped to bring Cameroonians together, involve them in broad issues, and eventually lead them to self-government along modern lines.

Native authority was an important instrument of native administration and as defined, it was either an individual, an assembly of village headmen or a council, who constituted the governing body of each unit, a *sine qua non* of the native authority. The existence of such a body, which in some places presented numerous problems, led to official recognition by the colonial government. Once these bodies were recognised as native authorities, they received instruction and encouragement to engage in a form of native administration, and a degree of local government to the extent of their capabilities. The British established these guidelines for the instruction of native authorities:

> ... to educate the natives to manage their own affairs and to evolve from their own institutions a mode of government which (conformed) to civilised standards .... The evolution of indigenous institutions does not mean that those institutions are to be allowed to grow unchecked and uncontrolled. It implies close and continuous direction, supervision and guidance by administrative officers. It implies repression and excision of abuses.[41]

While some have argued that the introduction of native administration aimed at preventing shocking abuses to Africans, and at cushioning the economic impact on the colonial government budget, the cited excerpt suggests that the colonial administrators also saw native authorities, the key instruments of native administration, as a vital medium of institutional evolution.

To the colonial administrators, native authorities became an essential part of the government. Traditional rulers were a link in the colonial administrative chain. As the popular *Political Memoranda* noted:

> there (were) not two sets of rulers – British and Native – working either separately or in co-operation, but a single Government in which the Native Chiefs have well-defined duties and an acknowledged status equally with the British officials.[42]

If, as this quotation suggests, it had been intended to create a government of whites and blacks, in practice, native administration remained distinct from colonial administration. While the colonial government was independent, initiated major policies, and controlled the instruments of policy implementation, native administration, in all respects, remained subordinate. Native administration managed what were known as 'native affairs' while the colonial administration managed matters at a broader level. A clear distinction also existed between the status of the European and that of the 'native'. The Europeans hoped to avoid any subordination to Africans so the concept of an integrated government or the equality of colonial and native officers could not materialise. Therefore, native administration did not integrate with the colonial government, but remained its instrument.

Indirect rule was proclaimed for Cameroon in October 1921.[43] As a planned policy it was easier to implement in some regions than in others. As F.H. Ruxton, Resident of Buea, in 1921, confirmed, 'progress on the lines of Indirect Administration would be quicker and easier in the grasslands than in Mamfe and Kumba Divisions'.[44] The policy began in Cameroon in early 1922, patterned after the Nigerian models. Indeed, it was often one and the same policy, since the practitioners were often officers who had served in Nigeria.[45] Thus, their experimentation with indirect rule in Nigeria dictated its adoption in Cameroon.

With experience in indirect rule elsewhere, colonial administrators in Cameroon were able to employ the system more cautiously and most profitably. Britain recognised indigenous institutions which were relatively well developed by the time of the British takeover, and constituted them as native authorities, although the terms of establishment differed from region to region. In many regions of Bamenda, chiefs and district heads were more readily available and these became native authorities. In the coastal region, where less-centralised political structures existed, the basis for indirect rule existed in councils of clan elders, which had become entrenched under appointed chiefs in the German period. Victoria and Buea represented examples of this conciliar system.

In addition to setting up native authorities the colonial administration created native courts and native treasuries. The system of native treasuries went into effect in Cameroon on 1 April 1922.[46] At its inception, unlike the system of native authorities, only four native treasuries were established, one in each division. Also, unlike native authorities, the native treasury was under the direct control of the DO. The system ensured that a certain proportion of the revenue collected was spent in the area from which it was derived for the benefit of those who contributed the revenue. Native treasury monies also maintained prisoners convicted in native courts but jailed in government jails. Even more importantly, colonial administrators provided the native authorities with a means of financial management since they saw such management as a lesson in local self-government. But until later, when a few native authorities received control of their native treasuries, financial management by native authorities remained theoretical.

With native courts, the third component of native administration, native authorities had more instruction. The proclamation of 10 June 1916 brought the Native Courts Ordinance of Nigeria into force in Cameroon.[47] The courts set up by the Resident, 'to meet the needs of the different districts', administered 'native law and custom'. Like native authorities, native courts opened in different parts of the country at different times. In some places either lack of traditional rulers to man the courts or want of colonial administrators to guide them hindered their creation and progress. Hence, in the early 1900s, when the establishment of native courts received colonial administrative priority, Victoria Division flourished with native courts while the more inland regions did not. By the end of 1917, Victoria Fako Division had fourteen native courts, while the other divisions had much fewer.[48]

Although native courts were more numerous and popular among the coastal peoples, the colonial administration found that native authority participation, without colonial involvement, functioned better in the Bamenda Grasslands where chiefs were 'more powerful ... and had been accustomed to dealing with cases'.[49] The grassland courts, however, lacked trained Cameroonian court clerks while the coastal courts had them. The courts also differed in the extent of judicial powers conferred upon them; but all provided a medium of instruction to native authorities in both civil and criminal cases. These leaders dealt with matrimonial matters, debts, and land, which formed the bulk of civil cases. While the Mamfe courts took the lead in the number of matrimonial and debt cases, and Bamenda courts in land cases, all courts had examples of each. The native authorities also examined such criminal cases as mayhem, stealing, and resistance to authority, which was a dominant feature of Bamenda native courts.[50] Through the courts native authorities learned to adjudicate numerous cases along Western lines.

Native courts were also the economic backbone of native administration. The courts, through fines and fees, initially provided much of the revenue which was required to support the chiefs, councillors, court clerks, and messengers who ran the courts. They also contributed to those projects which fell under the jurisdiction of native administration. The number of courts created reflected the economic importance of the courts. By the end of 1916, Victoria Division which included the Kumba region had 30 courts. A brief period of amalgamation of courts followed, but from the early 1920s a steady growth occurred in the number of these courts. Table I illustrates this growth.

It was important that the colonial administration should encourage the growth of courts and participation in them. An examination of the native treasury revenue records shows that native courts were next to taxes in swelling the native treasuries.[51] The chiefs and councillors who presided over the native courts worked to increase the intake of the native treasuries which was a major source of their income. So in this way, native authorities used native courts and treasuries to foster native administration.

Undoubtedly, since the system progressed at different rates, some

Table I: Growth of Courts

Year	Number of Courts	Year	Number of Courts
1922–3	23	1933	64
1924–5	28	1934	62
1926	30	1935	77
1927	38	1936	82
1928	39	1937	85
1929–31	40	1938	90
1932	42		

Source: Colonial Reports, 1922–1938.

native authorities benefited more from it than others. Some chiefs became quite involved in national politics while others did not. But all of them, by engaging in native administration, received exposure to much broader issues than in the past. Many had to re-orient themselves from tribute to tax.[52]

Since one of the objectives of native administration was to federate the native authorities, the system afforded power to individual leaders in varying degrees. Some leaders, such as those of Victoria and Bali, gained more than those of Buea or Bafut. The key question was to what extent did native administration bring the intended shift towards self-government? What changes occurred in the basic structure of the system? An overview of native administration from its formation in the early 1920s to the mid-1950s provides some guidelines.

Native administration: an overview
Prescribed and structured by the colonial administration to carry out their orders 'without incidents', native administration received high priority in the early 1920s. The system was encouraged in all the regions. But just as the response of the population differed from place to place, so did the progress. A divisional year-by-year analysis of native administration in Cameroon will show its evolution over time, and indicate those areas which progressed and those which did not. It will also expose the problems of the system.

In the first few years of native administration in Cameroon, colonial administrators conducted assessments to establish viable indigenous institutions which could constitute and control native administration. In 1923, for example, the DO for Mezam reported that areas were being marked out for native administration. B. Sharwood-Smith, the ADO for Mamfe in 1923, complained after his assessment that except for the Bangwa and the Nkongkwa, all indigenous internal administrative machinery lacked executive power. Sharwood-Smith, therefore, concentrated his efforts on education for native administration. In Kumba Division, F.B. Carr (ADO), found out that there was little traditional basis to build up native administration. As an initial step, he suggested that each village be organised as a native administrative area and then, as a next step, that two ethnic groups be integrated together, each with a council. In 1924, F.B. Carr, who had complained earlier about the fragmentation of the area, adopted a policy of fusion. He disregarded the ethnic question and attempted association. Dividing the division into twenty village areas, each under a salaried village head, Carr argued that 'the obvious policy was to work towards fusion of these clans disregarding the Ekumbe and Barombi ... who could not be considered independently'.[53]

In Mamfe, in 1923, training in native administration continued and ADO Rutherford was pleased that, except for Nsanakang and Menka, the other seven native administrations had recognised the importance of native administration. In 1924, the government arbitrarily divided Victoria Division, with its immigrant population, into two native districts – Buea and Victoria (Limbe) – and placed each under a district head. The arbitrary placement of immigrants under these district heads, coupled with the heads' high level of sophistication, might have seemed a positive advancement towards federation and/or national integration. But as some of the inhabitants of Victoria demonstrated, Cameroonians were not yet prepared for an arrangement which gave immigrants many land, political, economic and other rights.

But, whatever problems resulted from the attempt to set up native administration districts the increased responsibility which the native authorities had by the late 1920s contributed to 'progress' in native administration. This progress appeared first in Victoria Division, with its literate district heads and heterogeneous population. In 1931, a deliberative council was established in Victoria with a permanent council hall in which the three district heads of Victoria, Buea and Balong met to discuss financial and other administrative matters.[54]

A key feature of native administration in the early 1930s, especially beginning in 1932, was the attempt to enlist, or at least engage, the educated element in native administration. In addition to the literate district heads of Victoria Division, noteworthies included Chief Fominyen of Meta, a graduate of Bamenda Government School, and the chief of Babungo, a Basel Mission catechist, educated mainly in mungaka but who could understand English.[55] Many higher school graduates were not inclined to engage in native administration, a system which they saw as aristocratic, undemocratic, and unprogressive, so the colonial administration sought to fill this void.

To the colonial administrators 1932 was the year of the emergence of 'literate and semi-literate classes'. By this period the graduates of the first senior primary schools and of Kake (the teacher training college, near Kumba) had formed a core of the educated class. Small in number, this class of people felt alienated from the aristocratic system. This attitude not only compelled colonial administrators to solicit their participation in native administration, but actually encouraged new investigations into the status of this class.[56] This policy of keeping a watchful eye on the educated element was not to ensure the 'sympathies' of these people as colonial reports noted. The educated element, to be sure, felt alienated from the unprogressive, aristocratic system but they wanted involvement in the colonial administrative system rather than in native administration.

To accommodate these new developments, in 1932 new methods of applying the policy of native administration developed. That year there was a leap towards federation. The rationale for federation, as the colonial administrators perceived it, was to broaden the basis of native administration so that the varying elements within an administrative division would combine for the common weal. Thus 1932 became a year of reassessment, a year to take inventory of the progress of native administration. Now accepting, or at least, recognising the inadequacies of the system, the colonial administration expanded the native administrative system to bring it 'more into line with the indigenous system and (at the same time) ensuring that the sympathies of no classes were alienated'.

This meant that the chiefs were to 'share' executive power with members of the native administration. In an attempt to share power in the Bamenda Grasslands, traditional practices were curbed to accommodate the literate classes. In the past, traditional organisations, for example *kwi'fon*, and *nyamkwe*, were the main advisory bodies to the chiefs. Beginning in the early 1930s, the government no longer recognised or accepted the advisory function of these groups. By this time the colonial administration tended to listen to the many inhabitants of the coastal regions who desired a more democratic system − a system which would accommodate the many immigrants and literates of the divisions.

Although 1932 seemed to have sparked the beginning of a revolution in native administration, the colonial administrative device of setting up a compromise to enlist the educated elements prevailed upon a more revolutionary process. In most places the idea of councils instead of sole authorities with executive power flourished. This trend led the colonial administration to report, with delight, at the end of 1932, that 'no active discontent' existed in Cameroon. So, as long as Cameroonians were 'content' or quiet about the situation the colonial administration waited and watched. Nonetheless, the idea of councils became an important feature of native administration after 1932.

One setback in the organisation of native administration in the early 1930s stemmed from the economic depression. Everywhere there were reductions in the numbers of native administration staff. For example, before the depression 725 Africans were employed, but the number had declined to 328 in 1933.[57] The decrease in the number of staff, did not, however, discourage early native authorities such as those of Bali, Bafut, Nso, and Kom from selecting advisers from a wider field than that in the traditional past. In the post depression period, the government still encouraged the native administrations to establish councils, broaden their scope and instruct their members in the new concepts of law and order, sanitation and taxation.

To broaden the native administrative system within each administrative unit, the native authority was required to maintain the obedience of the people under its control. Modifications were made 'to conform with modern requirements'; thus chiefs or elders who were seen to be more modernising often advanced beyond the more traditional ones. To curb any extant autocratic tendencies, chiefs were made to work with a council and although they chaired meetings, they had to act through councils. Each council consisted of two representatives from each village. The Native Authority Council, as the central one was called, met (sometimes fortnightly, as that of Buea, or when necessity arose) to deliberate on matters ranging from village headship and family disputes to the appointment of court messengers. This conciliar function operated best with the native court system, in which each village was permitted a court but all villages met, once a month at a clan court to discuss 'local' affairs.[58] As intended by the colonial administration the conciliar system was a compromise between the traditional, conservative classes and those who represented the modern point of view.

By the late 1930s, shifts in favour of corporate responsibility led the colonial administration to entrust native administrations with a more direct interest in the development of the territory. The government gave native authorities more responsibility for financial management, and then embarked on education in revenue and expenditure, believing, as observed earlier, that it was an essential step towards self-government. By the end of the 1930s the native authorities of Nso, Victoria, Buea, Balong, and Kembong controlled their own treasuries.[59] In addition to instruction through treasuries, in 1937, the colonial government decided that, beginning in April 1938, each native authority would receive a larger share of the direct taxes, thus providing them with greater financial responsibilities. In Kumba division, where cocoa prospered, the native administrative schools attempted to train future native authority personnel in budget planning. But the outbreak of World War II interfered with many such designs. Like most institutions, native administration suffered neglect during the war years and, as Mackenzie, the DO for Bamenda, noted in 1943; 'Native authorities existed in name only and seldom met except when visited by an administrative officer'.[60]

Following World War II another major development in native administration occurred. At a meeting in Mamfe, in May 1946, native administrative members proposed that two provincial meetings be established – one for the Bamenda and Mamfe areas and the other for the Kumba and Victoria divisions.[61] The decision favoured only one provincial meeting and each division selected representatives for the first provincial meeting held on 27 and 28 November 1946, in Buea.[62] At this significant meeting divisional representatives selected Chief Manga Williams, already the Cameroonian representative to the Nigerian Legislative Council, and *fon* Galega II of Bali, to represent Cameroon in the Eastern House of Assembly, Enugu, Nigeria.[63] The provincial meeting also provided the occasion for some of those attending to go beyond their boundaries for the first time. Since they met in the coastal region, the grassland members lost no time in availing themselves of the opportunity to visit the sea, see the ships, and tour other facilities in Victoria division.

In the post-World War II era, the establishment of divisional and provincial committees provided a broad base of operation and also led to new progressive policies. The new procedure, introduced at the provincial meetings for selection of provincial members to represent Cameroon in Nigeria, was based upon a majority vote, prescribed by the Rules of Procedure adopted by the first provincial meeting of November 1946.[64] This was a departure from the usual selection process for representatives.

In keeping with the post-World War II developments, the colonial administration gave new attention to critics of the European system of native administration. Since most of the criticism emanated from the educated persons, the colonial administration accelerated changes and modified the method of selection of council and committee members to give the educated progressive class a greater say in council and committee affairs.

Thus, by the end of the 1940s, literacy was increasingly a necessary qualification for appointment to council or committee membership. The theory of native administration was no longer maintained only on existence of inherited authority. Native administration, to be successful, had to extend beyond the family, clan, and ethnic group. It had to include the small but growing progressive and educated class to whom broader issues of westernisation were becoming more important. Both the native administration and the colonial administration had to reckon with the aspirations of this class in the government services. While the question of advancing Cameroonians in government service was undoubtedly significant in its own right, it was even more consequential because it raised a new problem for the colonial administration in regard to the status of the native administration.

Native administration, from its inception, was an instrument or process through which Africans were to gain experience in self-governance. In the late 1940s the literate persons shunned native administration and preferred inclusion and advancement in the colonial government service as the only means to affect policy and to achieve self-government according to modern concepts. This situation caused the Europeans to realise that by establishing two administrative systems – one local or native and the other central or colonial – they had created a problem, if not for themselves, then for the Africans who would have to decide, upon independence, how to integrate native administration with central or national administration. Since the new elite insisted upon entering colonial service, the colonial administration, as earlier, had to compromise. In the late 1940s a Local Government Board, which would accommodate the progressive and educated Cameroonians, was proposed.[65]

In June 1949, a provincial conference, comprising members of the provincial meeting, and representatives of ethnic unions and youth organisations, converged in Mamfe. The conference was important, among other reasons, because it brought together people who represented traditional institutions as well as those who favoured government along modern lines. It was even more significant because it demanded separate regional status for Cameroon in Nigeria. Although this proposal was rejected because, as it was claimed, it was 'politically and economically unsound', it reflected the advanced state of political thinking of the educated Cameroonians and the issues with which the colonial administration now had to contend.[66]

The colonial administration in the early 1950s continued to encourage (through legislation) educated Cameroonians to participate in local affairs, which now had the word, 'public' inserted to read, 'local public affairs.' On the other hand, this educated class had induced native administrations to become involved in issues inconsistent with the objectives of the institution (as set out by the colonial administrators). R. Angeloni's complaint about the Victoria native administration in his division is illustrative.

> The major part of the deliberations of the Councils are taken up in discussing real or imaginary grievances against the stranger population, the Corporation (Cameroons Development Corporation) or the Companies, and the Central Government. The Native Authorities have become protective associations against encroachments which they consider to be contrary to the interests of the indigenous people.[67]

Regardless of how the colonial administration felt about either the educated class or the new concerns of native administration, the early 1950s were characterised by compromises which aimed to appease Cameroonians. By 1952, for example, not only were more literate men included in native administration but women were also encouraged to join.[68]

The colonial administration set out by 1953, with a greater vigor, to infuse new life into the declining native administrations. This was a definite need in Victoria division, where the inhabitants paid more attention to issues arising from plantations than to native administration. In the early 1950s, many administrators, including the Commissioner of Cameroon, believed that DOs should begin to remove themselves from 'obtrusive roles at the meetings of the native authorities'. They also agreed that decentralisation failed to attract the educated élite and was becoming outmoded in a modern world. To resolve this, the commissioner proposed a system of elective councils; but local councils now contained many people disinclined to revive a system which they detested. Many of these councils had become forums for public opinion and avenues for disseminating information. A fight to resuscitate native administrative institutions as they were in their glorious days was a losing battle. At best, the colonial administration had to concede that native administration and the central government had to co-exist and progress side by side. And so in October 1954, when the first Cameroonian House of Assembly convened in Buea, five native authority members became partners with the new élite in the House.[69]

Native administration and nationalism

The two men who represented Cameroon in the Eastern House of Assembly, Enugu, Nigeria, were traditional leaders – Chief J. Manga Williams of Victoria and *Fon* Galega II of Bali. Galega, who represented a centralised kingdom, was a relative newcomer to chieftaincy, and hence, to native administration. In 1946, when he and Chief Manga Williams were appointed Cameroonian represent-atives to Nigeria, he had been *fon* for approximately six years. He inherited the throne in 1940, following the death (many traditional peoples prefer the term 'loss') of *fon* Fonyonga II. Although he was relatively new to the throne, he, like Chief Manga Williams, was literate, which undoubtedly enhanced his appointment as a Cameroonian representative. He was also a former dispensary attendant.[70]

Unlike *Fon* Galega II, Chief Manga Williams entered national politics with a wealth of experience in native administration, years of contact with Europeans, and longevity in 'public' life. Thus much more has been noted about his public life than about that of any other traditional leader.[71] Chief Manga Williams, born about 1877, as explained earlier (in Chapter Three) was a descendant of Chief Bile (King William) of Bimbia, who in 1826, according to Leeming, surrendered Bimbia to the British 'in exchange for the title of King'.[72] King William, by this and other acts, enhanced the future relationship of his grandchild with Europeans. Not only was Chief Manga Williams educated and made district head of Victoria by the Germans (1908), but when the British took over in 1916, they extended his powers. In matters of native administration, Chief Manga Williams received sole authority.[73] Unlike Chief Endeley, his coastal counterpart at Buea, who worked through the conciliar system.

From the late 1920s Chief Manga Williams became more and more prominent and 'public'. In June 1928, as the Cameroonian representative, he read the welcome address to the visiting Governor of Nigeria, Sir Graeme Thomson. On this occasion, Chief Manga Williams was decorated with a Certificate of Honour.[74] In 1938, when the first federated council was established in Victoria, Chief Manga Williams became its first president. When the need arose in the early 1940s for a Cameroonian representative to the Nigerian Legislative Council, he was nominated, albeit against the wishes of some educated elements.[75] In 1946, he and the *Fon* of Bafut were honoured. But while the *Fon* received the Certificate of Honour, which Chief Manga Williams had been awarded seventeen years earlier, Chief Manga Williams was awarded the coveted Order of the British Empire (OBE) medal.[76] In the same year, he and Galega II were appointed to represent Cameroon in the Nigerian Eastern House of Assembly. In the summer of 1949, 'as a guest of the British Council', he visited England and while there, attended a board meeting of the Cameroon Development Corporation, a position which he acquired that same year.[77] Undoubtedly, these reflect the credentials of one who had emerged as the single most popular, if not significant, personality in Cameroonian emerging nationalism. Indeed, this portfolio earned him the popular title 'father of the House of Assembly'.[78]

While the chiefs' acquisition of power encouraged some sort of autocracy which distanced the chiefs from many people, the very nature of the native administrative system and the outlook of chiefs presented sources of conflict. Indeed, the conservatism of the system, particularly of the natural leaders in the Bamenda Grasslands, contributed to the discontent between them and the educated or progressive elements. And thus, by the time the Cameroonian House of Assembly was established in 1954, the natural leaders had formed a lobby group − the Conference of Chiefs and Natural Rulers − to forestall the nationalist activities of the Western educated élites.[79] But even if the educated people preferred more modern and lucrative jobs and a democratic government to the less cumbersome but autocratic native administration, many of them were either by birth relatives of chiefs (as was Dr Endeley), or by upbringing traditional enough to compromise with the traditional system and leadership (as was Dr Foncha). Hence, by this inclination, some of the politicians moved in favour of a future house of chiefs.[80] Although they made the motion in the 1950s, the chiefs were not to realise such a house until the early 1960s.[81]

The chiefs, in the early 1970s, found out that the education which they had supported had ousted them from a significant role in leadership. But if this turn of events was a surprise to the chiefs, it probably was not to the more informed colonial administrators, who after World War II, came to believe that the chief, especially the illiterate one, had no future in national politics. E.S.B. Tagart's advice to the colonial administrators was representative of this view. Commenting on the role of the chief, Tagart wrote:

> I would say, then, ... that while we should do what is possible to preserve the dignity of the chiefs of our native peoples, we should not expect those chiefs in return to perform executive functions as agents of a European Government.[82]

Whether or not Tagart's view became policy, it showed that there was no scheme within the native administrative system to accommodate the traditional and the modern. Possibly, some administrators privately hoped, a new form of government would evolve from the native administrative system. But unfortunately for the natural rulers, instead of an evolution, a revolution occurred. They discovered upon independence that although introduced into the modern political system because of their experience, they were to be removed from national politics because of the unsuitability of traditional institutions as an instrument of modernisation.

Notes

1   The phrase 'growth of nationalism' has been used in this study to imply also the growth of a Cameroonian nation although the creation of a nation precedes nationalism.

2   The French, who proposed the administrative system which became known as a condominium, soon brought their own trained personnel. See V.T. LeVine, *The Cameroons: From Mandate to Independence*, Los Angeles, 1964, pp. 31–32.

3   The Supreme Council had, in May 1919, allocated the various German colonies to their conquerors as Mandates. Although the Council confirmed the status it permitted the powers to decide on the status of their respective territories. On the Mandate, see Q. Wright, *Mandates Under the League of Nations*, Chicago, 1930. We shall refer to the second administrative period as the period of Provisional Administration.

4   Ba 1917/1, p. 1. (The Ba file series are found in the National Archives, Buea).

5   The Native Courts Ordinance of 1914 and the Native Authority Ordinance of 1916 were proclaimed in Cameroon in May 1916. See Elizabeth M. Chilver, 'Native Administration in West Central Cameroons, 1902–1954', in K. Robinson and F. Madden (eds.), *Essays in Imperial Government: Presented to Margery Perham*, Oxford, 1963, p. 100.

6   Ba 1917/1, pp. 4, 13; also Ba 1919/1, p. 1. Kumba was still considered part of Fako (Victoria) Division. Courts were opened in 1917, in Mamfe and Bamenda.

7   Ba 1921/1, p. 8. The few experienced administrators came and went with such frequency that they did not have time to draw up, if they wanted to, an administrative guide.

8   Ba 1921/1, p. 8. In fact, earlier, the governor-general of Nigeria, in 1916, had issued orders instructing administrative officers in Cameroon to use as the basis of administration existing German laws but failing those laws they should apply the laws of that part of Nigeria in which the officer served. See Chilver, 'Native Administration . . .', p. 100.

9   One of the early nationalists – P.M. Kale – explained that prior to this split 'Cameroonians from the coast to the interior had been mixing freely in schools and all walks of life' and this changed with the balkanisation of Cameroon into British and French spheres. See P.M. Kale's *Political Evolution in the Cameroons*, Buea, 1967, p. 86. In discussing the impact of World War I in this section, I am largely concerned with those aspects that had a bearing on British administration. The Francophones, especially the Duala, more so than the Anglophones (in the inter-war years), made an issue of this split. See LeVine, *Cameroons*, pp. 38, 111–117.

10   Elizabeth Dunstan, 'A Bangwa Account of Early Encounters with the German Colonial Administration', *Journal of the Historical Society of Nigeria*, 3, 1965, p. 413.

11   Ba 1921/1, p. 11. It is also likely, as some scholars have suggested, that Asonganyi's behaviour was a response to the German advice that Cameroonian Chiefs refrain from future European wars and that they should accommodate themselves to the British but the memory of the maltreatment, imprisonment and killings of Africans was sufficient to invoke such a response. See Chilver, 'Native Administration . . .', p. 99.

12   E.M.L. Endeley, 'Political History in West Cameroon', Unpublished manuscript, p. 5.

13   Ba 1920/5, p. 70; also LeVine, *The Cameroons*, p. 32

14   Cb 1917/1.

15   Ba 1929/1, p. 3. Although the colonial officers were generally given instruction in agricultural, legal, economic, historical, geographical, and anthropological studies, a year's instructions and the problems attendant with pioneers hardly qualified them as masters in those fields. See Ba 1954/1, p. 23.

16   J. Davidson from 1 January 1921 to 13 February 1921; Capt. G. Anderson from 14 February 1921 to 17 June 1921; Major F.H. Ruxton from 17 August 1921 to 31 December 1921. Between 18 June 1921 and 16 August 1921 the post was vacant, although the divisional officer, N.C. Duncan deputised. Ba 1921/1, pp. 1 and 3. For a typical frequency in change, see Ba 1928/1, pp. 3–4 also B. Booth, *A Comparative Study of Mission and Government Involvement in Educational Development in West Cameroon, 1922–1969*, Ph.D. thesis, University of California, Los Angeles, 1973.

17   Ba 1924/1, p. 2.

18   Ba 1926/1, pp. 3–4. Duala grammar was already in print. Mamfe seemed to have been caught in the middle (Banyang and Keaka were suggested) see Ba 1926/1, p. 4.

19   Many more joined the list. Ba 1954/1, pp. 1–3. Although these officers were referred to as ADOs their function in the early period was indistinguishable from that of the DOs. It seems Cameroon received many cadets because of the general calm, and the disposition of the Cameroonians, as a DO noted, to be submissive to the British. Cameroonians had been 'pacified' during the 30 years of German rule. Britain's prized officers went to India and Sudan. Those next in importance went to such colonies as Nigeria; see R.O. Collins, 'The Sudan Political Service', *African Affairs*, 71, 1972, pp. 293–303; A.H.M. Kirk-Greene, 'The Sudan Political Service: A Profile in the Sociology of Imperialism' (Manuscript), 1981.

20   Ba 1928/1, p. 2.

21   Ba 1920/5, p. 69. In his study of native administration in Bussa, Nigeria, Michael Crowder adds that recurrent illness and much paper work hampered administrative efficiency. See his *Revolt in Bussa*, London, 1973, p. 66.

22   Cb/1916/2

23   Kumba was so called because whenever there was a shortage of staff it was the last to be considered; see Ba 1921/1, p. 16.

24   See the case of Rex vs. Tabi and 43 others. Case No. 80/1929 Pc/b 1933/1. British appointment was not only based upon inaccurate information, it was based, sometimes, on those appointees who were amenable.

25   Ba 1920/5, p. 17; For a study of this Duala man, see R. Joseph's critical views 'The Royal Pretender: Prince Douala Manga Bell in Paris, 1919–1922', *Cahiers d'Etudes Africaines*, 54, XIV, 2 (1974): 339–358.

26   *Ibid.* Joseph argues that Bell's 'positive' contribution to French Cameroonian

nationalism was minimal; see his *Radical Nationalism in Cameroon*, Oxford, 1977, p. 80.

27   Ba 1920/5, p. 17.

28   Ba 1920/5, p. 18.

29   Cf/a (1928); also Gardinier, 'The British . . .'. pp. 524–525; Rubin, *Cameroun*, pp. 199–203.

30   Ba 1920/5, p. 66. In 1919; H.W.V. Temperly had proposed the concept of a Cameroonian-Nigerian 'administrative, fiscal, or customs union'. See Gardinier, 'The British . . .'. p. 522.

31   Until 1921 there were only three divisions – Victoria, Mamfe, and Bamenda as the Germans had them. In 1921, Kumba, hitherto a part of Victoria Division, received divisional status. Ba 1921/1, p. 16.

32   Gardinier, 'The British . . .'. p. 528.

33   For some of the British defences, see Colonial Report for 1930, pp. 4–5; Colonial No. 153 (1937), p. 77.

34   *Renascent Africa*, New York, Negro University Press, 1937, p. 172.

35   Ba 1942/2, p. 1.

36   *Ibid*. It seems that the Pioneer Corps was first created in Victoria in 1942; see Ba 1942/2; Ba 1944/1.

37   Ba 1943/1, pp. 6ff.; Interview with Mr Toromiro, Victoria, Cameroon, summer, 1979.

38   For some of these changes, see E. Chiabi, '*Background to Nationalism in Anglophone Cameroon, 1914–1954*, University of California, Santa Barbara, 1982, section on Cameroon: A UN Trusteeship.

39   Edinburgh, 1922. (Reprint) London, 1965, Examples of other works which treat the subject include, Margery Perham, *Native Administration in Nigeria*, London, 1962; William M. Hailey (Lord Hailey), *Native Administration in the British African Territories*, 5 vols., London, 1950–53; Raymond L. Buell, *The Native Problem in Africa*, 2 vols., London, (1965, edition); Michael Crowder, *Revolt in Bussa: A Study of British Native Administration in Nigerian Borgu*, 1902–1935, London, 1973. The concept of native administration may be traced to Sir George Goldie of the Royal African Company. Mary Kingsley also urged the English to acquire a 'wider knowledge of the facts of African life' and that 'goodwill' should be the basis of colonial rule (see Lord Hailey, *An African Survey*, London, 1938, pp. 133–134).

40   Although a fine distinction may be made between native administration (the structure) and indirect rule (the method), in this study the words native administration, indirect rule, and indirect administration will be used interchangeably.

41   Colonial No. 16 (1924), p. 45.

42   Quoted in Buell, *Native Problem*, p. 688.

43   Ba 1921/1, p. 3. Prior to the early 1920s, the policy, as DO N.C. Duncan stated, was 'individual and uncontrolled'; *Ibid*., p. 8.

44   *Ibid*., p. 7. This was because of the centralised kingdoms of Bamenda Grass-lands.

45   The importation of the model was not wholesale, since the colonial administration in Cameroon had to rebuild the ethnological institutions which had been destroyed during World War I, and had to be aware of the dangers of applying indirect rule in areas with no traditional foundations, a lesson they had learned in Southern Nigeria; see for example, Gardinier, 'The British in the Cameroons, 1919–1939', P. Gifford and W.R. Louis, (eds.), *Britain and Germany in Africa: Imperial Rivalry and Colonial Rule*, New Haven, 1967, p. 545, for the modifications which were adopted in Cameroon.

46   Colonial Report for 1922, p. 58.

47   *Ibid.* p. 37
48   Ba 1917/1. Kumba was still considered part of Victoria Division. Bali, with a centralised *fondom*, did not receive a warrant for a Native Court until 1925. See Colonial No. 30 (1926), p. 21.
49   *Ibid.*, p. 13.
50   The Courts were limited to hear and determine only civil cases and approximately 90 per cent of criminal cases. See Cmd. 1647 (1921), pp. 50 and 55; Colonial reports for the years 1926–1930.
51   For example, the 1924/25 revenue for Victoria showed native courts fees and fines to be £1034, next to Poll tax which was £2757. In Kumba, for the same period, court revenue was £1125 while Poll tax was £3720. The other revenues – interest on investment, school fees, market tolls, and miscellaneous – only totalled £79. In Mamfe in the same period, court revenues were even closer to taxes than in other divisions. But in all divisions including Bamenda, and for most of the period into the early 1950s, court-related revenues remained a major source of revenue second only to direct taxes. See Colonial Reports for 1926, 1950, and 1952.
52   For such an orientation, see Phyllis M. Kaberry and Elizabeth Chilver, 'From Tribute to Tax in a Tikar Chiefdom', in *Africa*, 30, 1 January 1960, pp. 1–19.
53   Ba 1924/1, pp. 20–21.
54   Colonial No. 76 (1931), p. 5; Ba 1931/3.
55   Ba 1932/1, p. 54
56   Ba 1932/1, pp. 54–55.
57   These numbers included all Africans and Native Administration staff of the then Northern Cameroons. See the Colonial Report for those years. It is interesting to observe that the number of courts did not decline (of course, they were a source of income).
58   See the example of Balong which adopted the Conciliar system in 1935, Colonial No. 131 (1936), p. 17.
59   Colonial No. 153 (1937), p. 8–9. Nso had theirs since 1932. The other areas had a central treasury controlled by district officers.
60   Ba 1943/1, p. 4.
61   Ba 1946/2, pp. 3ff. It is interesting that this proposal preceded the provincial division into the Southern and Bamenda Provinces in 1949.
62   *Ibid.*
63   As we shall see in the next section, these members of the native administration became among the first to participate in national politics, especially in the early period of administrative integration with Nigeria.
64   Colonial No. 221 (1947), p. 22
65   Colonial No. 244 (1948), p. 44.
66   Colonial No. 262 (1949), pp. 2 and 33.
67   Ba 1950/1, p. 21.
68   Colonial No. 299 (1952), p. 44. Nso had taken the lead earlier by requesting and having some royal women made members of the Native Court. See Ba 1940/1, p. 5.
69   The five members were Chiefs S. Asungna Foto of Mamfe, J. Manga Williams of Victoria, and Mformi of NKambe and Messrs A.N. Jua of Wum and M.T. Monju of Bamenda. Kumba was yet to elect a representative. Mr H.N. Mulango was later elected. See Colonial No. 325 (1955), p. 32. Both Monju and Jua were educated, progressive elements.
70   Ba 1940/1, p. 4.

71   However, his biography still awaits a biographer, while more details have been written on other Cameroonian chiefs. See Williams' 'portrait' in *West Africa*, October 8, 1949, p. 944. Popular literature on chiefs include Rebecca Reyher, *The Fon and His Hundred Wives*, New York, 1952; R.E. Ritzenthaler and Pat Ritzenthaler, *Cameroons Village: An Ethnography of the Bafut*, Milwaukee, 1962; Pat Ritzenthaler, *The Fon of Bafut*, New York, 1966. These are on chieftaincy in the northwest province. Among dissertations on the subject are S.W. Russell, *Aspect of Development in Rural Cameroon: Political Transition Among the Bali of Bamenda*, Boston, 1980; B.M. Masquelier, *Structure and Process of Political Identity: Ide, A Polity of the Metchum Valley (Cameroon)*, University of Pennsylvania, 1978; P.N. Nkwi, *Traditional Government and Social Change: A Study of the Political Institutions Among the Kom of Cameroon Grassfields*, Fribourg, 1976; and Michael T. Aletum, *Political Conflicts Within the Traditional and the modern Institutions*, Louvain, 1973.

72   A.J. Leeming, 'A Historical Sketch of Victoria, British Cameroons', *Nigerian Field*, 16, 1 January, 1951; p. 185. Edwin Ardener places Williams's birthdate between 1876 and 1879. See his *Coastal Bantu*, p. 25.

73   Regarded as most able he was put in charge of the heterogeneous Victoria population of immigrants. Colonial No. 118 (1935), pp. 10–11; E. Ardener, *Coastal Bantu*, p. 25. The special privilege did not, however, prevent the British from imprisoning Chief Williams's brother, Fritz in 1916.

74   Ba 1932/1, p. 11; Colonial No. 42 (1928), p. 13. The first reference gives the month of award as May and the second as June.

75   Chief Manga Williams was appointed in 1942. See Ba 1942/2, p. 1. In March 1943 he attended the Legislative Council Budget Meeting, Ba 1943/1, p. 2; Ba 1949/1, pp. 18ff.

76   Ba 1942/2, p. 4. In 1931, The *Fon* of Bali, Fonyonga II had been awarded a similar certificate, Ba 1940/1, p. 4.

77   Ba 1942/2, p. 4; Ba 1949/1, pp. 18–19.

78   Southern Cameroons, Government, *Introducing the Southern Cameroons*, Lagos, 1958, p. 32; also, Ikoyn, 'Politics and Personalities in the Cameroons', *West African Review*, 26, 1955, p. 19. Chief Manga Williams epitomised the successful example of Native Administration integration. But had he lived past 1959, one wonders whether he would have fared better than his colleagues after 1972, when the House of Chiefs was abolished.

79   It seems that the chiefs had wanted the nationalists to press for the creation of a House of Chiefs. See E.W. Ardener, 'The Political History of Cameroon', *The World Today*, 18, 1962, p. 345; Chilver, 'Native Administration . . .' p. 138.

80   By so doing the Cameroonian nationalists, as did Ghana's CPP, agreed that while realising the outdatedness of native administration in political concepts, sentimental attachments prevented total denunciation of the system. For the Ghana example, see D. Brokensha, 'Chieftaincy at Larteh', in M. Crowder and O. Ikime, *West African Chiefs*, p. 402. Dr John Ngu Foncha has been noted as a foremost traditionalist. He moved for the House of Chiefs.

81   The House of Chiefs was established in 1960 and dismantled in 1972.

82   Tagart, *The African Chief*, p. 74.

Bibliography

1 Books and articles in English

Abubakar, Sa'ad. *The Lamibe of Fombina: A Political History of Adamawa 1809–1901*, London, Ahmadu Bello University Press and Oxford University Press, 1977.

Anene, J.C. *The International Boundaries of Nigeria 1885–1960: The Framework of an emerging African Nation*, London, Longman, 1970.

Ardener, E.W. *Coastal Bantu of the Cameroons*, London, International African Institute, 1956.

Historical Notes on the Scheduled Monuments of West Cameroon, Buea, Government Press 1969.

'The Political History of Cameroon' *The World Today*, 18, 8, 1982.

'Documentary and Linguistic Evidence for the Rise of the Trading Polities between Rio del Rey and Cameroon 1500–1650', in Lewis, I.M. (ed.) *History and Social Anthropology*, no. 7, London, Tavistock, 1968.

'The nature of the reunification of Cameroon', in Hazelwood, A. (ed.) *African Integration and Disintegration*, London, 1967.

Ardener, E.W. and S.S. and Warmington, W.A. *Plantation and Village in the Cameroons*, Oxford University Press, 1960.

Ardener, Shirley G. *Eye-Witnessess to the Annexation of Cameroon 1883–1887*, Buea, Government Press, 1968.

Ardener, Shirley and Ardener, Edwin. 'Wovea Islanders', *Nigeria*, 59, 1958.

Austen, R.A. 'Duala versus Germans in Cameroon: economic dimensions of a political conflict', *Revue Française d'Histoire d' Outre-mer*, LXIV 237, 1977.

'Slavery among Coastal Middlemen: The Duala of Cameroon', in Kopytoff, I. and Miers, Suzanne, (eds.) *Slavery in Africa*, Madison, University of Wisconsin, 1977.

Barth, H. *Travel and Discoveries in North and Central Africa 1849–1855*, London, Longman, 5 vols. 1857: Reprinted by Frank Cass Ltd., Centenary edition 1955.

Bederman, S.H. *The Cameroon Development Corporation: Partner in National Growth*, Bota, 1968.

Bender, C.J. *Religious and Ethical Beliefs of African Negroes: Douala and Wakweliland*, Girard, Kansas, Haddeman–Julius, 1926.

Betley, J.A. 'Stefan Szole Rogozinski and the Anglo-German Rivalry in the Cameroons', *Journal of the Historical Society of Nigeria*.

Brackenbury, E.A. 'Notes on the Bororo Fulbe or Nomad Cattle Fulani', *Journal of the African Society*, 23, 91, 1924; 23, 92, 1924.

Brain, R. *Bangwa Kinship and Marriage*, Cambridge University Press.

Burnham, P. *Opportunity and Constraint in a Savannah society: The Gbaya of Meiganga Cameroon*, Oxford University Press, 1980.

'Raiders and Traders in Adamawa', in Watson J. (ed.) *Asia and African Systems of Slavery*, Oxford, Basil Blackwell and Mott, 1981.

Burton, R.F. *Abeokuta and the Cameroons Mountain*, 2 vols, London, Tinsley Brothers 1963.

Buttner, T. 'On the Social-Economic Structure of Adamawa in the 19th Century: Slavery or Serfdom', in Markov, W. (ed.) *Afrika-Studien*, 1967.

Chem-Langhëë, B. 'The Question of Native Administration in Mamfe Division Between the Wars', *Habaru*, vol. III, 2, 1980.

'The British and the Northern Kamerun Problem 1919–1961', *Abbia*, 38–39–40, 1982.

'The Origins of the Southern Cameroons House of Chiefs', *International Journal of African Historical Studies*, vol. 16, 4, 1983.

'Southern Cameroons Traditional Authorities and the Nationalist Movement 1953–1961', *Afrika Zamani*, 14, 1984.

Chem-Langhëë, B. and Fomin, E.S.D. 'The Banyang Slave System: Social Differentiation and Citizenship', *Annals of the Faculty of Letters and Human Sciences*, 1, 1985.

Chem-Langhëë, B. and Njeuma, M.Z. 'The Pan-Kamerun Movement, 1949–1961', in Kofele-Kale, N. (ed.) *An African Experiment in Nation Building: The Bilingual Cameroon Republic since Reunification*, Colorado, Westview Press, Boulder, 1980.

Chilver, E.M. 'A Bamileke Community in Bali-Nyonga: A Note on the Bawok', *African Studies*, 23, 3/4, 1964.

'Chronological Synthesis: The Western region, comprising the Western Grassfields, Bamum, the Bamileke chiefdoms and the central Mbam', in Tardits, C. (ed.) *The Contribution of ethnological research to the history of Cameroon cultures*. Paris, CNRS, 1981.

'Meta Village Chiefdoms of Bome Valley in the Bamenda Prefecture of West Cameroon', *Nigerian Field*, 30, 1, 1965; 30, 2, 1965.

'Native Administration in the West Central Cameroons, 1902–1954', in Robinson, K., and Madden, F., (eds.) *Essays in Imperial Government presented to Margery Perham*, Oxford, Blackwell, 1963.

'Paramountcy and Protection in the Cameroons: The Bali and the Germans 1889–1913', in Gifford, P. and Louis, W.R. (eds.) *Britain and Germany in Africa: Imperial Rivalry and Colonial Rule*, New Haven and London, Yale University Press, 1967.

'The Bangwa and the Germans: a tailpiece', *Journal of the Historical Society of Nigeria*, Vol 4, 1, 1967.

The History and Custom of Ntem, Oxford, Oxonian Press 1961.

Zintgraff's Exploration in Bamenda, Adamawa and Benue Lands 1889–1892, Buea, Government Printing Press, 1966.

Chilver, E.M., and Kaberry, P.M. 'The Kingdom of Kom in West Cameroon', in Forde, D. and Kaberry, P.M. (eds.) *West African Kingdoms in the Nineteenth Century*, Oxford University Press, 1967.

Traditional Bamenda: The Pre-colonial History and Ethnography of the Bamenda Grassfields, Buea, Government Printing Press, 1967.

'Traditional Government in Bafut, West Cameroon', *Nigerian Field*, 28, 1, 1963.

'Sources of the 19th Century Slave Trade: The Cameroon Highlands, *Journal of African History*, 6, 1, 1965.

Comber, T.J. 'Explorations Inland from Mt Cameroons and Journey through Congo to Makuta', *Proceedings of the Royal Geographical Society*, vol. 1, 1879.

Delancey, M. and Delancey, V. *A Bibliography of Cameroon*, New York, African Publishing Company, 1975.

Denham, D. and Clapperton, H. *Narrative of Travels and Discoveries in Northern and Central Africa*, London, 1826.

Dillon, R.G. *Ideology, Process, and Change in Precolonial Meta Political Organisation*, Ann Arbor University Microfilms, 1974.

Dugast, I. 'Banen, Bafia, and Balom', in McCulloch, M., Littlewood, and Dugast, I. (eds.) *Peoples of the Central Cameroons*, London, 1954.

Dunstan, Elizabeth. 'A Bangwa Account of Early Encounters with the German Colonial Administration', *Journal of the Historical Society of Nigeria*, 3, 2, 1965.

East, R.M. *Stories of Old Adamawa: A collection of Historical Texts in the Adamawa Dialect of Fulani*, Lagos, London, 1934.

Ejedepang-Koge, S.N. *The Tradition of a people, Bakossi: A Historico-Socio-Anthropological Study of One of Cameroon's Bantu Peoples*, Yaoundé, 1972.

Elango, Lovett Z. 'Franco-Cameroonian wartime and postwar co-operation, 1939–1945: prelude to the politics of emancipation', *Annals of the Faculty of Letters and Human Sciences*, 1987.

The Anglo-French 'Condominium' in Cameroon 1914–1916. History of a Misunderstanding, Limbe, Navi-Group Publications, 1987.

'The Anglo-French "Condominium" in Cameroon 1914–1916: the Myth and the reality'. *International Journal of African Historical Studies*, 18, 4, 1985.

The Cameroon Coast in Maritime History. c. 1472 to the Present, Douala, Editions CAPE, 1985.

'The Councils of Notables and the politics of control in Cameroon Under French rule, 1925–1949'. *Journal of Eastern African Research and Development and Trans-African Journal of History*, vol. 16, 1987.

Epale, S.J. 'The Impact of Early English Christian Missionary Contact on Economic Growth in Cameroon, 1800–1884', in Haberland, E. *et. al.*

(eds.) *Symposium Leo Frobenius, Deutsche Unesco-Kommission*, Köln, No. 25, München 1974.

Eyongetah, J. and Brain. R. *A History of Cameroon*, London, Longman 1974.

Fanso, V.G. 'Background to the Annexation of Cameroon 1875–1885', *Abbia*, 29–30, 1975.

Fonlon, B. 'The Language Problem in Cameroon: An Historical Perspective', in Smock, D.R. and Bentsi-Enchil, K. (eds.) *The Search for National Integration in Africa*, New York, The Free Press, 1975.

Gardinier, D.E. *Cameroon: United Nations Challenge to French Policy*, Oxford University Press, 1963.

'The British in the Cameroons 1919–1939', in Gifford, P. and Louis, W.R. (eds.) *Britain and Germany in Africa: Imperial Rivalry and Colonial Rule*, New Haven and London, Yale University Press, 1967.

'Urban Politics in Douala, Cameroon, 1944–1955. Douala Reactions to Proposed Municipal Reforms', *African Urban Notes*, 4, 3, 1969.

Geary, Christraud, *Things of the Palace. A Catalogue of the Bamum Palace Museum in Foumban (Cameroon)*, Wiesbaden, Franz Steiner Verlag GMBH, 1983.

(ed.) 'Ludwig Brandt's Historical Notes on the Kingdom of Kom', *Paideuma*, 26, 1980.

Geary, Muhle C. 'The Historical Development of the chiefdom of We (Southern Fungom)' in Tardits, C. (ed.) *Contribution. . . .* (Paris 1981).

Geschiere, P. *Village communities and the State: Changing relations among the Maka of Southeastern Cameroon since the colonial conquest*, London, Kegan Paul, 1982.

Gifford, P. and Louis, R. *Britain and Germany in Africa, Imperial Rivalry and Colonial Rule*, New Haven, Yale University Press, 1967.

Gorges, E.H.F. *The Great War in West Africa*, London, Hutchinson, 1927.

Grassfields Working Group. 'Palaces and Chiefly Households in the Cameroon Grassfields', *Paideuma*, 31, 1985.

Harris, Rosemary. 'The History of Trade at Ikom, Eastern Nigeria', *Africa*, 42, 2, 1972.

Haywood, A. and Clarke, F.A.S. *The History of the Royal West African Frontier Force*, Aldershot, Gale and Polden, 1964.

Henderson, W.O. 'British Economic Activity in the German Colonies, 1884–1914', *Economic History Review*, 15, 1/2, 1945.

Horner, G.R. 'The Allocation of Power and Responsibility in Bulu Society' *Cahiers d'Etudes Africaines*, 4, 3, 1964.

'The Bulu Response to European Economy' in Bohannan, P. and Dalton, G. (eds.) *Markets in Africa*, Illinois, Evanston, 1962.

Horner, N.A. *Cross and Crucifix in Mission: a Comparison of Protestant-Roman Catholic Missionary Strategy*, New York, Abingdon Press, 1965.

Hutchinson, T. *Ten Years Wandering Among the Ethiopians*, New Impression, London, Frank Cass, 1967.

Jeffreys, M.D.W. 'A Genealogy of the Bamum Kings and Queens', *Afrika und Ubersee*, 54, 1/2, 1971

'Banyo, a local Historical Note', *Nigerian Field*, 18, 2, 1953.

'The Bamum Coronation Ceremony, as Described by King Njoya', *Africa*, 20, 1, 1950.

'Traditional Sources Prior to 1890 for the Grassfield Bali of Northwestern Cameroons', *Afrika und Ubersee*, 46, 3, 1962, and 47, 4, 1963.

'The Wiya Tribe', *African Studies*, 21, 2, 34, 1962.

Jeffreys, M.D.W. and Kaberry, P.M. 'Nsaw History and Social Categories: Notes', *Africa*, 22, 1, 1952.

Johnson, W.R. *The Cameroon Federation: Political Integration in a Fragmentary Society*, New Jersey, Princeton University Press, 1970.

Johnston, H.H. 'Explorations in the Cameroons District of Western Equatorial Africa', *Scottish Geographical Magazine*, 4, 10, October 1888. *George Grenfell and the Congo*, 2 vols. London, Hutchinson and Company, 1908.

Joseph, R.A. *Radical Nationalism in Cameroon: Social Origins of the UPC. Rebellion*, Oxford University Press, 1977.

'The Royal Pretender: Prince Douala Manga Bell in Paris, 1919–22', *Cahiers d'Etudes Africaines*, XIV, 54, 1974.

'The German Question in French Cameroun, 1919–1939', *Comparative Studies in Society and History*, 17, 1975.

Kaberry, P.M. 'Retainers and Royal Households in the Cameroons Grassfields', *Cahiers d'Etudes Africaines*, 3, 2, 1962.

'Some Problems of Land Tenure in Nsaw, Southern Cameroons', *Journal of African Administration*, 12, 1, 1960.

'Traditional Politics in Nsaw', *Africa*, 29, 4, 1959.

Women of the Grassfields: A Study of the Economic Position of Women in Bamenda, British Cameroons. London, H.M. Stationery Office. 1952 & reprinted, New York, Humanities Press, 1969.

Kaberry, P.M. and Chilver, E.M. 'An Outline of the Traditional Political System of Bali-Nyonga, Southern Cameroons', *Africa*, 31, 4, 1961.

Kale, P.N. *A Brief History of the Bakweri*, Lagos, Tika-Tore Press, 1939. *Political Education in the Cameroons*, Buea, Government Press, 1967.

Kaspi, A. 'French War Aims in Africa 1914–1919' in Gifford, P. and Louis, R. (eds.) *France and Britain in Africa*, New Haven, Yale, 1971.

Kingsley, Mary. *Travels in West Africa: Congo Français, Corisco and Cameroons*, London, Macmillan, 1897; reprinted in London, by Frank Cass, 1965.

Kirk-Greene A.H.M. *Adamawa, Past and Present*, Oxford University Press, 1958.

Kofele-Kale, N. *The Political Culture of Anglophone Cameroon: A Study of the Impact of Environment on Ethnic Group Values and Member Political Orientations*, Ann Arbor, University Microfilms, 1974.

'Reconciling the Dual Heritage: Reflections on the Kamerun Idea', in Kofele-Kale, N. (ed.) *An African Experiment in Nation Building: The Bilingual Cameroon Republic since Reunification*, Boulder, Colorado, Westview Press 1980.

Kumm, K. 'From Housaland to Egypt, Through the Sudan', *The Geographical Journal*, 36, 2, 1910.

Leeming, A.J. 'A Historical Sketch of Victoria, British Cameroons', *Nigerian Field*, 15, 4, 1950; 16, 1, 1951.

Lenfant, P. 'From the Atlantic to the Chad by the Niger and the Benue', *Scottish Geographical Magazine*, 20, 6, 1900.

Le Vine, V.J. 'A Contribution to the Political History of Cameroon: the United Nations and the (Internal) Policies of Decolonization; the Termination of the British Cameroons Trusteeship', *Abbia*, 24, 1970.

The Cameroons from Mandate to Independence, Berkeley, and Los Angeles, University of California Press, 1964.

Le Vine, V.T. and Nye, R.P. *Historical Dictionary of Cameroon*, Metuchen, N.J., Scarecrow Press, 1974.

Lewis, T. *These Seventy Years: An Autobiography*, London, The Carey Press, 1927.

Littlewood, Margaret, *et al.* *Peoples of the Central Cameroons*, London, International African Institute, 1954.

Macleod, O. *Chiefs and Cities of Central Africa, Across Lake Chad by Way of British, French and German Territories*, London, W. Blackwood, 1912. Reprinted by Libraries Press, Freeport, New York, 1971.

Malcolm, L.W.G. 'Notes on the Religious Beliefs of the Eghap, Central Cameroon', *Folk-Lore*, 33, 4, 1922.

'The socio-political organization of the Eghap', *Anthropos*, 21, 1/2, 1926.

Mbum, M.F. and Turner, Frank L. *The Economic Potential of West Cameroon — Priorities of Development. Supplement I Gazetteers of Place Names in West Cameroon*, California, Stanford Research Institute, Menlo Park, 1964.

McCullouch, M. and Dugast, I. *et al.* 'Peoples of Central Cameroons', *Part IX of Western Africa, Ethnographic Survey of Africa*. Forde, Daryll (ed.) London, International African Institute, 1954.

Meek, C.K. *A Sudanese Kingdom: An Ethnographical Study of the Jukun — Speaking Peoples of Nigeria*. First edition 1931; reprinted New York, Negro University Press, 1969.

Tribal Studies in Northern Nigeria, 2 vols. London, Kegan Paul, 1931.

Migeod, F.W.M. *Through British Cameroons*, London, Heath Cranton 1965.

Mosima, F.M. 'Imperial Business in Cameroon under United Kingdom Administration', *Afrika Zamani, Revue d'Histoire Africaine*, Yaoundé 1981.

Njeuma, M.Z. 'Adamawa and Mahdism: The Career of Hayatu Ibn Said in Adamawa, 1878–1898', *Journal of African History*, XII, 1, 1971.

Fulani Hegemony in Yola (Old Adamawa) 1809–1902, Yaoundé, Centre d'Edition et de Production pour l'Enseignement et la Recherche, 1978.

'Notes on the Sources of Cameroon History from Pre-historic to colonial Times', *Annals of the Faculty of Letters and Human Sciences*, no., II, 1984.

'Some observations on the Chronology of North and Central Cameroon from Ethnological data', in Tardits, C. (ed.) *Contribution* ..., Paris. 1981.

'The Ancient History of Bamun from its Origin to Sultan Njoya', in Haberland, E. *et al.* (eds.) *Symposium Leo Frobenius*, Deutsche UNESCO – Kommission, Köln. no. 25, Pullach bei München, 1974.

'The Emergence of the Kingdom of Mandara from Origins to 1600', *Habaru: Journal of the Department of History*, University of Yaoundé, vol. 2, 1978.

The Origins of Pan-Cameroonism Buea, Government Press, 1964.

Nkwi, P. *Traditional Government and Social Change: A Study of the Political Institutions among the Kom of the Cameroon Grassfields*, Switzerland, University of Fribourg, 1976.

'Cameroon Grassfield Chiefs and Modern Politics' *Paideuma*, 25, 1979.

Oshuntokun, J. 'Anglo-French Occupation and the Provisional Partition of the Cameroons 1914–1916', *Journal of the Historical Society of Nigeria*, 7, 4, 1975.

Plessis, J. du. *Thrice Through the Dark Continent: A Record of Journeyings across Africa during the Years 1913–1916*, London, Longman, 1917.

Prescott, J.R.V. *The Evolution of Nigeria's International and Regional Boundaries 1861–1971*, Vancouver, Tantalus Research Ltd., 1917.

Price, D. 'Who are the Tikar Now?', *Paideuma*, no. 25, 1979.

Quinn, F. 'An African Reaction to World War I: the Beti of Cameroon', *Cahiers d'Etudes Africaines*, 52, 1981.

'Beti Society in the Nineteenth Century', *Africa*, London, 50, 3, 1980.

'The Beti and the Germans (1887–1916)' *Afrika und Ubersee*, vol. 56, 1/2, 1972; 3, 1973.

Ritzenthaler, P. *The Fon of Bafut*, London, Cassell and Company Ltd., 1967.

Ritzenthaler, Robert and Ritzenthaler, Pat, *Cameroons Village: an Ethnography of the Bafut*, Milwaukee Public Museum, 1962.

Rowlands, M.J. 'Local and Long Distance Trade and Incipient State Formation on the Bamenda Plateau in the late 19th Century', *Paideuma*, 25, 1979.

Rubin, N. *Cameroon: An African Federation*, New York, Praeger Publishers, 1971.

Rudin, H.R. *Germans in the Cameroons: 1884–1914. A Case Study in Imperialism*, New Haven, Yale University Press, 1938.

Ruel, M. *Leopards and Leaders: constitutional politics among a Cross River people*, London, Tavistock, 1969.

Russell, A. 'The Colas of Nigeria and the Cameroons', *Tropical Agriculture*, vol. 32, 1955.

Saker, Emily M. *Alfred Saker of Cameroons*, London, The Carey Press, 1929.

Schultze, A. 'German Congo and South Cameroon' in Friedrich, Adolf (ed.) *From the Congo to the Niger and the Nile: An Account of the German Central African Expedition of 1910–1911*, vol. 2, London, 1913.

Sharwood, S.B. *Recollections of British Administration in the Cameroons and Northern Nigeria, 1921–1957*, Durham, North Carolina, Duke University Press, 1969.

Underhill, E.B. *Alfred Saker, Missionary to Africa*, London, The Carey Press, 1844; reprinted by CMS 1958.

Vandercook, J.W. 'The French Mandate of Cameroon: A Vast African Territory Ruled by Petty Sultans Under French Sway', *National Geographical Magazine*, 59, 2, 1931.

Vaughan, J.H. Jr. 'Culture, History, and Grass-Roots Politics in a Northern Cameroon Kingdom', *American Anthropologist*, 66, 5, 1964.

Vernon-Jackson, H.O.H. 'A Chronology of the History of Academic Education in Cameroon 1844–1940', *Abbia*, no. 3. 1963.

Victoria Centenary Committee, *Victoria, Southern Cameroons, 1858–1958*, Victoria, 1958.

Warnier, J-P. 'Trade guns in the Grassfields of Cameroon', *Paideuma*, 26, 1980.

and Fowler, I. 'A Nineteenth Century Ruhr in Central Africa', *Africa*, 49, 4, 1979.

Whitelock, G.F.A. 'The Yola Cross River Boundary Commission, Southern Nigeria', *Geographical Journal*, 36, 4, 1910.

2   Ouvrages et articles en Français

Abbo, H. 'Robinson, M. et Lebeuf, J-P. 'L'origine et les souverains du Mandara (Texte Arabe, traduction et commentaire)', *Etudes Camerounaises*, 11, 3/4, 1949; aussi *BIFAN*, 18, Series B, 1/2 1956.

Abwa, D. 'La diplomatie dans l'Afrique Pré-Coloniale: le cas du pays Banen au Cameroun'. *Afrika Zamani, Revue d'Histoire Africaine*, 16–17, 1985.

'L'école française dans le Lamidat de Ngaoundéré de 1917 à 1945', *Annales de la Faculté des Lettres et Sciences Humaines*, 11, Yaoundé, 1984.

Adier, A. 'Le royaume Moundang de Léré au XIXe siècle', in Tardits, C., *Contribution . . .*, Paris, 1981.

Albert, A. *Au Cameroun français: Bandjoun*, 2nd. ed. Montréal, Edition de l'Arbre, 1943.

Alexandre, P. et Binet, J. *Le groupe dit Pahouin (Fang-Boulou-Beti)*, Paris, Press Universitaires de la France pour International African Institute 1958.

Atangana, C. 'Une étude sur la Chefferie', *Abbia*, 23, 1969.

Aymerich, J. *La Conquête du Cameroun, 1er août 1914–20 février, 1916*, Paris, Payot, 1933.

Azoulay, L. 'Hutter, Franz: exploration dans l'hinterland septentrional de la colonie du Cameroun', *Bulletin de Mémoirs de la Socièté d'Anthropologie de Paris*, 4, 5th Series, 1903.

Bah, T.M. 'Contribution à l'étude de la résistance des peuples africains à la colonisation: Karnou et l'insurrection des Gbaya', *Afrika Zamani*, no. 3, 1974.

'Les armées peuls de l'Adamaoua au 19e siècle', *Journal of International African Institute*, Zaria, 1979.

Bakari, Modibbo. 'Histoires des Sultans de Maroua', *Abbia*, 3, 1963.

Bassoro, Mal Hammadou. 'Un manuscrit peul sur l'histoire de Garoua', *Abbia* 8, 1965.

Bayart, J.F. 'Les rapports entre les églises et l'Etat au Cameroun de 1958–1971', *Revue Française d'Etudes Politiques Africaines*, 80, 1972.

'L'Union Nationale Camerounaise', *Revue Française de Sciences Politiques*, 20, 4, 1970.

'Presse écrite et développement politique au Cameroun', *Revue Française d'Etudes Politiques Africaines*, 88, 1973.

Bekombo, Manga. 'Notes sur le temps, conceptions et attitudes chez les Douala', *Ethnographie*, 60/61, 1966–1967.

Bekombo-Priso, M. 'Essai sur le peuplement de la region côtière du Cameroun: les populations dites duala', in Tardits, C. *Contribution* ..., Paris 1981.

Berger, R.P. 'Les missions catholiques au Cameroun', in Ambrière, F. (ed.) *Afrique Centrale; Les Républiques d'Expression Française*, Paris, 1962.

Bouchaud, J. *La Côte du Cameroun dans l'histoire et la cartographie, des origines à l'Annexion allemande* (1884), Paris, 1952.

Briault, M. *Mission de Foumban des Prêtres du Sacré-Coeur de Saint-Quentin*, Paris, 1931.

Brussaux, E. 'Notes sur les Moundang', *Bulletin de la Société d'Anthropologie*, 5e series, 1907; aussi dans *Bulletin de la Société des Recherches Congolaises* 1, 2, 1922.

'Notes sur la Race Baya', *Bulletin et Mémoires de la Société d'Anthropologie de Paris*, 5e séries, 9, 1908.

Brutsch, J.R. 'Autour du Procès de Rudolf Douala Manga', *Études Camerounaises*, 51, 1966.

'Les Débuts du Christianisme au Cameroun', *Études Camerounaises*, 4, 33/34, 1951.

'Les Traités Camerounais, recueillis, traduits et commentés', *Études Camerounaises*, 47/48, 1955.

Bureau, R. 'Ethno-sociologie religieuse des Douala et apparentés', *Recherches et Études Camerounaises*, 7/8, 1962.

'Influence de la Christianisation sur les institutions traditionnelles les ethnies côtières du Cameroun', in Baeta, C.G. (ed.) *Christianity in Tropical Africa*, Oxford University Press 1968.

Cardaire, M.P. *Contribution à l'étude de l'Islam Noir*, Memorandum 11, Centre IFAN Cameroun, 1949.

Cheuveau, J. 'Mizon à Yola'. *Revue d'Histoire des Colonies*, XL1, 1954.

Clozel, F. *Les Bayas*, Paris, J. André, 1896.

Copet, E. 'Les Kaka', in Tardits, C. *Contribution* ..., Paris, 1981.

Crowther, S. 'Trois états foulbés du Soudan Occidental et Central: la

Fouta, la Macina, l'Adamaoua', *Annales de l'Université de Grenoble*, 8, 1896.

Costedoat, R. *l'Effort français au Cameroun: le Mandat français et la réorganisation des territoires du Cameroun*, Besançon, Imprimerie Jacques et Demontrond, 1930.

De Garine, I. 'Contribution à l'histoire du Mayo Danaye (Massa, Toupouri, Moussey et Mousgoum)', in Tardits, C. *Contribution* ..., Paris, 1981.

'*Les Massa du Cameroun: Vie Economique et Sociale*, Paris, Press Universitaires de France, 1964.

Despoirs J. 'Des Montagnards au Pays Tropical: Bamiléké et Bamoun, *Revue de Géographie Alpine*, 4, 1945.

Dikoume, A.F. '*Native Baptist Church*', *messianisme ou syncrétisme*: Paris, Edition Harmattan, 1987.

'Du portage comme point de départ de l'economie coloniale au Cameroun', *Annales de la Faculté des Lettres et Sciences Humaines*, Série Sciences Humaines, 2, 1985.

Dippold, M.F. *Une Bibliographie du Cameroun (les écrits en langue allemande)*, Imprimerie Otto Book Burgan, 1971.

Dubie, P. 'Christianisme, Islam et Animisme chez les Bamouns', *Bulletin de I.F.A.N.*, XIX, 3/4, 1957.

Dugast, I. *Inventaire ethnique du Sud-Cameroun*, I.F.A.N. Contre du Cameroun, Series Population, 1949.

'Le peuplement du Sud-Cameroun' in *Encyclopédie de l'Afrique Française, Cameroun-Togo*, Paris, 1951.

Etoga, E.F. *Sur les Chemins du développement: essai d'histoire des faits économiques du Cameroun*, Yaoundé, C.E.P.E.R. 1971.

Faraut, F. 'Les Mboum', in Tardits, C. (ed.) *Contribution* ..., Paris 1981.

Farrely, M. *Chronique du pays banen (au Cameroun)*, Paris, Société des Missions Évangeliques, 1948.

Ferrandi, J. *Conquête du Cameroun-Nord, 1914–1915*, Paris, Charles-Lavanzelle, 1928.

Fondjo, T. *Album des 75 ans de l'église catholique au Cameroun*, Yaoundé, Imprimerie St-Paul, 1966.

Froelich, J.C. 'Le commandement et l'organisation sociale chez les Fali', *Etudes Camerounaises*, 49, 1956.

'Le Commandement et l'organisation sociale chez les Foulbé de l'Adamaoua', *Etudes Camerounaises*, 45/46, 1954.

Les musulmans d'Afrique noire, Paris, 1962.

'Ngaoundéré: la vie économique d'une cité Peul', *Etudes Camerounaises*, 43/44, 1954.

'Notes sur les Mboum du Nord-Cameroun', *Journal de la Société Africaniste*, 29, 1959.

Gaudemet, P.M. 'L'Autonomie Camerounaise', *Revue Française de Science Politique*, 8, 1, 1958.

Geschiere, P.L. 'Remarques sur l'histoire des Maka', in Tardits C. (ed.) *Contribution* ..., Paris 1981.

Ghomsi, E. 'La naissance des chefferies bamiléké et les relations entre les divers groupements avant la conquête allemande'. *Revue Camerounaise d'Histoire*, I, I. 1971.

'Resistance africaine á l'impérialisme européan: le cas des Douala du Cameroun', *Afrika Zamani, Revue d'Histoire Africaine*, Yaoundé, 11, 1976.

Gomsu, J. 'L'autorité coloniale allemande et les systèmes poliques traditionnels au Cameroun (1884–1914)'. *Cahiers d'Allemand et d'Etudes Germaniques*, Université de Yaoundé, 1, 2, 1985.

'La formation de Camerounais en Allemagne pendant la période coloniale', *Cahiers d'Allemand et d'Etudes Germaniques*, Université de Yaoundé, 1, 2, 1985.

Gonidec, P.F. 'De la dépendance à l'autonomie: L'etat sous tutelle du Cameroun', *CNRS, Annuaire Français de Droit International, III, 1957*, Paris, 1958.

Grall, F. 'Etudes anthropologiques, ethniques et démographiques des Kirdi Matakam et des Kirdi Kapsiki de la circonscription Mokolo', *L'anthropologie*, 1936.

Heberle, G. *L'église Catholique au Cameroun et les missions des prêtres du Sacré-Coeur de Saint Quentin*, Issy-les Moulineaux, Imprimerie Saint Paul, 1960.

Hilberth, J. *Les Gbaya*, Uppsala, Hakam Ohlssons, 1962.

Hilberth, E. and Hilberth, J. *Contribution à l'ethnographie des Gbaya*, Uppsala: Studia Ethnoloaphique Uppsaliensia, 1968.

Homont, A. 'L'application du régime de la tutelle aux territoires sous Mandat', *Revue Juridique et Politique*, 6, 2, 1952.

Joos, L. 'Traité Germano-Peul de Tibati (11–9–1899)', *Etudes Camerounaises*, 51, 1956.

Juillerat, B. 'Eléments d'ethno-histoire des Muktele et du Mandara Septentrional', in Tardits, C. (ed.) *Contribution* ..., Paris 1981.

Kange, E.F. *La politique dans le système religieux catholique romain en Afrique de 1815 à 1960*, Paris, Honoré Champion, 1976.

Kaptue, L. 'L'administration coloniale et la circulation des indigènes au Cameroun', *Afrika Zamani: Revue d'Histoire Africaine*, 10/11, 1979.

'Les conditions d'existence des travailleurs manuels au Cameroun sous régime français jusqu'en 1952', *Habaru*, III, 2, 1980.

'Réflexions critiques sur la recherche de solutions au problème de la main-d'oeuvre au Cameroun sous régime français, 1916–1960', *Habaru*, III, 1, 1980.

Keller, J. 'Les églises et les missions protestantes au Cameroun et en Afrique Central', in Ambrière, F. (ed.) *Afrique Centrale; les Républiques d'Expression Française*, Paris, 1962.

Kouo F. 'Les répercussions de la crise économique de 1929 au Cameroun', *Afrika Zamani; Revue d'Histoire Africaine*, 1979.

Laburthe-Tolra, P. *À travers le Cameroun du Sud au Nord (Voyages et explorations dans l'arrière-pays de 1888 à 1891)*. Publication de la Sorbonne, Série 'Afrique', Paris, introduction de Curt von Morgen, *Durch Kamerun von Sud nach Nord*, Leipzig, Brockhaus, 1893.

'Essai de synthèse sur les populations dites "beti" de la région de Minlaba (sud du Nyong)', in Tardits, C. (ed.) *Contribution* . . . , Paris, 1981.

'Le So des Beti selon M. Hubert Onana', *Annales de la Faculté, de Lettres et Science Humaines.* Yaoundé, 1, I. 1969.

Yaoundé d'après Zenker (1895), Dijon, Imprimerie Darantiere, 1970.

Lacroix, P-F. 'Matérieux pour servir à l'histoire de Peuls de l'Adamaoua', *Etudes Camerounaises*, 37/38, 1952; 39/14, 1953.

'Islam Peul de l'Adamaoua', in Lewis, I.M. (ed.) *Islam in Tropical Africa*, London, 1966.

Landeroin. 'Du Tchad au Niger, notice historique', in *Documents scientifiques de la mission Tilho (1906–1909)*, vol. II, Paris, Imprimerie Nationale 1911.

Lebeuf, Annie. *Les principautés kotoko: essai sur le caractère sacré de l'autorité*, Paris, Université de Paris, 1969.

Lebeuf, J-P. *L'habitation des Fali montagnards du Cameroun Septentrional: technologie, sociologie, mythologie, symbolisme*, Paris, Librairie Hachette, 1961.

Lecoq, R. *Les Bamilékés: Une Civilisation Africaine*, Paris, Presence Africaine, 1953.

Lembezat, B. *Les populations païennes du Nord-Cameroun et de l'Adamaoua*, Paris, Presses Universitaires de France, 1961.

Lemoigne, J. 'Les pays conquis du Cameroun Nord', *L'Afrique Française Renseignements coloniaux*, 1918 pp. 94–114 et 130–153.

Lenfant, E.A. *La grande route du Tchad: mission de la société de Géographie*, Paris, Librairie Hachette, 1905.

Lestringant, J. *Les pays de Guider au Cameroun: essai d'histoire régionale*, Versailles, 1964.

Madiba, E. 'La France et la redistribution des territoires du Cameroun (1914–1916)'. *Afrika Zamani, Revue d'Histoire Africaine*, Yaoundé, 12/13, 1981.

Maitre, C. *À travers l'Afrique centrale, du Congo au Niger (1892–1893)*, Paris, Hachette 1895.

Mangongo-Nzambi, A. 'La délimitation des frontières du Gabon', *Cahiers d'Etudes Africaines*, 9, 1, 1969.

Martin, J.Y. 'Essai sur l'histoire pré-coloniale de la société Matakam', in Tardits, C. (ed.) *Contribution* . . . , Paris 1981.

Les Matakam du Cameroun: essai sur la dynamique d'une société pré-industrielle, ORSTOM 41, Paris 1970.

Martin, M. 'Le pays des Banen et le Sultan Njoya', *Etudes Camerounaises*, 4, 33/34, 1951.

Michel, M. 'Les plantations Allemandes du Mont Cameroun (1885–1914)', *Revue Française d'Histoire d'Outre-Mer*, 57, 1969.

Mohamadou, E. 'Introduction historique à l'étude des sociétés du Nord-Cameroun'. *Abbia*, 12/13, 1966.

Le royaume du Wandala où Mandara au XIXe siècle, Bamenda, ONAREST, 1975.

Les royaumes foulbé du plateau de l'Adamaoua au XIXe siècle, ILCAA, Tokyo, 1978.

'L'histoire des lamidat foulbé de Tchamba et Tibati'. *Abbia*, 6, 1964.

L'histoire des peuls férobé du Diamaré, Maroua et Petté, ILCAA, Tokyo, 1976.

'L'implantation des Peuls dans l'Adamaoua (approche chronologique)', in Tardits, C. (ed.) *Contribution* . . ., Paris 1981.

'Pour servir à l'histoire du Cameroun: la chronique de Bouba Njidda Rey', *Abbia*, 4, 1963.

'Pour une histoire du Cameroun central: les traditions historiques des Vouté ou "Babouté",' *Abbia*, 16, 1967.

Ray ou Rey-Bouba. Traditions historiques des Foulbé de l'Adamaoua, Edition du CNRS, Paris, 1979.

Mouchet, J. 'Note sur la conversion à l'Islam, en 1715 de la tribu Wandale', *Bulletin de la Société d'Etudes Camerounaises*, 15/16, 1946.

Moume-Etia, L. *Sites historiques de Douala*, 1ère partie, 2e edition, Douala, Imprimerie Commercial, 1940.

Muston, E. 'Petit journal de la mission de délimitation Congo-Cameroun. Mission Moll au Sangha-Tchad 1905−1906−1907', *Bulletin de la Société des Recherches Congolaises*, 19, 1933.

Mveng, E. *Histoire du Cameroun*, Paris, Présence Africaine, 1963.

Mveng-Ayi, M. 'Echanges précoloniaux et diffusion des plantes au Sud-Cameroun', in Tardits, C. (ed.) *Contribution* . . ., Paris, 1981.

'La formation et l'equipement des armées beti au début du XXIe siècle', *Revue Camerounaise d'Histoire*, 1, 1971.

'Notes sur l'emigration des Camerounais à Fernando Po entre les Deux Guerres Mondiales', *Abbia*, 23, 1969.

Ngoa, H. 'Situation historico-généalogique des Ewondo', *Abbia*, 22, 1966.

Nicol, Yves, *La tribu des Bakoko: un stade de l'évolution d'une tribu noire au Cameroun*, Paris, Larose, 1919.

Njoya, I.A. *Histoire et coutumes des Bamoun*, Yaoundé, IFAN, 1952.

Nkwenga, J. 'Histoire de la chefferie de Banganté', *Abbia*, 9−10, 1965.

Owona, A. 'A l'aube du nationalisme Camerounais: la curieuse figure de Vincent Ganty', *Revue Française d'Histoire d'Outre-Mer*, 56, 204, 1969.

'La naissance du Cameroun (1884−1914)', *Cahiers d'Etudes Africaines*, 13, 1, 1973.

Pave, I. 'Les Allemands à Foumban', *Abbia*, 12/13, 1966.

Pontié, G. *Les Guiziga du Cameroun septentrional. L'Organisation traditionnelle et sa mise en contestation*, ORSTOM, 65, Paris, 1973.

'Quelques éléments d'histoire Guiziga', in Tardits. C. (ed.) *Contribution* . . ., Paris, 1981.

Pouka, L.M. 'Les Bassa du Cameroun', *Cahiers d'Outre-Mer*, 3, 10, 1950.

Pradelles de Latour Dejean, C-H. 'Quelques données historiques sur la Chefferie Bangwa (Bamiléké Orientaux)', in Tardits, C. (ed.) *Contribution* . . ., Paris 1981.

Richard, Madeleine. 'Histoire, tradition et promotion de la Femme chez les Batanga (Cameroun)', *Anthropos*, 65, 3/4, 1970.

Roche, J.B. *Au pays des Pahouins: du Rio Mouny au Cameroun*, Paris, la Vanzelle, 1904.

Rodinson, M., et Lebeuf, J-P. 'L'Origine et les Souverains du Mandara'. *Bulletin de l'IFAN*, 18, 1/2, 1956.

Santerre, R. *Pédagogie musulmane d'Afrique noire*, Les Presses de l'Université de Montréal, 1973.

Siran, J-L. 'Elément d'ethnographie vouté pour servir à l'histoire du Cameroun Central', in Tardits, C. (ed.) *Contribution* ..., Paris 1981.

Slageren, Jaap Van. *Les origines de l'église evangélique du Cameroun: missions européennes et christianisme autochtone*, Leiden, E.J. Brill, 1972.

Strumpel, K. *Histoire de l'Adamaoua d'après les traditions orales*. Traduction Française du Cap, Lemoigne Archives Nation Yaoundé, 1912.

Tardits, C. *Contribution à l'étude des populations Bamiléké de l'Ouest du Cameroun*, Paris, Berger-Leurault, 1960.
Contribution de la recherche ethnologique à l'histoire des Civilisations du Cameroun, 2 vols., Edition CNRS, Paris 1981.

Tardits, C. *'L'implantation des populations dans l'Ouest Cameroun'*, in Tardits C. (ed.) *Contributions* ..., Paris, 1981.
Le Royaume Bamoun, Paris, Librairie Armand Colin, 1980.

Tilho, A.J-M. *Documents Scientifiques de la Mission Tilho, 1906−1909*, Paris, Imprimerie Nationale, 1910−1914, 3 vols.

Van Beek, W.E.A. 'Les Kapsiki', in Tardits, C. (ed.) *Contribution* ..., Paris 1981.

Vincent J-P 'Eléments d'histoire des Mofu, montagnards du Nord-Cameroun', in Tardits, C. (ed.) *Contribution* ..., Paris, 1981.

Vossart, J. 'Histoire du Sultanat du Mandara, province de l'empire du Bornou', *Etudes Camerounaises*, 4, 35, 1952.

Warnier, J-P. 'L'histoire précoloniale de la chefferie de Mankon (Département de la Mezam)', in Tardits, C. (ed.) *Contribution* ..., Paris, 1981.

Weber, P. *Notes sur les échanges précoloniaux dans le Dja et Lobo*, ORSTOM, Yaoundé, 1973.

Wilhem, H. 'Le Commerce précolonial de l'Ouest (Plateau Bamiléké − Grassfield, région bamoum et bafia')', in Tardits, C. (ed.) *Contribution* ..., Paris, 1981.

Wirz, A. 'La Rivière de Cameroun: commerce précolonial et contrôle du pouvoir en Société lignagère', *Revue Française d'Histoire d'Outre-Mer*, LX, no. 219, Paris, 1973.

Zang-Atangana, J.M. 'Les partis politiques Camerounais', *Recueil Penant*, 70, 684, 1960.

Zeltner, J.C. 'L'installation des Arabes au Sud du Lac Tchad', *Abbia*, 16 1967.
'Le May Idris Alaoma et les Kotóko', *Revue Camerounaise d'Histoire*, 1, 1971.
'Notes relatives à l'histoire du Nord Cameroun', *Etudes Camerounaises*, 4, 35/36, 1953.

3 Quellen-und Literaturverzeichnis auf Deutsch

Ankermann, B. 'Bericht über eine ethnographische Forchungsreise Ins Graslands von Kamerun', *Zeitschrift für Ethnologie*, 42, 1910.

Autenrieth, Fr. *Ins Inner-Hochland von Kamerun*, Stuttgart, Holland und Jotenhaus, 1900, reprinted, 1909, 1913.

Barth, H. *Reisen und Entdeckungen in Nord-und Zentralafrika 1849–55*, 5 Bde., Gotha, 1857/58.

Baumann, H. und Vajda, L. 'Bernhard Ankermann's Völker Kundliche Aufzeichnungen im Grasland von Kameron 1907–1909', *Baessler-Archiv*, Neue Folge. Bd. VII, 1959.

Bauer, F. *Die deutsche Niger-Benue – Tschadsee – Expedition 1902–03*, Berlin, 1904.

Braukämper, U. *Der Einfluss des Islam auf die Geschichte und Kulturentwicklung Adamauas. Abriss eines afrikanischen Kulturwandels*, Wiesbaden, 1970.

Briesen, V. (Oberleutn). 'Beiträge zur Geschichte des Lamidates Ngaoundere', *Mitteilungen aus den deutschen Schutzgebieten* (MDS), 27, 1914.

Büttner, Thea. 'Die Sozialökonomische Struktur Adamauas im 19. Jahrhundert', *Wissenschaftliche Zeitschrift der Karl-Marx-Universiät*, Leipzig, 4/5, 1969.

'Zu Problemen der Stoatenbildung der Fulbe in Adamaua', *Wissenschaftliche Zeitschrift der Karl-Marx-Universität*, Leipzig, 13, 1964.

Chamier-Glisczinski, H. von. '*In Kamerun: Reise und Expeditionsskizzen eines ehemaligen Schutztruppenoffiziers*, Berlin, Reimar Hobbing, 1925.

Conrau, G. 'Bei den nordöstlichen Bangwa und im Lande der Kabo und Basosi' *Mitteilungen aus den deutschen Schutzgebieten*, 12, 1899.

Damis, F. *Auf dem Moraberge: Erinnerungen an die Kämpfe der 3 Kompanie der ehemaligen Kaiserlichen Schutztruppe für Kamerun*, Berlin, Deuss, 1925.

Danchelmann, A.S.F.E. *Das Kamerun-Abkommen vom 4. November 1911 im Reichstag und in der Budgetkommission*, Berlin, Selbstverlag. 1922.

Dominik, H. *Kamerun: Sechs Kriegs-und Friedensjahre in den Deutschen Tropen*, Berlin, E.S. Mittler und Sohn, 1901.

Vom Atlantik Zum Tschadsee: Kriege – und Forschungs-fahrten in Kamerun, Berlin, E.S. Mittler und Sohn, 1901.

Dominik A. und Ramsay, Hans von. 'Kamerun' in Schwabe K., (Hsg.) *Die deutschen kolonien*, Bd. 1, Berlin, 1909.

Duisburg, A. von. 'Zur Geschichte der Sultanate Bornu und Wandala (Mandara), *Anthropos*, 22, 1/2 1927.

Emouts, J. *Ins Steppen – und Bergland Innerkameruns*, Aachen, Xavierers, 1922.

Full, A. 'Kamerun', *Koloniale Rundschau*, 9/10, 1932.

Gardi, R. *Kirdi: Unter den heidnischen Stämmen in den Bergen und Sümpfen Nord-Kameruns*, Düsseldorf, Deutscher Bücherbund, 1960.

Geary, C. *We: die Genese eines Häuptlingstums im Grasland von Kamerun*, Studien zur Kulturkunde 38, Wiesbaden, Franz Steiner, 1976.

Hausen, Karin. *Deutsche Kolonialherrschaft in Afrika. Wirtschaftsinteressen una Kolonialverwaltung in Kamerun von 1914*, Zurich, Atlantis, 1970.

Hirschberg, W. 'Die Stammtafel der Bamum-Könige', *Archiv für Völkerkunde*, 17/18, 1962–1963.

Hutter, Franz. *Wanderungen und Forschungen im Nord-Hinterland von Kamerun*, Bravorschweig, Vieweg, 1902.

Ittman, J. 'Der Kultische Geheimbund Djengu und der Kameruner Küste' *Anthropos*, 52, 1/2, 1957.

Volkskundliche und religiöse Begriffe in nördlichen Waldland von Kamerun, Berlin, D. Reimer, 1953.

Jaeck, H-P. 'Die Deutsche Annexion', in Stoecker, H. (Hsg.) *Kamerun unter Deutscher Kolonialherrschaft*, Bd. 1, Berlin, VEB, 1960.

Kaeselitz, R. 'Kolonialeroberung und Widerstandskampf in süd-Kamerun (1884–1907)'. In Stoecker, H. (Hsg.), *Kamerun unter ... *Bd. 2 (Berlin: VEB, 1968).

Kemner, W. *Kamerun, dargestellt im Kolonialpolitischer, historischer, verkehrstechnischer, rassenkundlicher und rohstoffwirtschaftlicher Hinsicht*, Berlin, Freiheitsverlag, 1937.

Lieb, A. *Deutsche Kolonialarbeit und zehn Jahre Mandatsherrschaft in Kamerun*, Schwarzenbach, Weigand, 1932.

Mansfeld, A. *Urwald-Dokumente: Vier Jahre Unter den Cross-Flussnegern Kameruns*, Berlin, Dietrich Reimer, 1908.

Mentzel, H. *Die Kämpfe in Kamerun, 1914–1916: Vorbereitungen und Verlauf*, Berlin, Junker und Dunnhaupt, 1936.

Morgen, C. von. *Durch Kamerun von Süd nach Nord*: Reisen und Forschungen im Hinterlande, 1889 bis 1891, Leipzig, Brockhaus, 1893.

Oppenheim, M. *Rabeh und das Tschadseegebiet*, Berlin, D. Reimer, 1902.

Passarge, S. *Adamaua: Bericht über die Expedition des Deutschen Kamerun-Komitees in den Jahren 1893/94*, Berlin, D. Reimer, 1895.

Priester, A. *Kamerun als deutsches Schutzgebiet*, Aschaffenburg, Selbstverlag, 1960.

Puttkamer, J. von. *Gouverneursjahre in Kamerun*, Berlin, Georg Stilke, 1912.

Raaflaub, F. *Die Schulen der Basler Mission in Kamerun: Ihre Geschichte und Gegenwartsaufgabe*, Basel, Basler Missionsbuchhandlung, 1984.

Der bliebende Auftrag: 150 Jahre Basler Mission, Stuttgart, Evangelischer Missionsverlag, 1965.

Rein-Wuhrmann, Anna. *Fumban, die Stadt auf dem Schutte: Arbeit und Ernte im Missionsdienst in Kamerun*, Basel, Basler Missionsbuchhandlung, 1948.

Mein Bamunvolk in Grasland von Kamerun, Stuttgart und Basel, Evangelischer Missionsverlag, 1925.

Richter, M. *Durch Kamerun von der Küste bis zum Tschadsee zur Frühzeit der Deutschen Herrschaft*, Köln, Schaffstein, 1926.

Ritter, A. *Frieden und Krieg in Kamerun: Ein Erlebnisbericht*, Suhl, Strom, 1939.

Rueger, A. 'Die Duala und die Kolonialmacht 1884–1914: Eine Studie über die historischen Ursprünge des afrikanischen Antikolonialismus', in Stoecker, H. (Hsg.) *Kamerun unter.* ..., Bd. 1, Berlin, 1960.

'Die Entstehung und Lage der Arbeiterklasse unter dem Deutschen Kolonialregime in Kamerun (1895–1905) in Markov, W. (Hsg.) *Afrika – Studien*, Leipzig, 1967.

Scheve, E. *Die Mission der Deutschen in Kamerun, von 1884 bis 1901*, Berlin, Missionsgesellschaft der Deutschen Baptisten, 1901.

Schlunk, M. *Die Schulen für Eingeborene in den deutschen Schulzgebieten*, Hamburg, L. Frienderichsen, 1914.

Schmidlin, J. *Die Katholischen Missionen in den Deutschen Schutzgebieten*, Münster, Aschendorffsche Verlagsbuchhandlung, 1913.

Schnee, H. *Deutsches Kolonial-Lexicon*, 3 Bd., Leipzig, Quelleu Meyer, 1920.

Schomann, H. *Der Eisenbahnbau in Kamerun unter deutscher Kolonial-herrschaft.* Berlin, Humboldt-Universität, 1965.

Seidel, A. 'Das Bakwiri-Volk in Kamerun', *Beiträge zur Kolonial-politik und Kolonialwirtschaft*, 3, 1902, pp. 149–172, 193–210.

Skolaster, H. *Die Pallotiner in Kamerun: 25 Jahre Missions arbeit*, Limburg, Pallotine, 1925.

Steiner, P. *Unsere Kamerun-Mission bis zum Ausbruch des Weltkrieges*, Basel, Missionsbuchhandlung, 1915.

Stoecker, H. (Hsg.) *Kamerun unter Deutscher Kolonialherrschaft*, 2 Bde., Berlin, Rütten und Loening, 1960/68.

Strümpell, K. *Blätter aus der Geschichte der Schutztruppe für Kamerun*, Heidelberg, Carl Pfeffer, 1926.

'Die Geschichte Adamauas nach mündlichen Überlieferungen', *Mitteilungen der Geographischen Gesellschaft*, Hamburgs, 26, 1912.

Student, E. *Kameruns Kampf, 1914–16*, Berlin, Bernhard und Graefe, 1937.

Tessmann, G. *Die Bafia und die Kultur der Mittel-Kamerun-Bantu*, Stuttgart, Strocker und Schröder, 1934.

'Die Mbaka – Limbe, Mbum and Lakka', *Zeitschrift für Ethnologie*, 60, 4/6, 1926.

Tessmann, G. *Die Pangwe: völkerkundliche Monographie eines Westafrika-nischen Negerstammes. Ergebnisse der Lübecker Pangwe – Expedition 1907–1909 und früherer Forschungen 1904–1907*, 2 Bde. Berlin, Ernst Wasmuth, 1913.

Thorbeche, F. *Im Hochland von Mittel-Kamerun*, 3 Bde., Hamburg, L. Friederichsen, 1914–1929.

Vietor, J.K. *Geschichtliche und Kulturelle Entwicklung unserer Schutzgebiete*, Berlin, 1913.

Wirz, A. *Vom Sklavenhandel zum Kolonialen-Handel: Wirtschaftsräume und Wirtschaftsformen in Kamerun vor 1914*, Zürich und Freiburg, Atlantis, 1972.

Zenker, G. 'Jaunde', *Mitteilungen aus den deutschen Schutzgebieten*, 8, 1895.

Zimmermann, O. *Durch Busch und Steppes von Campo bis zum Schari, 1892–1902: ein Beitrag zur Geschichte der Schutztruppe von Kamerun.* Berlin, E.S. Mittler, 1909.

Zimmermann, Emil. *Neu-Kamerun. Reiserlebnisse und wirtschafts, Politische Untersuchungen. 1 Vom Dume zum Lobay und Kongo. Reiseberichte*, Berlin, E.S. Mittler, 1913.

Zintgraff, E. *Nord-Kamerun: Schilderung der im Auftrag des Auswärtigen Amtes zur Erschliessung des nördlichen Hinterlandes von Kamerun während der Jahre 1886–1892 unternommenen Reisen*, Berlin, Paetel, 1895.

4   Unpublished doctoral theses, History Department, University of Yaoundé

Abwa, D. 'Le Lamidat de Ngaoundéré de 1915 à 1945', Université de Yaoundé, 1980

Awasom, N.F. 'The Hausa and Fulani in the Bamenda Grasslands 1903–1960', Université de Yaoundé, 1985.

Bah, T.M. 'Architecture militaire traditionnelle et poliorcétique dans le Soudan Occidental du XVIe à la fin du XIXe siècle', Université de Paris I, 1970.

Che-Mfombong, W. 'Bamenda Division under British Administration 1916–1961: From Native Administration to Local Government', Université de Yaoundé, 1980.

Chem-Langhëë, B. 'The Kamerun Plebiscites 1959–1961: Perceptions and Strategies', University of British Columbia, 1976.

Chiabi, E. 'Background to Nationalism in Anglophone Cameroon: 1916–1945', University of California, Santa Barbara, 1982.

Dikoume, A.F. 'Les transports au Cameroun du 1884 à 1975', Université de Paris 1, 1982.

Efoua-Mbozo'o, S. 'La Mission Presbytérienne Américaine et les mutations religieuses et sociales chez les peuples du Sud-Cameroun (1919–1939)', Université de Lyon, 1981.

Elango, L.Z. 'Britain and Bimbia in the Nineteenth Century 1843–1878: A Study in Anglo-Bimbia Trade and Diplomatic Relations', Boston University, 1974.

Essomba, B., 'Sucre mediterranéen, sucre atlantique et commerce du nord Européen aux XVe et XVIe Siède', Université de Paris 1, 1981.

Essomba J-M. 'L'histoire ancienne des abords du lac Tchad et ses problèmes (exemple les Zaghwa du Kanem et les rapports possible entre les abords nord et sud du Tchad d'après les géographes et historiens arabes du VIIè au XVIé siècle, la tradition orale et archèologie', Universitè de Paris, 1975.

Fanso, V.G. 'Inter-Frontier Relations and Resistance to Cameroun – Nigeria Colonial Boundaries, 1916–1945', Université de Yaoundé, 1982.

Fomin, E.S.D. 'Slavery in Cameroon: Case Studies in Slavery in Selected Centralised and Non-centralised Polities', Université de Yaoundé, 1984.

Ghomsi, E. 'Histoire des Bamiléké des origines à 1920', Université de Paris 1, 1972.

Gomsu, J. 'Colonisation et organisation sociale. Les chefs traditionnels du Sud-Cameroun pendent la periode coloniale allemande (1884–1914)', Saarbrüken 1982.

Koufan, J. 'La vie politique au Cameroun sous l'occupation française 1916–1923', Université de Paris 1, 1986.

Mveng, E. 'Les Sources grecques de l'histoire négro-africaine, depuis Homère jusquà Strabon', Université de Paris 1, 1970.

Ndi, A. 'Mill Hill Missionaries and the Southern Cameroons. 1922–1962', University of London, 1983.

Ngoh, V.J. 'The United States and the Nigerian Civil War: An Analysis of the American Policy towards the War, 1967–1970', University of Washington, Seattle, Washington, 1982.

Njiasse-Njoya, A. 'Naissance et evolution de l'Islam en pays Bamun (Cameroun)', Université de Paris I, 1981.

Nkili, R. 'Maroua la ville et sa region des origines à 1919', Université de Paris IVe, 1977.

Sah, L.I. 'Contribution à l'histoire de la presse de langues françaises et locales au Cameroun des origines à l'autonomie', Universitè de Paris 11, 1975.

Sonne, W. 'Action Sanitaire publique et auxiliaires au Cameroun sous administration française, 1916–1945', Université de Yaoundé, 1983.

Index

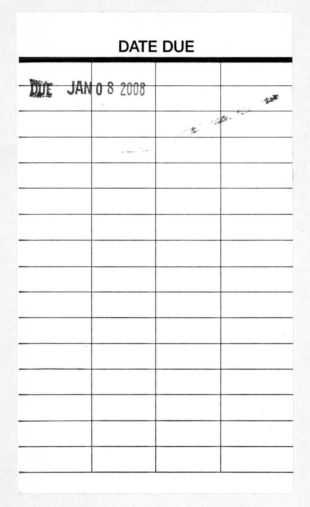

DATE DUE